Solicitors' Accounts—
A Practical Guide

put your knowledge into practice

- **Business Law**
  J. Scott Slorach and Jason G. Ellis

- **Legislation for Business Law**
  Rachel Cooper

- **Foundations for the LPC**
  George Miles *et al.*

- **Lawyers' Skills**
  Julian Webb *et al.*

- **Solicitors' Accounts**
  Dale Kay and Janet Baker

- **Criminal Litigation Handbook**
  Martin Hannibal and Lisa Mountford

- **Civil Litigation Handbook**
  Susan Cunningham-Hill and Karen Elder

- **Property Law Handbook**
  Robert Abbey and Mark Richards

- **A Practical Approach to Civil Procedure**
  Stuart Sime

- **A Practical Approach to Conveyancing**
  Robert Abbey and Mark Richards

- **Family Law Handbook** (*coming soon*)
  Jane Sendall

- **Commercial Law**
  Robert Bradgate and Fidelma White

- **Employment Law**
  James Holland and Stuart Burnett

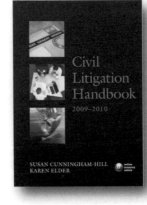
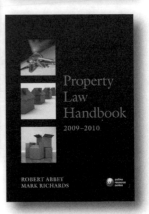

Solicitors' Accounts—
A Practical Guide

Dale Kay
Solicitor (Hons)

and

Janet Baker
LLB (Hons), Solicitor

OXFORD
UNIVERSITY PRESS

OXFORD

UNIVERSITY PRESS

Great Clarendon Street, Oxford OX2 6DP

Oxford University Press is a department of the University of Oxford.
It furthers the University's objective of excellence in research, scholarship,
and education by publishing worldwide in

Oxford New York

Auckland Cape Town Dar es Salaam Hong Kong Karachi
Kuala Lumpur Madrid Melbourne Mexico City Nairobi
New Delhi Shanghai Taipei Toronto

With offices in

Argentina Austria Brazil Chile Czech Republic France Greece
Guatemala Hungary Italy Japan Poland Portugal Singapore
South Korea Switzerland Thailand Turkey Ukraine Vietnam

Oxford is a registered trademark of Oxford University Press
in the UK and in certain other countries

Published in the United States
by Oxford University Press Inc., New York

First edition 1997
Second edition 1998
Third edition 1999
Fourth edition 2000
Fifth edition 2001
Sixth edition 2002
Seventh edition 2003
Eighth edition 2004
Ninth edition 2005
Tenth edition 2006
Eleventh edition 2007
Twelfth edition 2008
Thirteenth edition 2009

British Library Cataloguing in Publication Data
Data available

Typeset by Laserwords Private Ltd., Chennai, India
Printed in Great Britain
on acid-free paper by
Ashford Colour Press Limited, Gosport, Hampshire

ISBN 978–0–19–957464–3

10 9 8 7 6 5 4 3 2 1

OUTLINE CONTENTS

DETAILED CONTENTS

PREFACE

Thanks to Janet Baker, whose original book still forms a basis for this Guide. My thanks also go to my husband, Roger, to all my former students and ex-colleagues for their constructive comments, and to all the helpful and supportive team at Oxford University Press, particularly Lucy Read and Helen Davis.

Dale Kay
April 2009
Manchester

ONLINE RESOURCES TO ACCOMPANY THIS BOOK...

Online Resource Centres are developed to provide students and lecturers with ready-to-use teaching and learning resources. They are free-of-charge, designed to complement the textbook and offer additional materials that are suited to electronic delivery. The Online Resource Centre to accompany this book can be found at:

www.oxfordtextbooks.co.uk/orc/solicitorsaccounts09_10

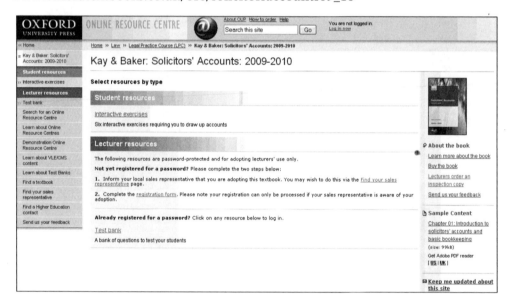

Lecturer resources

Password-protected to ensure only lecturers adopting this book can access these resources, each registration is personally checked to ensure the security of the site. Use these resources to complement your own teaching notes and the resources you provide for your LPC students.

Registering is easy: click on 'Lecturer Resources' complete a simple registration form which allows you to choose your own username and password, and access will be granted within 48 hours (subject to verification).

Test bank of multiple choice questions

Using your lecturer password, you can gain access to a fully customisable bank of multiple choice questions offering a versatile way to test your students' knowledge and understanding of the accounting methods and principles covered in this book. The questions are downloadable into Questionmark Perception, Blackboard, WebCT and most other virtual learning environments capable of importing QTI XML. The questions are also available in print format.

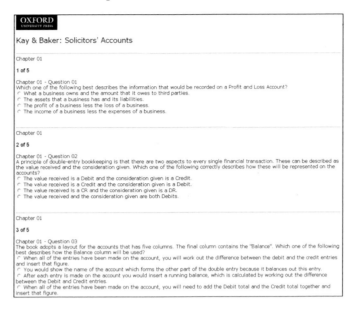

Student resources

Students can access several interactive exercises without the need for a password. These exercises offer an excellent interactive way to test your knowledge and understanding of the accounting principles.

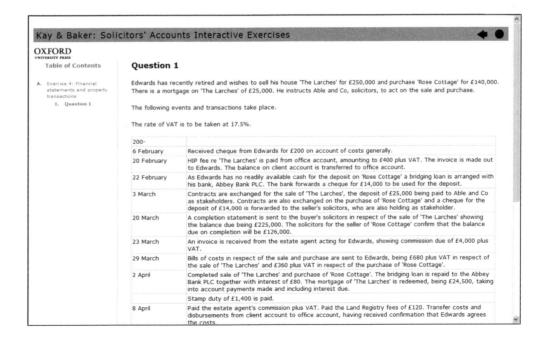

Introduction to solicitors' accounts and basic bookkeeping

1.1 Introduction

This chapter includes:

1. An overview of accounts;

2. The purpose of keeping accounts;

3. An explanation of the double-entry bookkeeping system, types of account and worked examples;

4. Reminder of key points;

5. Practical self-test exercises in drawing up accounts using the double-entry system.

! INTENDED OUTCOME

An understanding of:

1. The need for accounts;

2. The principles of bookkeeping, evidenced by the ability to draw up simple accounts using the double-entry bookkeeping system.

1.2 Overview of accounts

This book covers the areas required on both the old and the new Legal Practice Course. A word of encouragement at the start. Although initially Accounts can seem daunting, most students do well, and even manage to enjoy the time they spend on Accounts. Do not worry if you did not enjoy GCSE maths; the only maths involved here is very basic arithmetic.

Do practice using the exercises in the book and those given to you on your course. This is the best way to come to grips with the subject. The questions at the end of each chapter are graded, starting with easier exercises and working up to more challenging questions.

The following websites may be useful to you, and will also be mentioned in the relevant chapters:

<http://www.sra.org.uk> and <http://www.lawsociety.org.uk> in respect of solicitors' accounts;
<http://www.companieshouse.gov.uk> in respect of company accounts;
<http://www.berr.gov.uk/> in respect of company accounts;
<http://www.hmrc.gov.uk> HM Revenue & Customs in respect of VAT, Inland Revenue.

1.2.1 Why study Accounts?

You may think that Accounts is the last subject a prospective solicitor needs to know. However, there are very good reasons why it is included. Solicitors can be struck off as solicitors if they breach the Solicitors' Accounts Rules—have a look in the Law Society's *Gazette* and see how often this is a reason. Some examples of the Solicitors' Disciplinary Tribunal cases are shown in Chapter 11, para 11.2.2. Solicitors look after large sums of money on behalf of their clients, and must be trusted to do so. They are ultimately responsible and cannot totally rely on the skill or honesty of others.

Solicitors are also running a business; they must be able to understand how the accounts are kept, and, as partners, be able to read their Profit and Loss accounts and Balance Sheets each year.

Often an understanding of accounts will be useful when giving advice, whether to corporate clients, or, for example, to matrimonial clients when advising on asset distribution.

1.2.2 How to study Accounts

Accounts is a practical subject, it involves understanding the principles and applying them. The best way to do this is by reading the explanation and then working through the exercises. Only when you are satisfied that you understand what you are doing should you move on to the next section. Repetition of exercises will consolidate your understanding. Once you understand the basic principles the later sections should fall into place.

1.2.3 The main areas of study

Accounts on this course falls into two main sections:

1. Business Accounts;
2. Solicitors' Accounts.

Business Accounts

This includes basic double-entry bookkeeping, the Trial Balance, and preparation of final accounts, being the Profit and Loss and Balance Sheet. The final accounts can be prepared for a sole owner, a partnership, or a company. Analysis and interpretation of simple final accounts is expected on the new Legal Practice Course.

Solicitors' Accounts

This covers the Solicitors' Accounts Rules, the difference between office and client account, and the bookkeeping entries required. It also covers how to prepare a simple financial statement for a client, and the particular bookkeeping entries required for certain types of work, for example property or probate work.

1.3   The purpose of keeping accounts

All businesses need to keep a day-to-day record of all their financial transactions, so that they can see what is happening. From these records they will be able to draw up final accounts.

These fall into two main sections:

The Profit and Loss account

This will record all income less expenses, to give the profit or loss for the period.

The Balance Sheet

This will show what the business OWNS—its assets—and what the business OWES—its liabilities.

Note that different people will use the accounts for different purposes, for example:

The owners—will need to know what is happening financially, this will help them with planning for the business;

HM Revenue & Customs—for tax purposes;

Any person or company that has lent money to the business, for example the bank;

A buyer of the business;

A new partner coming into a partnership.

1.4   An introduction to double-entry bookkeeping

Basic accounts are merely records or histories of financial transactions. The normal method of keeping day-to-day accounts is that of double entry, which will be used in this book. This means that **TWO** entries are made for every **SINGLE FINANCIAL TRANSACTION**.

1.4.1   The principle of double-entry bookkeeping

The system of double-entry bookkeeping operates on the basis that when the business is involved in a transaction there are two sides to the transaction:

1. The business receives value from the transaction;
2. The business gives consideration for the value received.

The double-entry system records both sides of the transaction so that somewhere in the accounts both parts of the transactions will be shown—the double entry.

For example, if a firm buys a computer for £1,000 cash, it has gained an asset, but has lost cash. If the business provides legal services and is paid £500, then it has gained cash of £500, but given consideration of the work done, which is the source of the income.

The benefit received is shown on the left-hand side of the account and called the **DEBIT** entry, the consideration given is shown on the right-hand side of the account, and called the **CREDIT** entry.

<table>
<tr><td align="center">**DEBIT**</td><td align="center">**CREDIT**</td></tr>
<tr><td align="center">**BENEFIT RECEIVED**</td><td align="center">**CONSIDERATION GIVEN**</td></tr>
</table>

This may seem strange or wrong at this stage, as you may associate credit with receipts, and debit with payments out, usually based on your bank statement sent out from the bank, where payments out of your account are shown as debit entries and receipts are shown as credit entries.

EXAMPLE

Jane Morris pays £1,000 into her bank account with the Northern Bank PLC. The Northern Bank will draw up its accounts as follows:

Northern Bank PLC Cash account

	Benefit received Debit	Consideration given Credit	Balance
Jane	1,000		1,000 DR

Jane Morris account

	Benefit received Debit	Consideration given Credit	Balance
Cash		1,000	1,000 CR

The bank has followed the rules given above, but all Jane sees is her account, which is one part of the double entry. From Jane's point of view the credit entry records a receipt. From the Bank's point of view the receipt was **debited** on the Bank's Cash account and Jane's account was **credited** to show that Jane has given the cash. Jane is a creditor of the Bank—see later.

Remember that the two entries made DO record the same SINGLE transaction. The principle of double-entry bookkeeping is therefore: **for every debit entry in one account there must be a corresponding credit entry in another account.**

1.4.2 The layout of an account

There are several methods of drawing an account. The method adopted in this book is as follows.

Name of account

Date	Details	DR	CR	Balance

Note the following:

(a) This layout has five columns.

(b) There is one column each for date and details. Note that the details column must indicate clearly the name of the account which forms the other part of the double entry.

(c) The column headed 'DR' (abbreviation of debit) is always on the LEFT. Debit entries are made in this column.

(d) The column headed 'CR' (abbreviation of credit) is always on the RIGHT. Credit entries are made in this column.

(e) There is a balance column which gives a running balance on the account after each transaction is completed. The balance is the difference between the debit and credit entries. If the debit side is heavier than the credit side then there is a debit balance, and vice versa.

Note that for solicitors, rule 32(5) of the Solicitors' Accounts Rules 1998 imposes an obligation to show the current balance on each client's ledger, or the balance must be readily ascertainable from the records kept. See also Chapter 11, para 11.2.3(f).

1.4.3   An example of double-entry bookkeeping

On 1 March the business buys a car for £3,000 and pays by cheque drawn on the firm's bank account. The two sides to this transaction are:

1. The receipt of value in the form of an asset acquired by the business, ie the car;
2. The giving of consideration, ie reducing the firm's bank balance by £3,000.

To record this transaction the firm will use two accounts:

1. The Motor cars account;
2. The Cash account.

Motor cars account

Date	Details	DR	CR	Balance
1 March	Cash—purchase of car	3,000		3,000 DR

Cash account

Date	Details	DR	CR	Balance
		(Received)	(Paid)	
1 March	Motor cars		3,000	3,000 CR

1.5   Classification of accounts

All financial transactions will therefore need to be recorded by double entry in the ledger (day-to-day) accounts of a business. These ledger accounts can be divided into three groups:

1. Personal accounts—accounts for each individual, business or company dealing with the business;
2. Asset (real) accounts—accounts showing each asset or set of assets (for example cars) of the business;
3. Nominal accounts:
   (a) Income accounts name the source of the income;
   (b) Expense accounts name the source of the loss.

Using the double-entry system there are set rules for these accounts, set out below. These rules can be memorised, and followed for every entry made on ledger accounts. Once you have used these rules for some time, you will find that the accounts do always follow the twofold aspect of benefit and consideration mentioned previously.

A summary of the rules for these groups of accounts is set out briefly below, then a more detailed explanation is given.

1. PERSONAL accounts

   DEBIT—the personal account which receives goods, cash, or services from the business.

   CREDIT—the personal account which has given goods, cash, or services to the business.

2. ASSET (real) accounts

   DEBIT when business receives an asset or assets are increased.

   CREDIT when the business disposes of an asset or if the assets are reduced.

3. Nominal INCOME or EXPENSE accounts

   CREDIT Income accounts—they name the source of the income.

   DEBIT Expense accounts—they name the source of the loss.

1.5.1 Personal accounts

A separate account must be kept for each person, firm, or company with which the business has dealings, for example, each debtor and creditor.

The rule for making entries in a personal account is:

DEBIT   When goods, cash, or services are received by that person or company from the business, ie they are being charged for the goods, etc.
(They are then a DEBTOR)

CREDIT When that person or company gives goods, cash, or services to the business, ie the business owes them money for the goods, etc.
(They are then a CREDITOR)

1.5.2 The personal accounts of the business owner

As the accounts look at a transaction from the point of view of the business, the business and its owner are treated as separate entities. See Chapter 7, para 7.2.1. This principle holds good for a solicitor's practice. The accounts which record transactions between the business and its owner are personal accounts. These accounts are:

1.5.2.1 The owner's Capital

When a person sets up in business he or she will usually introduce assets, for example money, premises, car, and equipment. When this happens:

(a) DEBIT the relevant asset account;

(b) CREDIT the Capital account, which will show the amount due to the owner.

EXAMPLE

On 1 January Harry starts up in practice as a sole practitioner. He introduces £8,000 cash, a car valued at £5,000, and office equipment worth £2,000. These opening entries will be recorded as follows:

Cash account—Asset account/personal account with bank

Date	Details	DR	CR	Balance
		(Received)	(Paid)	
1 Jan	Capital introduced by Harry	8,000		8,000 DR

Car account—Asset account

Date	Details	DR	CR	Balance
1 Jan	Capital introduced by Harry	5,000		5,000 DR

Office equipment account—Asset account

Date	Details	DR	CR	Balance
1 Jan	Capital introduced by Harry	2,000		2,000 DR

Capital account—personal account of the owner

Date	Details	DR	CR	Balance
1 Jan	Cash		8,000	8,000 CR
	Car		5,000	13,000 CR
	Office equipment		2,000	15,000 CR

1.5.2.2 Drawings account

From time to time the owner will take money out of the business either in cash or by paying private expenses, for example, a home gas bill. These are called drawings and are usually recorded in a personal account, the drawings account.

The drawings account will always be DEBITED.

EXAMPLE

On 31 January Harry draws £1,000 out of the firm's bank account for his own use and pays his personal tax of £500. The entries to record these transactions are as follows:

Drawings account—Harry—personal account

Date	Details	DR	CR	Balance
31 Jan	Cash—drawings	1,000		
31 Jan	Cash—personal tax	500		1,500 DR

Cash account—Asset/personal account with bank

Date	Details	DR	CR	Balance
	Balance			8,000 DR
31 Jan	Drawings—cash		1,000	7,000 DR
	Drawings—personal tax		500	6,500 DR

The credit balance on the capital account shows the amount which the business owes to its owner, ie the amount he has invested. The debit balance on the drawings account shows the amount the owner owes the business.

1.5.3 Asset/real accounts

These will show the assets at the price paid for them (cost price).

It is not always easy to decide whether a purchase should be recorded as an asset, or as an expense. For example, if the business buys office furniture, this is likely to last for some time and so will be recorded as an asset. However, if the business buys stationery, this will be used up in a fairly short time, and so it will be recorded as an expense.

The cash account

This is not only a real account; it is also a personal account with the bank.

The business will usually place most of its cash in the bank; it will pay all cheques received into the bank, and make most payments out by cheque or transfer. Any cash in the bank will be an asset. However, if the business went overdrawn at the bank, then the overdraft would be a liability.

The petty cash account

This deals with cash payments made by the firm. A cash sum will be taken out of the bank each week as a cash float. This can be used to make payments out, and topped up when required.

The rule for making entries in an asset account is:

DEBIT   receipt of an asset.

CREDIT   reduction of an asset.

EXAMPLE ASSET ACCOUNTS

Assume that a firm has £10,000 cash in the bank.

The firm purchases office furniture for £2,000.

DEBIT the increase/receipt on the office furniture account.

CREDIT the decrease/payment out on the Cash account.

Office furniture account

Date	Details	DR	CR	Balance
	Cash	2,000		2,000 DR

Cash account

Date	Details	DR	CR	Balance
	Balance			10,000 DR
	Office furniture		2,000	8,000 DR

The balances on the accounts show the shift in assets from cash to office furniture; at first the firm had £10,000 cash, now it has £8,000 cash and office furniture worth £2,000.

1.5.4 Income and expense accounts

(a) INCOME ACCOUNTS These record the receipt of income by the firm, they name the source of the income. The following are examples of income accounts kept by a solicitor:

   (i)   Profit Costs account—this account shows the amounts charged to clients. It is based on the bills sent to clients.

   (ii) Interest received account—this account shows interest received by the firm on money held in a deposit account.

   (iii) Rent received account—this account shows rent received by the firm if it leases out any of its surplus office accommodation.

NB Income accounts are CREDITED with income received and will therefore always have CREDIT balances.

EXAMPLE

A firm lets its surplus office premises for which it receives rent of £800 per month. On 1 January the firm receives the first month's rent.

CREDIT   Rent received account.

DEBIT   Cash account.

Rent received account

Date	Details	DR	CR	Balance
1 Jan	Cash		800	800 CR

Cash account

Date	Details	DR	CR	Balance
1 Jan	Rent received	800		800 DR

EXAMPLE

The firm does work for Basil, for which the charge is £500. When the bill is sent to Basil, the income (billed work done) account will be credited; it shows what the business has given in return for the gain. Note that in solicitors' firms the income account, based on the bills sent out, is usually called the Profit Costs account. Basil's personal account will be debited, showing that Basil has received £500 worth of services. The debit balance will show that Basil is a debtor of the firm; he owes £500.

CREDIT   Profit Costs account.

DEBIT   Basil account.

Profit Costs account (work done account)
Income

Date	Details	DR	CR	Balance
	Basil—bill		500	500 CR

Basil account (personal account)

Date	Details	DR	CR	Balance
	Profit costs—bill	500		500 DR

When Basil pays the bill, the entries will be:

DEBIT   The Cash account (real account).
CREDIT   Basil's account.

Cash account

Date	Details	DR	CR	Balance
	Balance, say			8,000 DR
	Basil	500		8,500 DR

Basil account

Date	Details	DR	CR	Balance
	Balance			500 DR
	Cash you		500	—

The debt of £500 due from Basil has been paid and converted into cash.

Note: the balance on Basil's account was £500 debit, the balance is now nil as the amount owed has been paid.

(b) EXPENSE ACCOUNTS These record the payment of business expenses, naming the source of the loss:

    (i)   A separate expense account is opened for each type of expense which the firm has; for example, most firms will have rent, council tax, electricity, telephone, and salaries accounts.

    (ii) An expense account is DEBITED each time the firm pays a business expense.

EXAMPLE

On 30 November the firm pays an office electricity bill of £600.

DEBIT   Electricity account.

CREDIT   Cash account.

Electricity account

Date	Details	DR	CR	Balance
30 Nov	Cash	600		600 DR

Cash account

Date	Details	DR (Received)	CR (Paid out)	Balance
	Balance, say			5,000 DR
30 Nov	Electricity		600	4,400 DR

Payments made under any leasing or rental agreement are business expenses and are recorded in an expense account.

EXAMPLE

A firm leases word processors from Computer Supplies Ltd. The quarterly rental is £100. On 1 April the first instalment is paid. Assume the firm has a cash balance of £5,000 at the bank.

DEBIT   Rental account.

CREDIT Cash account.

Word processors rental account

Date	Details	DR	CR	Balance
1 Apr	Cash	100		100 DR

Cash account

Date	Details	DR	CR	Balance
	Balance			5,000 DR
1 Apr	Word processors rental		100	4,900 DR

NB Expense accounts are DEBITED and will always have DEBIT balances.

1.5.5 Trading accounts

Manufacturing and trading accounts are dealt with in more detail in Chapter 7, where the same principles apply. Where goods are purchased as part of the trading cycle, for example goods are purchased for £6,500 cash, the entries would be:

CREDIT the Cash account £6,500.

DEBIT the Purchases (expense account) £6,500.

On the assumption that the firm starts with £16,500 cash then the accounts would be as follows:

Cash account

Date	Details	DR	CR	Balance
	Balance			16,500 DR
	Purchases		6,500	10,000 DR

Purchases account

Date	Details	DR	CR	Balance
	Cash	6,500		6,500 DR

When the goods are sold a separate sales account will be opened. This will be CREDITED.

EXAMPLE

Assume the business has £10,000 cash.
Goods are sold for £9,000 cash.

DEBIT   the Cash account £9,000.

CREDIT   the Sales account (an income account) £9,000.

Cash account

Date	Details	DR	CR	Balance
	Balance			10,000 DR
	Sales	9,000		19,000 DR

Sales account (nominal income account)

Date	Details	DR	CR	Balance
	Cash		9,000	9,000 CR

1.5.6 Solicitors and accounts

Note that as solicitors will usually be holding large sums of money on behalf of clients they will have at least two bank accounts, one dealing with the firm's own money, called OFFICE ACCOUNT and the other dealing with clients' money called CLIENT ACCOUNT. For further details see Chapter 11 onwards.

1.6   Worked example on double entry

Foster, a sole practitioner, sets up her practice on 1 February with £10,000 cash, office equipment worth £1,000, and premises valued at £140,000.

During the month of February the practice engages in the following transactions:

1. It pays her secretary's salary of £1,300.

2. It receives one month's rent from the tenant occupying part of the office premises—£800.

3. It buys a desk for £500.

4. It buys a car on credit from Karsales Ltd for £9,000.

5. Foster draws £1,000 out of the bank for her own use.

6. The firm sends a bill to Jarman for £500, re profit costs for work done.

7. Jarman pays the bill of £500.

Cash account

Date	Details	DR	CR	Balance
Feb	Capital introduced	10,000		10,000 DR
	Salaries		1,300	8,700 DR
	Rent received	800		9,500 DR
	Office furniture		500	9,000 DR
	Drawings (cash)		1,000	8,000 DR
	Jarman	500		8,500 DR

A real account/personal account with the bank.

Office equipment account

Date	Details	DR	CR	Balance
1 Feb	Capital introduced	1,000		1,000 DR

A real/asset account.

Premises account

Date	Details	DR	CR	Balance
1 Feb	Capital introduced	140,000		140,000 DR

A real/asset account.

Capital account

Date	Details	DR	CR	Balance
Feb	Cash		10,000	10,000 CR
	Office equipment		1,000	11,000 CR
	Premises		140,000	151,000 CR

A personal account.

Salaries account

Date	Details	DR	CR	Balance
Feb	Cash (secretary)	1,300		1,300 DR

A nominal expense account.

Rent received account

Date	Details	DR	CR	Balance
Feb	Cash		800	800 CR

A nominal income account.

Office furniture account

Date	Details	DR	CR	Balance
Feb	Cash (desk)	500		500 DR

A real/asset account.

Motor vehicles account

Date	Details	DR	CR	Balance
Feb	Karsales Ltd (car)	9,000		9,000 DR

A real/asset account.

Karsales Ltd account

Date	Details	DR	CR	Balance
Feb	Motor vehicles (car)		9,000	9,000 CR

A personal account.

Drawings account

Date	Details	DR	CR	Balance
Feb	Cash (drawings)	1,000		1,000 DR

A personal account.

Profit Costs income account

Date	Details	DR	CR	Balance
Feb	Jim—bill		500	500 CR

A nominal income account.

Jarman

Date	Details	DR	CR	Balance
Feb	Profit costs—bill	500		500 DR
	Cash you		500	—

A personal account.

1.7 Reminder of key points

1. The need for accounts:
    (a) Essential to ensure money held for clients is dealt with properly;
    (b) Necessary for solicitors in running their practice as a business;
    (c) Needed when advising clients, for example corporate clients or matrimonial clients, on financial aspects.
2. The double-entry system—used to give complete information.

    For ONE financial transaction there will be TWO entries—

a DEBIT ENTRY on one account; and

a CREDIT ENTRY on another account.

3. The main types of account are:

INCOME accounts and EXPENSE accounts

For example, income from work done for clients or from trading;

expenses could include rent payable, salaries to staff;

ASSET (REAL) accounts

Examples include cash at the bank, cars, office premises;

PERSONAL accounts for each person/company dealing with the business

4. The rules:

CREDIT INCOME accounts;

DEBIT EXPENSE accounts;

ASSET accounts:

DEBIT when assets are acquired;

CREDIT when assets are disposed of.

The above entries on asset accounts may well seem wrong to you; they may appear to be the wrong way round, but you will find that they are right and the system does work.

PERSONAL accounts:

DEBIT when the person receives goods or services (they are then debtors);

CREDIT when the person gives the business goods or services (they are then creditors).

 online resource centre Now try the self-test exercises following and try the multiple choice questions online which are available through your tutor via the Online Resource Centre that accompanies this book. You may find these useful as another method of testing your understanding. When you have completed the exercises move on to the Trial Balance in Chapter 2.

1.8 Exercises on double-entry bookkeeping

1. Allow 5 to 10 minutes for this.

State the double entry that would be made in the following transactions:

(a) Khan starts a business and introduces cash of £5,000.

(b) Little and Co. receive cash of £600 in payment of work done.

(c) North pays out £300 in respect of an electricity bill.

(d) Fishwick pays an employee's salary of £500.

(e) Grayling draws £1,000 from her business for her own use.

(f) Morris purchases a car for his business for £15,000 on credit from Stockton Garage Ltd.

2. Allow 5 to 10 minutes for this.

Blears starts in business on 1 January as a solicitor, and introduces cash of £6,000 and office furniture worth £4,000. Show the accounts to record this.

3. Allow 10 minutes for this.

Latter starts a business with £5,000 cash on 10 November. He then buys a computer for £800 on 11 November. He sends a bill for £1,000 to a customer, Howard, for work done on 20 November.

Show the accounts to record this.

4. Allow 20 to 30 minutes for this.

Rahman starts in practice as a solicitor on 1 July with cash of £10,000, a car worth £16,000 and premises worth £128,000. During the month of July the following transactions occur:

1 July	Pays council tax £900.
3 July	Buys office furniture £1,800. Pays by cheque.
8 July	Pays secretary's salary £1,500.
10 July	Receives £12,500 as a loan from NatWest.
14 July	Draws £2,500 for his own use.

Prepare accounts to record the above transactions.

1.9 Suggested answers to exercises on double-entry bookkeeping

1 (a) DEBIT the Cash account £5,000.

CREDIT the Capital account (for Khan) £5,000.

(b) DEBIT the Cash account £600.

CREDIT the Profit Costs (work done) account (income account) £600.

(c) CREDIT Cash account £300.

DEBIT Electricity account (expense account) £300.

(d) CREDIT Cash account £500.

DEBIT Salaries account (expense account) £500.

(e) CREDIT Cash account £1,000.

DEBIT Drawings account (personal account) £1,000.

(f) DEBIT Car account (asset account) £15,000.

CREDIT Stockton Garage Ltd account (personal account) £15,000.

2 **Cash account**

Date	Details	DR	CR	Balance
1 Jan	Capital	6,000		6,000 DR

Office furniture account

Date	Details	DR	CR	Balance
1 Jan	Capital	4,000		4,000 DR

Blears Capital account

Date	Details	DR	CR	Balance
1 Jan	Cash		6,000	6,000 CR
	Office furniture		4,000	10,000 CR

3 Cash account

Date	Details	DR	CR	Balance
10 Nov	Capital	5,000		5,000 DR
11 Nov	Computer		800	4,200 DR

Capital account

Date	Details	DR	CR	Balance
10 Nov	Cash		5,000	5,000 CR

Computer account

Date	Details	DR	CR	Balance
11 Nov	Cash	800		800 DR

Howard account

Date	Details	DR	CR	Balance
20 Nov	Profit costs–bill	1,000		1,000 DR

Profit costs

Date	Details	DR	CR	Balance
20 Nov	Howard–bill		1,000	1,000 CR

4 Cash account

Date	Details	DR	CR	Balance
1 July	Capital	10,000		10,000 DR
	Council tax		900	9,100 DR
3 July	Office furniture		1,800	7,300 DR
8 July	Salary		1,500	5,800 DR
10 July	Loan: NatWest	12,500		18,300 DR
14 July	Drawings		2,500	15,800 DR

Car account

Date	Details	DR	CR	Balance
1 July	Capital	16,000		16,000 DR

Premises account

Date	Details	DR	CR	Balance
1 July	Capital	128,000		128,000 DR

Capital account

Date	Details	DR	CR	Balance
1 July	Cash		10,000	10,000 CR
	Car		16,000	26,000 CR
	Premises		128,000	154,000 CR

Council tax account

Date	Details	DR	CR	Balance
1 July	Cash	900		900 DR

Office furniture account

Date	Details	DR	CR	Balance
3 July	Cash	1,800		1,800 DR

Salaries account

Date	Details	DR	CR	Balance
8 July	Cash (secretary)	1,500		1,500 DR

Loan account: NatWest

Date	Details	DR	CR	Balance
10 July	Cash		12,500	12,500 CR

Drawings account

Date	Details	DR	CR	Balance
14 July	Cash	2,500		2,500 DR

2

The Trial Balance

2.1 Introduction

This chapter includes:

1. The purpose of the Trial Balance;
2. Preparation of the Trial Balance;
3. Use of Suspense accounts;
4. Errors not revealed by the Trial Balance;
5. Reminder of key points;
6. Exercises on double-entry bookkeeping and Trial Balances.

> **!** **INTENDED OUTCOME**
>
> An understanding of how accounting data are used to prepare a Trial Balance, evidenced by the ability to draw up a Trial Balance from balances on the accounts.

2.2 The Trial Balance

Note that this is only a LIST of all the balances at the end of each account—it is not an account.

2.2.1 Purpose of the Trial Balance

The Trial Balance is used:

1. To check the accuracy of the double-entry bookkeeping;
2. As a first stage in drawing up the final accounts.

2.2.2 Preparation of the Trial Balance

As two entries are always made for each single transaction, one debit and one credit, then all the debit entries must equal all the credit entries. Provided all the entries are correct, then all the debit balances at the end of the accounts should equal all the credit balances at the end of the accounts.

To check the accuracy of the double entries that have been made a Trial Balance is drawn up. This will be done regularly and also before the final accounts are prepared. All the balances at the end of each account are listed. There will be one column for all the debit balances and one column for all the credit balances. Each column will be added up and the total of the Debit column should equal the total of the Credit column.

On the Trial Balance

The DEBIT column will show EITHER assets OR expense accounts.
The CREDIT column will show EITHER liabilities OR income accounts.

EXAMPLE TRIAL BALANCE

On 31 October the bookkeeper extracts the following balances from the accounts of A. Mulligan Solicitor:

Profit costs	16,000
Capital account	15,000
Motor cars account	20,000
Office furniture account	5,000
Rent paid account	1,300
General expenses account	200
Council tax account	1,250
Postage account	100
Stationery account	80
Salaries account	1,600
Drawings account	800
Cash account	4,500 DR
Petty cash account	170
Loan account	4,000

The following trial balance is then prepared.

A. Mulligan Solicitor: Trial Balance as at 31 October

Name of account	DR	CR
Profit costs—income		16,000
Capital amount due to owner—liability		15,000
Motor cars—asset/real	20,000	
Office furniture—asset/real	5,000	
Rent—expense	1,300	
General expenses—expense	200	
Council tax—expense	1,250	
Postage—expense	100	
Stationery—expense	80	
Salaries—expense	1,600	
Drawings—amount taken out by owner—personal	800	
Cash—asset/real	4,500	
Petty cash—asset/real	170	
Loan—liability		4,000
Totals	35,000	35,000

You can see from the above example that the DEBIT balances show either ASSET accounts or EXPENSE accounts. The CREDIT balances show either LIABILITIES (for example, due to the owner of the business or creditors) or INCOME accounts.

2.2.3 Suspense accounts

If the debit and credit columns do not agree, even after checking all the entries, it may be necessary to adjust for the difference by opening a Suspense account until the difference can be found. Thus, if the credit balances exceed the debit balances by £100 a Suspense account can be opened with a debit balance of £100.

2.2.4 Errors not revealed by the Trial Balance

The fact that the total debit and total credit balances agree does not necessarily mean that the bookkeeper has not made any mistakes. There are some errors which will not be revealed by the trial balance, for example:

(a) Errors of entry—the same incorrect entry is made in both accounts used to record the transaction.

EXAMPLE

The firm buys a typewriter for £500. The bookkeeper inadvertently makes a debit entry in the office equipment account of £50 and a credit entry of £50 in the Cash account. The accounts used are correct, the amount shown is not.

(b) Compensating errors—the bookkeeper makes two separate errors which cancel each other out.

EXAMPLE

The bookkeeper incorrectly totals one account by £100 too much on the Credit side and another by £100 too much on the Debit side.

(c) Errors of omission—the bookkeeper leaves out both parts of the double entry from the accounts.

(d) Errors of commission—the bookkeeper makes the right entry but in the wrong account.

EXAMPLE

The firm buys office equipment costing £1,000. Instead of debiting the office equipment account with £1,000 the bookkeeper debits the stationery account.

(e) Errors of principle—the bookkeeper makes an entry in the wrong type of account.

EXAMPLE

The purchase of office equipment is shown in the general expenses account, ie a nominal instead of a real account. If this error remains undetected at the time the firm's final accounts are prepared the business expenses will be overstated in the Profit and Loss account and the value of the assets will be understated in the Balance Sheet.

2.3 Reminder of key points

1. The nature of the Trial Balance.

    It is just a list of the balances on all the accounts of the business at a given time.

2. Although intended as a check to make sure that the double entries made are correct, it does not necessarily pick up all errors made.

3. The Trial Balance will have a column showing all the debit balances on the accounts, and a column showing all the credit balances on the accounts:

    (a) the Debit column lists all asset accounts and expense accounts;

    (b) the Credit column lists all liability accounts and income accounts.

online resource centre

Now try the self-test exercises at the end of this chapter and remember to try the online multiple choice questions for Chapter 2 available through your tutor via the Online Resource Centre that accompanies this book. Then move on to final accounts in Chapter 3.

2.4 Exercises on double-entry bookkeeping and Trial Balance

1 **Allow 10 to 15 minutes for this exercise.**

The bookkeeper has extracted the following balances from the accounts of Hooper, a sole practitioner, on 30 September. From the balances you are asked to prepare a Trial Balance. State what each account is, for example an asset account, a personal account, or an income or expense account.

Salaries	1,000
Leasehold property	15,000
Capital	35,000
Drawings	2,000
Administration expenses	4,000
Motor cars	12,500
Cash account	500 DR

2 **Allow 15 to 20 minutes for this exercise.**

From the following information, extracted as at 30 June, prepare a trial balance for Tahir, a sole practitioner.

General expenses	200
Salaries	1,200
Drawings	4,000
Rent	1,250
Council tax	150
Electricity	800
Creditors	2,500
Office furniture	7,000
Bank overdraft	2,300
Loan account	9,000
Car	7,700
Capital	8,500

3 **Allow 20 to 25 minutes for this exercise.**

The bookkeeper has extracted the following balances from the accounts of Sally Jones, a sole practitioner, on 31 January. From the balances you are asked to prepare a Trial Balance.

Salaries	3,000
Office equipment	15,000
Freehold property	235,000
Capital	220,000
Drawings	13,200
Midshire Bank—loan account	20,000
Cash—office account	1,000 DR
Cash—client account	125,000 DR
Council tax	900
General expenses	1,400
Debtors	2,000
Creditors	1,500
Rent received	2,000
Profit costs	30,000
Due to clients	125,000
Bank interest paid	2,000

2.5 Suggested answers to exercises on Trial Balance

1 **Hooper: Trial Balance as at 30 September**

Name of account	DR	CR
Salaries—expense	1,000	
Leasehold property—asset	15,000	
Capital—personal		35,000
Drawings—personal	2,000	
Administration expenses—expense	4,000	
Motor cars—asset	12,500	
Cash account—asset/personal	500	
Totals	35,000	35,000

2 **Tahir: Trial Balance as at 30 June**

Name of account	DR	CR
General expenses	200	
Salaries	1,200	
Drawings	4,000	
Rent	1,250	
Council tax	150	
Electricity	800	
Creditors		2,500
Office furniture	7,000	
Bank overdraft		2,300
Loan account		9,000
Car	7,700	
Capital		8,500
Totals	22,300	22,300

3   **Sally Jones: Trial Balance as at 31 January**

Name of account	DR	CR
Salaries	3,000	
Office equipment	15,000	
Freehold property	235,000	
Capital		220,000
Drawings	13,200	
Loan account		20,000
Cash (office)	1,000	
Cash (client)*	125,000	
Council tax	900	
General expenses	1,400	
Debtors	2,000	
Creditors		1,500
Rent received		2,000
Profit costs		30,000
Due to clients*		125,000
Bank interest paid	2,000	
Totals	398,500	398,500

* NB The amount due to clients equals the amount held at the bank for clients.

2.6 Full exercise on double-entry bookkeeping and Trial Balance

Allow about 40 minutes to complete this exercise.

A Janik starts in practice as a solicitor on 1 January. She introduces £15,000 into the firm's bank account and a car worth £8,200. During the month of January the following transactions take place:

4 January	Pays rent of £1,000.
5 January	Pays salary £1,200 to secretary.
6 January	Buys a computer costing £650 on credit from Wylie Ltd.
22 January	Buys stationery for £80.
24 January	Pays instalment of £65 to Wylie Ltd.
25 January	Draws £1,600 for her own use.

Prepare accounts to record the above transactions, and prepare a Trial Balance as at 31 January.

2.7 Suggested answers to exercise on double-entry bookkeeping and Trial Balance

Cash account

Date	Details	DR (Receipts)	CR (Payments out)	Balance
1 Jan	Capital	15,000		15,000 DR
4 Jan	Rent		1,000	14,000 DR
5 Jan	Salaries		1,200	12,800 DR
22 Jan	Stationery		80	12,720 DR
24 Jan	Wylie Ltd		65	12,655 DR
25 Jan	Drawings		1,600	11,055 DR

Capital account

Date	Details	DR	CR	Balance
1 Jan	Cash		15,000	15,000 CR
	Car		8,200	23,200 CR

Car account

Date	Details	DR	CR	Balance
1 Jan	Capital	8,200		8,200 DR

Rent account

Date	Details	DR	CR	Balance
4 Jan	Cash	1,000		1,000 DR

Salaries account

Date	Details	DR	CR	Balance
5 Jan	Cash (secretary)	1,200		1,200 DR

Office equipment account—computer account

Date	Details	DR	CR	Balance
6 Jan	Wylie Ltd (computer)	650		650 DR

Wylie Ltd

Date	Details	DR	CR	Balance
6 Jan	Office equipment		650	650 CR
24 Jan	Cash	65		585 CR

Stationery account

Date	Details	DR	CR	Balance
22 Jan	Cash	80		80 DR

Drawings account

Date	Details	DR	CR	Balance
25 Jan	Cash	1,600		1,600 DR

A. Janik: Trial Balance as at 31 January

Name of account	DR	CR
Cash	11,055	
Capital		23,200
Car	8,200	
Rent	1,000	
Salaries	1,200	
Office equipment	650	
Wylie Ltd		585
Stationery	80	
Drawings	1,600	
Totals	23,785	23,785

Final accounts

3.1 Introduction

This chapter includes:

1. An explanation of the Profit and Loss account and the Balance Sheet;
2. Transferring the income and expense accounts to the Profit and Loss account;
3. The vertical form Profit and Loss account;
4. Definition of items in the Balance Sheet;
5. The vertical form Balance Sheet;
6. The solicitor and client money;
7. Reminder of key points;
8. Exercises on basic final accounts.

! **INTENDED OUTCOME**

An understanding of how accounting data are used to prepare the Profit and Loss account and the Balance Sheet, evidenced by the ability to draw up a simple Profit and Loss account and a Balance Sheet from a Trial Balance.

3.2 Final accounts

Basic final accounts consist of:

(1) the Profit and Loss account;
(2) the Balance Sheet.

Final accounts are usually prepared annually at the end of the firm's financial year.

Immediately before the final accounts are prepared a trial balance is drawn up listing the balances on the accounts. Each balance shown on the trial balance will EITHER be:

(a) transferred to the Profit and Loss account;

    OR

(b) shown on the Balance Sheet.

3.2.1 Profit and Loss account

Note that this is a double-entry account, ie it is part of the double-entry system.

Its function is to calculate the net profit or loss made by the practice during the financial year. It shows income less expenses.

3.2.2 Balance Sheet

The Balance Sheet is a statement of the firm's assets and liabilities on a given date, usually the last day of the financial year. It shows what the firm owns and what it owes.

The Balance Sheet is NOT an account and is therefore not part of the double-entry system. It is a list of the balances on the asset and liability accounts.

At any time the assets of a business should equal its liabilities. This is because each time the business acquires something of value it gives consideration.

EXAMPLE

Newman, a solicitor, commences in practice with £2,000 in cash which is placed in the firm's bank account. Immediately Newman has a Balance Sheet; it is:

Liability		**Asset**	
Capital	2,000	Cash at bank	2,000

Newman's practice is thus shown to own £2,000 cash (an asset) all of which is owed to Newman, the owner of the practice (a liability).

3.3 Closing the income and expense accounts

(a) Before preparing the Final accounts the Income and Expense accounts are closed by transferring the balance on each account to the Profit and Loss account.

(b) Expense accounts have DEBIT balances and so to transfer from an expense account to the Profit and Loss account, the bookkeeping entries are:

  (i) CREDIT the nominal expense account.

  (ii) DEBIT the Profit and Loss account.

All you have done is move the debit balance to the Profit and Loss account.

EXAMPLE

At the end of the year the firm's salaries account has a debit balance of £15,000. The balance is transferred to the Profit and Loss account on 31 December.

Salaries account

Date	Detail	DR	CR	Balance
	Balance			15,000 DR
31 Dec	Profit and Loss account: transfer		15,000	—

(c) Income accounts have CREDIT balances and so to transfer from an income account to the Profit and Loss account, the bookkeeping entries are:

   (i)   DEBIT the Income account.

   (ii) CREDIT the Profit and Loss account.

EXAMPLE

At the end of the year the firm's Profit Costs account has a credit balance of £300,000. On 31 December the balance is transferred to the Profit and Loss account.

Costs account

Date	Detail	DR	CR	Balance
	Balance			300,000 CR
31 Dec	Profit and Loss account: transfer	300,000		—

(d) These transfer entries close the Income and Expense accounts.

3.4 Presentation of final accounts

3.4.1 Vertical format: Profit and Loss account

There are two methods of presenting final accounts: the horizontal format and the vertical format. In this book, the vertical format will be used. A basic vertical format Profit and Loss account is shown in the following example:

Sally Jones: Profit and Loss account for the year ended 30 September 200—

INCOME		
Profit costs	300,000	
ADD ADDITIONAL INCOME		
Rent received	20,000	
TOTAL INCOME		320,000
LESS EXPENSES		
Salaries	60,000	
Rates	9,000	
General expenses	14,000	
Bank interest charged	2,000	85,000
NET PROFIT		235,000

This is only a very basic example of a Profit and Loss account. You will see in the next chapter that adjustments will be made to give a more accurate picture of the profit or loss.

3.4.2 Notes on the Profit and Loss account

(a) As shown in para 3.3 above at the end of the financial year the Income and Expense accounts are closed. The credit balances from the Income accounts are transferred to the Income part of the Profit and Loss account. The debit balances from the Expense accounts are transferred to the Expenses part of the Profit and Loss account.

(b) The balance left after deducting total Expenses from total Income is net profit (or loss). If a profit is made this is credited to the Capital account in the case of a sole owner. If a loss is made this is debited to the Capital account. For the position in the case of a partnership see Chapter 6.

(c) Note that drawings made by the owner are appropriations of profit, NOT business expenses. Thus the balance on the Drawings account is NOT transferred to the Profit and Loss account, but will be shown on the Balance Sheet.

3.5   The Balance Sheet

The Balance Sheet, unlike the Profit and Loss account, is not an account of double entry and so the balances on the asset and liability accounts are not transferred to the Balance Sheet. They are merely listed on the Balance Sheet. The asset and liability accounts are ongoing and will be kept open for as long as the asset is owned by the firm or for as long as the liability remains unsettled.

3.5.1   Definitions of items in the Balance Sheet

3.5.1.1   Assets

A business may own all kinds of assets, for example:

Premises—freehold or leasehold
Office furniture
Office equipment
Machinery
Stocks of goods
Cars
Work in progress (the value of work done but not yet billed)
Debtors (they will pay and convert the debts into cash)
Cash at the bank
Cash in hand (petty cash).
Note that assets are split into two groups:
FIXED ASSETS
CURRENT ASSETS.

Fixed assets
These are assets which are held long term, they are not part of the day-to-day working cycle. Examples would be:

Premises
Factory machinery
Office equipment
Office furniture
Library
Cars.

Current assets

Also known as circulating assets. These arise from the day-to-day trading or working cycle of the business; they represent cash, or are intended for conversion into cash, or they have a short life, for example stationery. They include: cash at the bank, petty cash, debtors, work in progress, and payments in advance (see later). If the firm is a trading one, then goods (stock) intended for resale will be a current asset.

Those assets which are cash, or assets which can be easily converted into cash, for example debtors, are known as liquid assets.

3.5.1.2 Liabilities

Money owed by the business in respect of loans to the business, for example capital, bank loans, mortgages, or money owed for goods or services supplied to the firm, ie creditors.

Like assets, liabilities can be broken down into groups:

(a) Capital;

(b) Long-term liabilities;

(c) Current liabilities.

3.5.1.3 Capital

This is the amount due to the owner of the business. It will include the value of any assets the owner introduced to the business. Any profit made will also belong to the owner, less any drawings that the owner has taken out over the year.

On the Balance Sheet this will be shown as follows:

For a sole owner

CAPITAL
PLUS PROFIT
LESS DRAWINGS
equals TOTAL DUE TO OWNER.

Note that the Drawings account is a personal account, showing that the proprietor is a debtor of the business. It is not an expense account and should never be shown on the Profit and Loss account. Think of it as a personal account which will reduce the amount due to the owner.

Long-term liabilities

Usually some formal loan from an individual, bank, or other financial institution, repayable over, or after, a stated number of years. These would include long-term bank loans (not usually overdrafts), private loans, mortgages.

Current liabilities

If a liability has to be settled in the short term, then it is a current liability. Current liabilities include: creditors, bank overdrafts, outstanding expenses.

3.5.2 The form of the Balance Sheet

The form more commonly used now is the vertical form. The Balance Sheet is in two parts.

The first part will show NET ASSETS.
The second part will show THE TOTAL DUE TO THE OWNER.
The two totals should be equal.

3.5.3   Listing assets and liabilities on the Balance Sheet

There is a common set order in listing the assets and liabilities on the balance sheet.

Assets

Fixed assets are shown first and then Current assets. The general rule is that you start at the top with the most permanent asset and work down to the least permanent. The top asset on the list will be the most difficult to turn into cash, the bottom will be the most liquid asset, for example cash itself. (The order of liquidity is reversed.)

For example, fixed assets may start with premises, which are usually the most permanent fixed asset belonging to the firm, and end with motor cars which are usually the least permanent fixed asset. Current assets start with work in progress which is the least liquid current asset, as it needs two stages to be converted into cash; first it would have to be billed, then the debtors will have to pay.

Liabilities

Current Liabilities are then deducted from the Current Assets, to give a figure known as Net Current Assets, or Working Capital, being that part of the capital invested in the business which is left to run the business after providing the Fixed Assets. This important figure is then added to the Fixed Assets.

Long-term Liabilities will then be deducted from this total, which gives the total Net Assets.

The total achieved should equal the Capital due to the owner of the business.

A summary of the vertical form Balance Sheet is as follows:

NAME OF BUSINESS

BALANCE SHEET as at 31 December 200—

FIXED ASSETS	
ADD	
NET CURRENT ASSETS	
(BEING CURRENT ASSETS	
LESS CURRENT LIABILITIES)	
	TOTAL
LESS LONG-TERM LIABILITIES	
	FINAL TOTAL, ie NET ASSETS
CAPITAL EMPLOYED	
CAPITAL	
ADD NET PROFIT	
	SUBTOTAL
LESS DRAWINGS	
	= FINAL TOTAL—AMOUNT DUE TO OWNER(S)

3.5.4   The solicitor and client money

When a solicitor handles money on behalf of his/her clients, it is the client's money and not the solicitor's. The Solicitors' Accounts Rules 1998 say that a solicitor must keep the records showing dealings with this money totally separate from the solicitor's own money. To do this the solicitor must have a separate bank account (or accounts) for clients' money called the Client Account. The money held in the client bank account(s) must always equal the amount that is shown due to clients.

This can be shown at the end of the Balance Sheet.

3.5.5 An example of vertical format: Balance Sheet

Sally Jones: Balance Sheet as at 30 September 200—

FIXED ASSETS			
Freehold property	235,000		
Office equipment	15,000		
			250,000
CURRENT ASSETS			
Debtors	20,000		
Cash (office bank account)	10,000	30,000	
LESS CURRENT LIABILITIES			
Creditors		15,000	
NET CURRENT ASSETS			15,000
			265,000
LESS LONG-TERM LIABILITIES			
Midshire Bank loan			40,000
TOTAL NET ASSETS			**225,000**
CAPITAL EMPLOYED			
Capital	200,000		
Add net profit	64,000		
		264,000	
Less drawings		39,000	
TOTAL DUE TO OWNER			**225,000**
CLIENT ACCOUNT			
Cash at bank client current account	300,000		
Deposit account	200,000	500,000	
Due to clients		500,000	

3.6 Reminder of key points

1. The nature of the Profit and Loss account and the Balance Sheet.

   The Profit and Loss account is part of the double-entry system—the balances from the Income and Expense accounts will be transferred to the Profit and Loss account. This will close the Income and Expense accounts for the year.

   Contrast the Balance Sheet—this is just a list of the assets and liabilities of the business on a particular date.

2. The vertical form Profit and Loss account.

   This will show all the income first and then list all the expenses.

   The total expenses are then deducted from the total income to give the net profit (or loss).

3. The vertical form Balance Sheet.

This is in two parts:

Part 1 NET ASSETS

which should equal

Part 2 AMOUNT DUE TO THE OWNER OR OWNERS.

The details are as follows:

Part 1

Fixed Assets total

then add Net Current Assets (being Current Assets less Current Liabilities)

less Long Term liabilities

Part 2

Capital due to the owner

plus net profit

less drawings (the amounts the owner has taken out of the business).

The total for Part 1 should equal the total for Part 2.

   Note: Solicitors must show the money they hold on behalf of clients separately from their own accounts. There will therefore be a separate section (usually at the end of the Balance Sheet) which will show the money held at the bank on behalf of clients, and will show the equal amount due to clients, this is in effect a mini Balance Sheet for client money.

4. Client money must be held and shown separately.

Now try the exercises on basic final accounts at the end of this chapter and try the online multiple choice questions available through your tutor via the Online Resource Centre that accompanies this book. Then move on to adjustments in the next chapter.

3.7 Exercises on basic final accounts

1 Allow 20 to 30 minutes for this.

From the following Trial Balance dated 31 December 200— draw up a Profit and Loss account and Balance Sheet for the owner, Mirza.

	DR	CR
Profit costs		82,500
General expenses	24,000	
Wages	22,000	
Drawings	34,000	
Cash at bank	5,250	
Freehold premises	150,000	
Capital		154,000
Creditors		2,950
Debtors	4,130	
Petty cash	70	
	239,450	239,450

2 Allow 30 to 35 minutes for this.

From the Trial Balance of North drawn up on 31 December 200— and set out below, draw up a Profit and Loss account and a Balance Sheet.

	DR	CR
Freehold premises	140,000	
Profit costs		62,920
Office furniture	5,000	
Car	15,000	
Interest received		1,450
Creditors		1,200
Cash at bank	2,500	
Petty cash	150	
Salaries	20,000	
Drawings	25,000	
Capital		110,000
General expenses	10,578	
Administrative expenses	4,642	
Debtors	1,700	
Long-term loan		49,000
	224,570	224,570

3 Allow about 45 minutes for this.

From the following balances extracted from the accounts of Alexandra on 30 September 200— prepare:

(a) a Trial Balance;

(b) a Profit and Loss account;

(c) a Balance Sheet.

Profit costs	130,000
Light and heat	3,600
Drawings	55,000
Creditors	4,969
Cash at bank (office)	19,230 DR
Cash at bank (client)	750,000 DR
Premises	220,000
Insurance commission received	3,000
Council tax	1,700
Salaries	48,000
Stationery	2,000
Capital	100,400
Bank loan	120,000
Debtors	7,960
Petty cash	879
Due to clients	750,000

3.8 Suggested answers to exercises on basic final accounts

1 **Mirza: Profit and Loss account for the year ending 31 December 200—**

INCOME		
Profit costs		82,500
ADD ADDITIONAL INCOME		—
LESS EXPENSES		82,500
General expenses	24,000	
Wages	22,000	
Total expenses		46,000
NET PROFIT		36,500

Mirza: Balance Sheet as at 31 December 200—

FIXED ASSETS			
Freehold premises			150,000
CURRENT ASSETS			
Debtors		4,130	
Cash at bank		5,250	
Petty cash		70	
		9,450	
LESS			
CURRENT LIABILITIES			
Creditors		2,950	
NET CURRENT ASSETS			6,500
			156,500
LESS LONG-TERM LIABILITIES			—
TOTAL NET ASSETS			**156,500**
CAPITAL EMPLOYED			
Capital		154,000	
ADD NET PROFIT		36,500	
		190,500	
LESS drawings		34,000	
TOTAL DUE TO OWNER			**156,500**

2 **North: Profit and Loss account for the year ending 31 December 200—**

INCOME		
Profit costs		62,920
ADD ADDITIONAL INCOME		
Interest received		1,450
		64,370
LESS EXPENSES		
General expenses	10,578	
Administrative expenses	4,642	
Salaries	20,000	
		35,220
NET PROFIT		29,150

North: Balance Sheet as at 31 December 200—

FIXED ASSETS

Freehold premises	140,000	
Office furniture	5,000	
Car	15,000	
		160,000
CURRENT ASSETS		
Debtors	1,700	
Cash at bank	2,500	
Petty cash	150	
	4,350	
LESS CURRENT LIABILITIES		
Creditors	1,200	
NET CURRENT ASSETS		3,150
		163,150
LESS LONG-TERM LIABILITIES		
Long-term loan		49,000
TOTAL NET ASSETS		**114,150**
CAPITAL EMPLOYED		
Capital	110,000	
ADD NET PROFIT	29,150	
		139,150
LESS drawings		25,000
TOTAL DUE TO OWNER		**114,150**

3 **Alexandra: Trial Balance as at 30 September 200—**

Name of account	DR	CR
Profit costs		130,000
Light and heat	3,600	
Drawings	55,000	
Creditors		4,969
Cash at bank (office)	19,230	
Cash at bank (client)	750,000	
Premises	220,000	
Insurance commission received		3,000
Council tax	1,700	
Salaries	48,000	
Stationery	2,000	
Capital		100,400
Bank loan		120,000
Debtors	7,960	
Petty cash	879	
Due to clients		750,000
Totals	1,108,369	1,108,369

Alexandra: Profit and Loss account for the year ended 30 September 200—

INCOME

Profit costs	130,000	
ADD ADDITIONAL INCOME		
Insurance commission received	3,000	133,000

LESS EXPENSES			
Light and heat		3,600	
Council tax		1,700	
Salaries		48,000	
Stationery		2,000	55,300
NET PROFIT			77,700

Alexandra: Balance Sheet as at 30 September 200—

FIXED ASSETS			
Premises			220,000
CURRENT ASSETS			
Debtors	7,960		
Cash (office bank account)	19,230		
Petty cash	879		
		28,069	
LESS CURRENT LIABILITIES			
Creditors		4,969	
NET CURRENT ASSETS			23,100
			243,100
LESS LONG-TERM LIABILITIES			
Bank loan			120,000
TOTAL NET ASSETS			**123,100**
CAPITAL EMPLOYED			
Capital	100,400		
ADD NET PROFIT	77,700		
		178,100	
LESS drawings		55,000	
TOTAL DUE TO OWNER			**123,100**
CLIENT ACCOUNT			
Client bank balance	750,000		
LESS due to clients	750,000		

Adjustments to final accounts

4.1 Introduction

This chapter includes:

1. The need for adjustments;
2. Outstanding expenses;
3. Payments in advance;
4. Closing stock;
5. Work in progress;
6. Summary of the adjustments—effect on the Profit and Loss account and the Balance Sheet;
7. Reminder of key points;
8. Exercises on adjustments and final accounts.

! INTENDED OUTCOME

An understanding of the need for adjustments generally.
An appreciation that adjustments will affect both the Profit and Loss account and the Balance Sheet and that they will be carried forward to the next accounting year, evidenced by the ability to use entries on the Trial Balance together with information supplied in respect of the above adjustments to draw up a Profit and Loss account and a Balance Sheet.

4.2 The need for adjustments

The balances on the income and expenses accounts do not show all the income earned, or all the expenses actually incurred during the year. Adjustments are made to make sure that:

1. Income includes the value of work done during the current year, even though it has not yet been billed;
2. Expenses include those which have been incurred in the current year, even though they have not yet been billed or paid;
3. Expenses do not include those which have been paid in the current year but which relate to the next year.

In this chapter we will look at the following adjustments:

(a) Outstanding expenses;
(b) Payments in advance;

(c) Closing stock;

(d) Work in progress.

Note that for all adjustments two entries are made on the same account; the first entry will affect the Profit and Loss account and the second will affect the Balance Sheet.

4.3 Outstanding expenses adjustment

There are expenses which have been incurred during the current financial year but where payment will not be made until the next financial year; for example, gas, electricity, and telephone charges.

At the end of the financial year, a provision is made for this. If a bill has not already been received the provision will be an estimate. The relevant expense will be INCREASED by the provision to give the true expense for the year.

Thus the adjustment is made on the relevant expense account by:

1. **DEBITING** the expense for the current year (increases the expense).

2. **CREDITING** the expense for the next year (reduces next year's expense).

These entries will therefore shift the expense from the next year to the current year.

The effect on the Profit and Loss account and the Balance Sheet for the current year will be:

1. **Profit and Loss account—increase** expenses;

2. **Balance Sheet**—show the outstanding expense as a **Current Liability.**

EXAMPLE

A solicitor prepares final accounts on 31 October. At that date the telephone account has a debit balance of £600. This represents cash paid for telephone charges over the year. It is decided to make a provision of £200 for telephone charges incurred but not yet paid. The provision carried down (1) will be debited to the telephone account.

Telephone account

Date	Details	DR	CR	Balance
	Balance			600 DR
31 Oct	Provision—outstanding expense c/d(1)	200		800 DR

The balance on the expense account, including the provision made at the end of the financial year, is then transferred to the Profit and Loss account and the nominal expense account is closed.

Continuing the example:

Telephone account

Date	Details	DR	CR	Balance
	Balance			600 DR
31 Oct	Provision—outstanding expense c/d(1)	200		800 DR
	Profit and Loss account: transfer		800	—

The provision made is brought down as a credit entry (2) in the expense account for the start of the next financial year. This provision will be set off against payment of the bill in the next financial year. Continuing the example, on 10 November the bill of £200 is paid.

Telephone account

Date	Details	DR	CR	Balance
31 Oct	Balance			600 DR
	Provision—outstanding expense c/d(1)	200		800 DR
	Profit and Loss account: transfer		800	—
1 Nov	Provision—outstanding expense brought down b/d(2)		200	200 CR
10 Nov	Cash—bill paid	200		—

Profit and Loss account for the year ended 31 October

EXPENSES

Telephones	600
Add outstanding expense	200
	800

The provision brought down for outstanding expenses will be shown on the Balance Sheet as a current liability because on the date on which the Balance Sheet is prepared, it is expenditure incurred but not yet paid.

Continuing the example:

Balance Sheet as at 31 October

FIXED ASSETS		XX
CURRENT ASSETS	XX	
LESS CURRENT LIABILITIES		
Outstanding expenses—telephone	200	
		XX
		XX
CAPITAL EMPLOYED		XX

4.4 Payment in advance

If a payment is made in the current financial year for a service which will not be used until the next financial year, for example, council tax, then, at the end of the financial year, the appropriate expense account is credited with the amount paid in advance. This has the effect of **reducing** the expenses and therefore increasing the profit. The corresponding debit entry is made in the same account at the start of the next financial year. This time the double entry shifts the expense out of the current year into the next year.

The adjustment is made on the relevant expense account by:

1. CREDITING the expense for the current year (reducing expenses);
2. DEBITING the expense for the next year (increasing next year's expenses).

The effect on the Profit and Loss account and the Balance Sheet for the current year will be:

1. **Profit and Loss account—reduce** expenses.
2. **Balance Sheet**—show as a **Current Asset.**

EXAMPLE

A solicitor pays council tax of £4,000 per annum by two equal instalments, in advance, on 31 March and 30 September each year. Final accounts are prepared on 31 December each year. Thus a payment in advance of £1,000 for council tax is being made because the £2,000 paid on 30 September is for council tax from 1 October to 31 March.

Council tax account

Date	Details	DR	CR	Balance
31 Mar	Cash	2,000		2,000 DR
30 Sept	Cash	2,000		4,000 DR
31 Dec	Payment in advance c/d(1)		1,000	3,000 DR

The balance on the expense account is transferred to the Profit and Loss account at the end of the year. Continuing the example:

Council tax account

Date	Details	DR	CR	Balance
31 Mar	Cash	2,000		2,000 DR
30 Sept	Cash	2,000		4,000 DR
31 Dec	Payment in advance c/d(1)		1,000	3,000 DR
	Profit and Loss account: transfer		3,000	—

Note that the firm is charging to the Profit and Loss account as a business expense only the amount incurred on council tax from 1 January to 31 December, ie in the current financial year.

The payment in advance is brought down as a debit entry on the expense account at the start of the next financial year, which is when the service that has been paid for in the current financial year will be used. Continuing the example:

Council tax account

Date	Details	DR	CR	Balance
31 Mar	Cash	2,000		2,000 DR
30 Sept	Cash	2,000		4,000 DR
31 Dec	Payment in advance c/d(1)		1,000	3,000 DR
	Profit and Loss account: transfer		3,000	—
1 Jan	Payment in advance b/d(2)	1,000		1,000 DR

Profit and Loss account for the year ending 31 December

EXPENSES

Council tax	4,000
Less payment in advance	1,000
	3,000

The payment in advance is shown on the Balance Sheet as a current asset. In theory the person to whom the payment has been made is a debtor of the firm for the service which is to be supplied. Continuing the example:

Balance Sheet as at 31 December

FIXED ASSETS			XX
CURRENT ASSETS			
Payments in advance			
Council tax	1,000		
		XX	
LESS CURRENT LIABILITIES			
		XX	
		XX	
CAPITAL EMPLOYED			
		XX	

4.5 Closing stock

Where a business has paid for items used over the year, for example stationery or pens, then only the cost of the items actually used during the year should be shown as an expense. Thus the value of any items left will be DEDUCTED from the relevant expense account, to give the true expense.

The adjustment is made on the relevant expense account by:

CREDITING the expense for the current year (thus reducing expenses).
DEBITING the expense for the next year (increasing next year's expenses).

Again this shifts the expense from the current year to the next year.
The effect on the Profit and Loss account and the Balance Sheet will be:

1. Profit and Loss account—**reduce** expenses.

2. Balance Sheet—show as a **Current Asset.**

EXAMPLE
During the year the firm pays the following amounts for stationery:

31 March	£40
16 October	£25
8 December	£35
Total	£100

Final accounts are prepared on 31 December. On 31 December the firm has a stock of stationery paid for but unused, valued at £30. The firm has therefore only used £70 worth of stationery.

Stationery account

Date	Details	DR	CR	Balance
31 Mar	Cash	40		40 DR
16 Oct	Cash	25		65 DR
8 Dec	Cash	35		100 DR
31 Dec	Closing stock c/d(1)		30	70 DR

At the end of the year the nominal expense account is closed and the balance on it is transferred to the Profit and Loss account. Continuing the example:

Stationery account

Date	Details	DR	CR	Balance
31 Mar	Cash	40		40 DR
16 Oct	Cash	25		65 DR
8 Dec	Cash	35		100 DR
31 Dec	Closing stock c/d(1)		30	70 DR
	Profit and Loss account: transfer balance		70	—

Thus only the cost of stationery actually used during the current financial year is transferred to the Profit and Loss account as a business expense.

The value of the closing stock is brought down as a debit entry in the expense account at the start of the next financial year.

Continuing the example:

Stationery account

Date	Details	DR	CR	Balance
31 Mar	Cash	40		40 DR
16 Oct	Cash	25		65 DR
8 Dec	Cash	35		100 DR
31 Dec	Closing stock c/d(1)		30	70 DR
	Profit and Loss account: transfer		70	—
1 Jan	Opening stock b/d(2)	30		30 DR

Note from the above account that at the start of the next financial year the closing stock from the previous year will be the opening stock.

Profit and Loss account for the year ending 31 December

EXPENSES
Stationery   100
Less closing stock   30
                                                            70

On the Balance Sheet the value of the closing stock is shown as a current asset.

Continuing the example:

Balance Sheet as at 31 December

FIXED ASSETS		XX
CURRENT ASSETS		
(Closing) Stock of		
Stationery	30	
		XX
LESS CURRENT LIABILITIES		
		XX
		XX
CAPITAL EMPLOYED		
		XX

4.6 Work in progress

For solicitors, the main source of income is from bills delivered in respect of work done for clients. The Profit Costs account will record all of the billed work. However, at the end of the year the firm will have done work for clients which has not yet been billed. As this work has been carried out in the current year it can be valued and shown as income earned during the year. This will be added to the current year's income and deducted from the next year's income.

The adjustment will be made to the Profit Costs account by:

CREDITING the account for the current year (increasing income);

DEBITING the account for the next year (reducing next year's income).

The effect on the Profit and Loss account and the Balance Sheet will be as follows:

Profit and Loss account;

INCREASE the Profit Costs by the Work in Progress for the end of the year.

Balance Sheet;

Show the Work in Progress at the end of the year as a CURRENT ASSET.

Year 2

As shown above, the Work in Progress brought forward reduces the Profit Costs income.

Thus the **Profit and Loss account for year 2** would show:

Profit Costs

LESS Work in Progress at the START of the year;

ADD Work in Progress at the END of the year.

This gives the VALUE OF WORK DONE during the year.

The **Balance Sheet** would show:

the Work in Progress at the END of the year as a CURRENT ASSET.

EXAMPLE YEAR 1

The firm prepares its final accounts on 31 December each year. On 31 December the Profit Costs account has a credit balance of £30,000. Work in Progress is valued at £5,000.

Profit Costs account

Date	Details	DR	CR	Balance
31 Dec	Balance			30,000 CR
	Closing Work in Progress c/d(1)		5,000	35,000 CR

At the end of the financial year the Profit Costs account is closed and the balance on the account is transferred to the Profit and Loss account. At the start of the new financial year the closing Work in Progress is brought down on the DR side as opening Work in Progress.

Continuing the example:

Profit Costs account

Date	Details	DR	CR	Balance
31 Dec	Balance			30,000 CR
	Closing Work in Progress c/d(1)		5,000	35,000 CR
	Profit and Loss account: transfer	35,000		—
1 Jan	Opening Work in Progress b/d(2)	5,000		5,000 DR

The value of the closing Work in Progress is shown on the Balance Sheet as a current asset.

Continuing the example:

Balance Sheet as at 31 December

FIXED ASSETS		XX
CURRENT ASSETS		
Work in Progress at the end of year	5,000	
	XX	
LESS CURRENT LIABILITIES		
	XX	
	XX	
CAPITAL EMPLOYED		
	XX	

Year 2

In the following year the Profit Costs account begins with the debit entry for opening Work in Progress. This reduces the income from profit costs in that year (as the profit costs figure includes bills delivered which include costs for work carried out in the previous year). The movement on the Profit Costs account will be shown in the Profit and Loss account, which will give the value of work done during the year.

EXAMPLE

Work in Progress at start of Year 2	£5,000	
Profit Costs for the year	£45,000	
Work in Progress at end of Year 2	£8,000	

Profit and Loss account for the year

INCOME

Profit Costs (based on bills delivered)	45,000	
ADD closing Work in Progress at 31 Dec	8,000	53,000
LESS opening Work in Progress at 1 Jan		5,000
VALUE OF WORK DONE		
		48,000

Note: only the Work in Progress figure at the end of the year is shown in the Balance Sheet.

Note: you should show each subtotal after adding the closing Work in Progress and then deducting the opening Work in Progress. Any additional income, for example rent received, interest received, insurance commission received, should be shown after the Work in Progress adjustments have been made.

4.6.1 Worked example on closing Work in Progress adjustment

A firm of solicitors prepares its final accounts on 30 June each year. The firm's Profit Costs account shows an opening debit balance on 1 July 2009 of £35,000. During the year ending 30 June 2010, bills have been delivered to clients totalling £175,000. The firm estimates that the value of work done during the year ending 30 June 2010, in respect of which bills have not yet been delivered, is £45,000. The accounts to record the above will appear as follows:

Profit Costs account

Date	Details	DR	CR	Balance
2009				
1 July	Opening Work in Progress b/d	35,000		35,000 DR
2010				
30 June	Sundry Profit Costs		175,000	140,000 CR
	Closing Work in Progress c/d(1)		45,000	185,000 CR
	Profit and Loss account: transfer	185,000		—
1 July 2010	Opening Work in Progress b/d(2)	45,000		45,000 DR

Profit and Loss account for the year ended 30 June 2010

INCOME	
Profit costs	175,000
ADD Closing Work in Progress	45,000
	220,000
LESS Opening Work in Progress	35,000
VALUE OF WORK DONE	185,000

Note: by convention the detailed movement on the Profit Costs account is shown on the Profit and Loss account.

Balance Sheet as at 30 June 2010

FIXED ASSETS		XX
CURRENT ASSETS		
Work in Progress (at end of year)	45,000	
	XX	

4.7 Summary of adjustments—effect on Profit and Loss account and the Balance Sheet

Outstanding expenses:

Profit and Loss account;

INCREASE expenses.

Balance Sheet;

CURRENT LIABILITY.

Payments in advance:

Profit and Loss account;

REDUCE expenses.

Balance Sheet;

CURRENT ASSET.

Closing stock:

Profit and Loss account;

REDUCE expenses.

Balance Sheet;

CURRENT ASSET.

Work in Progress:

Profit and Loss account;

DEDUCT Work in Progress at the START of the year from Profit Costs;

ADD Work in Progress at the END of the year to Profit Costs.

Balance Sheet;

Show Work in Progress at the END of the year as a CURRENT ASSET.

4.8 Reminder of key points

1. The reasons for adjustments:

   to give a true and fair view of the business—achieved by making sure that:

   (a) all income earned during the current year is shown, even though it may not have been billed;

   (b) expenses are adjusted to include those incurred in the current year even though not paid, and to take out those expenses which have been paid in advance for the next year.

2. Note that the adjustments made will affect both the Profit and Loss account and the Balance Sheet, and they will also be carried forward to the next accounting period;

3. Note the effect of each adjustment in this chapter on the Profit and Loss account and the Balance Sheet—see the summary in para 4.7 above.

online resource centre Now try the self-test exercises at the end of this chapter and the online multiple choice questions available through your tutor via the Online Resource Centre that accompanies this book, before moving on to the further adjustments in the next chapter.

4.9 Exercises on adjustments and final accounts

1 Allow 5 to 10 minutes.

On 31 October 200— the firm's light and heat account has a debit balance of £5,000. The firm estimates that a further £250 worth of gas has been used.

Show the state of the light and heat account on 1 November 200— and the entries which you would make in the final accounts which are prepared on 31 October 200—.

2 Allow 10 to 15 minutes.

The firm pays council tax of £1,000 on 1 April and on 1 October 2009 for the following six months. The payment in advance is therefore £500. The firm's final accounts are prepared on 31 December each year.

Show the rates account at 1 January 2010 and the entries you would make in the final accounts for the year ended 31 December 2009.

3 Allow about 10 minutes.

Final accounts are prepared on 30 June each year. On 30 June 2009 the stationery account shows a debit balance of £800. On checking the stationery it is discovered that there is £200 worth left.

Show the stationery account at 1 July 2009 and the entries in the final accounts for the year ended 30 June 2009.

4 Allow about 20 minutes.

At the end of its financial year, 31 December 2008, Grace & Co. had profit costs of £180,000 and its work in progress was valued at £18,000. At the end of its second year, 31 December 2009, the firm had delivered bills totalling £220,000 and its work in progress was valued at £25,000.

Show the Profit Costs account and also the final accounts for the year ended 31 December 2009.

5 Allow about 45 minutes.

The Trial Balance of Khan, a solicitor, is set out below.

	31 December 200—	
	DR	CR
Capital		65,000
Office equipment	6,330	
Car	14,900	
Leasehold property	95,000	
General expenses	38,290	

Rent paid	4,800	
Salaries	27,000	
Mortgage		45,000
Drawings	30,570	
Cash at bank office account	2,210	
Cash at bank client account	67,900	
Amount due to clients		67,900
Creditors		3,650
Amount due from clients (debtors)	2,000	
Profit costs		110,000
Work in Progress at 1 Jan 200—	5,000	
Commission received		2,450
	294,000	294,000

Work in Progress as at 31 December 200— is £6,000. Payments in advance are £1,200, and outstanding expenses are £540. Draw up the Profit and Loss account for the year ending 31 December 200— and the Balance Sheet as at that date.

4.10 Suggested answers to exercises on adjustments and final accounts

1 Light and heat account

Date	Details	DR	CR	Balance
200—				
31 Oct	Balance			5,000 DR
	Provision—outstanding expense: gas c/d	250		5,250 DR
	Profit and Loss: transfer		5,250	—
1 Nov	Provision—outstanding expense: gas b/d		250	250 CR

Profit and Loss account for the year ended 31 October 200—

INCOME		XX
LESS EXPENSES		
Light and heat	5,000	
Add outstanding expense	250	5,250

Balance Sheet as at 31 October 200—

FIXED ASSETS		XX
CURRENT ASSETS		XX
LESS CURRENT LIABILITIES		
Outstanding expense for light and heat	250	
		XX
		XX
CAPITAL EMPLOYED		
		XX

2 Council tax account

Date	Details	DR	CR	Balance
2009				
1 Apr	Cash	1,000		1,000 DR
1 Oct	Cash	1,000		2,000 DR
31 Dec	Payment in advance c/d		500	1,500 DR
	Profit and Loss: transfer		1,500	—
2010				
1 Jan	Payment in advance b/d	500		500 DR

Profit and Loss account for the year ended 31 December 2009

INCOME			XX
LESS EXPENSES			
Council tax	2,000		
Less paid in advance	500	1,500	

Balance Sheet as at 31 December 2009

FIXED ASSETS			XX
CURRENT ASSETS			
Council tax paid in advance	500		
		XX	
LESS CURRENT LIABILITIES			
		XX	
		XX	
CAPITAL EMPLOYED			
		XX	

3 Stationery account

Date	Details	DR	CR	Balance
2009				
30 June	Balance			800 DR
	Closing stock c/d		200	600 DR
	Profit and Loss: transfer		600	—
1 July	Opening stock b/d	200		200 DR

Profit and Loss account for the year ended 30 June 2009

INCOME			XX
LESS EXPENSES			
Stationery	800		
Less closing stock	200	600	

Balance Sheet as at 30 June 2009

FIXED ASSETS		XX
CURRENT ASSETS		
Closing stock of stationery	200	
		XX

4 Profit Costs account

Date	Details	DR	CR	Balance
2008				
31 Dec	Balance (bills delivered)			180,000 CR
	Closing Work in Progress c/d		18,000	198,000 CR
	Profit and Loss: transfer	198,000		—
2009				
1 Jan	Opening Work in Progress b/d	18,000		18,000 DR
31 Dec	Profit Costs		220,000	202,000 CR
	Closing Work in Progress c/d		25,000	227,000 CR
	Profit and Loss: transfer	227,000		—
2010				
1 Jan	Opening Work in Progress b/d	25,000		25,000 DR

Grace & Co.: Profit and Loss account for the year ended 31 December 2009

INCOME

Profit Costs	220,000	
ADD closing Work in Progress	25,000	
	245,000	
LESS opening Work in Progress	18,000	227,000
LESS EXPENSES		XX

Grace & Co.: Balance Sheet as at 31 December 2009

FIXED ASSETS		XX
CURRENT ASSETS		
Work in Progress	25,000	
		XX

5 Khan Profit and Loss account for the year ending 31 December 200—

INCOME

Profit costs		110,000
ADD Work in Progress at end of year		6,000
		116,000
LESS		
Work in Progress at start of year		5,000
VALUE OF WORK DONE		111,000
ADD ADDITIONAL INCOME		
Commission received		2,450
TOTAL INCOME		113,450
LESS EXPENSES		
General expenses	38,290	
Salaries	27,000	
Rent paid	4,800	
Outstanding expenses	540	
	70,630	
LESS payments in advance	1,200	
Total expenses		69,430
NET PROFIT		44,020

Khan: Balance Sheet as at 31 December 200—

FIXED ASSETS

Leasehold premises	95,000		
Office equipment	6,330		
Car	14,900		
			116,230

CURRENT ASSETS

Work in Progress	6,000		
Debtors (due from clients)	2,000		
Cash at bank	2,210		
Payment in advance	1,200		
		11,410	

LESS CURRENT LIABILITIES

Creditors	3,650		
Outstanding expenses	540		
		4,190	
NET CURRENT ASSETS			7,220
			123,450

LESS LONG-TERM LIABILITIES

Mortgage			45,000
TOTAL NET ASSETS			78,450

CAPITAL EMPLOYED

Capital	65,000		
ADD net profit	44,020		
		109,020	
LESS drawings		30,570	
TOTAL DUE TO OWNER			78,450

CLIENT ACCOUNT

Cash at bank client account		67,900	
Amount due to clients		67,900	

5

Further adjustments to final accounts

5.1 Introduction

This chapter includes:

1. Bad debts and provision for doubtful debts;
2. Depreciation and sale of assets;
3. Summary of the adjustments;
4. Reminder of key points;
5. Exercises on adjustments and final accounts.

> **!** **INTENDED OUTCOME**
>
> An understanding of bad debts and the need to make provision for doubtful debts and how these affect the Profit and Loss account and the Balance Sheet, together with an understanding of depreciation and how this affects the Profit and Loss account and the Balance Sheet, evidenced by the ability to use entries on the Trial Balance together with information supplied in respect of the above adjustments to draw up a Profit and Loss account and a Balance Sheet.

5.2 Bad debts and doubtful debts adjustments

5.2.1 Writing off bad debts

Debts owed to a business are assets. When the debtors pay, the debts will be converted into cash. However, some debtors will never pay and so the debts will be worthless. If a business knows that a particular debtor is never going to pay, for example the debtor has disappeared or is bankrupt, then the business will write off the bad debt, showing that it is worthless. The firm has lost that debt and it will be recorded as an expense.

To write off a bad debt:

1. CREDIT the debtor's account (this wipes out the debt).
2. DEBIT the Bad Debts account (this shows the loss/expense).

The effect on the Profit and Loss account and the Balance Sheet will be as follows:

1. Profit and Loss account—show the Bad Debts as an EXPENSE.

2. Balance Sheet—if the Trial Balance shows a figure for Bad Debts, then the debtor's figure will already have been reduced by the bad debts written off, so just use the debtor's figure shown.

    Note: if, however, you are asked to write off a bad debt AFTER the Trial Balance has been drawn up, then you would have to reduce the debtor's figure for the Balance Sheet, as well as showing the Bad Debt as an expense on the Profit and Loss account above.

EXAMPLE

A bill delivered to Jack for £235 (including £35 VAT) has not been paid. At the end of the financial year 31 October the debt was written off.

Jack's account

Date	Details	DR	CR	Balance
	Balance: amount due			235 DR
31 Oct	Bad debt: written off		235	—

Bad Debts account

Date	Details	DR	CR	Balance
31 Oct	Jack: debt written off	235		235 DR

Note that VAT relief for bad debts is dealt with in Chapter 13, para 13.7.

5.2.2 Recovery of a debt that has been written off

When a debt that has previously been written off as a bad debt is recovered, the following entries will be made in the account:

(a) DEBIT Cash account.

(b) CREDIT Bad Debts account.

Continuing the example, assume that in the year after the debt has been written off, Jack pays his bill.

Cash account

Date	Details	DR	CR	Balance
15 Jan	Bad debts (recovered from Jack)	235		235 DR

Bad Debts account

Date	Details	DR	CR	Balance
15 Jan	Cash (debt recovered from Jack)		235	235 CR

The credit entry on the Bad Debts account will reduce the expense of bad debts. No entry is made in Jack's account, although a note that he has paid could be useful.

5.2.3   Making a provision for doubtful debts

As well as writing off bad debts a business will also make provision for the debts that are unlikely to be paid. This provision is an estimated loss.

The provision is usually calculated as a percentage of the debtors figure, after bad debts have been written off.

1. Effect on Profit and Loss account—INCREASE expenses by this year's provision for doubtful debts.
2. Effect on Balance Sheet—REDUCE the debtors figure by this year's provision for doubtful debts.

The entries will be:

1. DEBIT the Bad Debts account with the provision at the end of the current financial year.
2. CREDIT the Bad Debts account with the provision at the start of the next financial year.

Note that the provision brought forward to the next year will reduce the expense of bad debts for the next year.

EXAMPLE

A solicitor prepares final accounts on 31 October. On that date the Bad Debts account has a debit balance of £1,500 in respect of bad debts written off during the year. Total debts owed to the practice amount to £20,000 and the solicitor decides to make a provision for doubtful debts of 5% of the total.

Bad Debts account

Date	Details	DR	CR	Balance
	Balance—bad debts previously written off			1,500 DR
31 Oct	Provision: doubtful debts c/d		1,000	2,500 DR

5.2.4   Effect of bad debts on final accounts

At the end of the financial year the Bad Debts account will be closed and the balance will be transferred to the Profit and Loss account. If, at the end of the financial year, the Bad Debts account has a debit balance this will be transferred to the Profit and Loss account as an expense by making the following entries in the accounts:

(a) CREDIT the Bad Debts account.

(b) DEBIT the Profit and Loss account.

Continuing the example above:

Bad Debts account

Date	Details	DR	CR	Balance
	Balance			1,500 DR
31 Oct	Provision: doubtful debts c/d	1,000		2,500 DR
	Profit and Loss account: transfer		2,500	—

Profit and Loss account for the year ended 31 October 200—

INCOME   —

Less EXPENSES
Bad debts   1,500
Provision for doubtful debts   1,000

                                                                        2,500

Note that at the start of the next financial year the provision will be carried down as a credit entry on the Bad Debts account. Continuing the example:

Bad Debts account

Date	Details	DR	CR	Balance
200—	Balance			1,500 DR
31 Oct	Provision: doubtful debts c/d	1,000		2,500 DR
	Profit and Loss account: transfer		2,500	—
1 Nov	Provision: doubtful debts b/d		1,000	1,000 CR

The provision for doubtful debts brought down at the end of the financial year is shown as a deduction from the debtors figure on the current assets part of the Balance Sheet. Continuing the example:

Balance Sheet as at 31 October 200—

FIXED ASSETS   XX
CURRENT ASSETS
Debtors   20,000
Less: Provision for doubtful debts   1,000
                                                            19,000
                                                            XX

Note: if the Bad Debts account has a credit balance at the end of the year because the firm has overestimated its provision for doubtful debts in previous years, then the credit balance is transferred to the Profit and Loss account as income by making the following entries:

(a) DEBIT Bad Debts account.
(b) CREDIT Profit and Loss account.

FULL EXAMPLE—BAD DEBTS AND PROVISION FOR DOUBTFUL DEBTS

At the start of the financial year, 1 January 200—, a provision of £3,000 is brought down from the previous year. During the year bad debts of £5,000 are written off. At the end of the financial year, 31 December 200—, total debtors amount to £40,000. It is decided to make a provision for doubtful debts of 10%.

Bad Debts account

Date	Details	DR	CR	Balance
200—				
1 Jan	Last year's provision b/d		3,000	3,000 CR
	Bad debts written off	5,000		2,000 DR
31 Dec	This year's provision c/d	4,000		6,000 DR
	Profit and Loss account:			
	transfer		6,000	—

Profit and Loss account for the year ended 31 December 200—

EXPENSES		
Bad debts	5,000	
ADD this year's provision	4,000	
	9,000	
LESS last year's provision	3,000	6,000

Balance sheet as at 31 December 200—

FIXED ASSETS			XX
CURRENT ASSETS			
Debtors	40,000		
Less this year's provision	4,000	36,000	

Only one method of providing for bad debts and doubtful debts has been shown in this book. There are other, equally acceptable methods in use.

5.3 Depreciation

5.3.1 Introduction

The asset accounts show the cost price of the assets. Over time the cost price of an asset is unlikely to be its true value, as many assets go down in value, through wear and tear or obsolescence. Instead of waiting until the asset is sold to find out the loss, the business can spread the fall in value over time, showing an expense of depreciation each year.

Calculating depreciation

There are different ways of doing this: the simplest is known as the straight-line method. Depreciation can be calculated as a percentage of the cost price each year. For example, if a car cost £20,000, the business could calculate depreciation at 20% each year, being £4,000 a year.

Alternatively the formula for calculating depreciation by the straight-line method is:

$$\frac{\text{Cost of asset–value of asset at end of its life}}{\text{life expectancy of asset}}$$

EXAMPLE

A firm buys a car for £5,500. The car has an estimated life of five years, at the end of which its sale value will be £500. The annual provision for depreciation using the straight-line method of calculating depreciation will be:

$$\frac{£5,500 - £500}{5} = £1,000 \text{ loss/depreciation per year}$$

A separate depreciation account should be opened for each class of fixed assets to be depreciated. Using the straight-line method, depreciation may be calculated as a percentage of the cost price of the asset.

EXAMPLE

A firm buys a car for £16,000. Depreciation is calculated at 15% per annum on the cost price. Thus each year the depreciation will be £2,400.

Note: a further alternative method is to depreciate on the reducing balance of the asset rather than the cost price, but you should depreciate using the straight-line method above.

5.3.2 Recording depreciation in the accounts

To record depreciation in the accounts at the end of the financial year, the following entries are made:

(a) CREDIT the appropriate accumulated depreciation account with depreciation charged on the fixed asset.

(b) DEBIT the Profit and Loss account with the current year's depreciation, as an expense.

Note that if an asset is bought part-way through the year, it is usual to depreciate it for a full year. Do this unless you are told otherwise.

EXAMPLE

The firm buys a car for £6,000 in March 200—. Depreciation on the car is 20% a year.
The firm's financial year ends on 31 December 200—.

Accumulated depreciation (Cars) account

Date	Details	DR	CR	Balance
200—				
31 Dec	Profit and Loss	1,200		1,200 CR

The accumulated depreciation is shown on the Balance Sheet as a deduction from the cost price of the asset. Continuing the example:

Profit and Loss account for year ended 31 December 200—

INCOME

—

LESS EXPENDITURE

Depreciation: motor cars   1,200

Balance Sheet as at 31 December 200—

FIXED ASSETS

Motor cars at cost   6,000

LESS accumulated depreciation   1,200

                                                                                      4,800

In year 2 the accounts would be shown as follows:

Accumulated depreciation (Cars) account

Date	Details	DR	CR	Balance
Year 1				
31 Dec	Profit and Loss		1,200	1,200 CR
Year 2				
31 Dec	Profit and Loss		1,200	2,400 CR

Profit and loss account for year 2

INCOME

—

LESS EXPENDITURE

Depreciation: motor cars

                                                                                      1,200

Balance Sheet as at end year 2

FIXED ASSETS

Motor cars at cost   6,000

LESS accumulated depreciation   2,400

                                                                                      3,600

5.4 Sale of assets

When an asset is sold an asset disposal account will be opened. The cost price of the asset and its accumulated depreciation to date will be transferred to this account, and the sale price will be recorded. From this account you will be able to see whether the business has made a 'profit' or a 'loss' on the sale.

For example, if a car had been purchased for £20,000 and the accumulated depreciation to date was £8,000, then the estimated current value of the car would be £12,000. If the car was sold for £13,000 a 'profit' of £1,000 has been made. This would be shown on the accounts as follows:

Car asset disposal account

Date	Details	DR	CR	Balance
200—	Cost price of car	20,000		20,000 DR
	Accumulated depreciation on car		8,000	12,000 DR
	Cash on sale		13,000	1,000 CR

The credit balance is a 'profit', which will be shown as INCOME on the Profit and Loss account.

If the account came out with a debit balance this would be a loss/EXPENSE for the Profit and Loss account.

5.5 Summary of adjustments—effect on Profit and Loss account and Balance Sheet

Bad debts

Profit and Loss Account
Show as an EXPENSE.

Balance Sheet
Only reduce the debtors figure by any bad debts which are written off after the Trial Balance. If bad debts are shown on the Trial Balance then the debtors figure has already been reduced; it should not be changed.

Provision for doubtful debts

This year's provision:
PROFIT AND LOSS ACCOUNT;
Show as an EXPENSE.
BALANCE SHEET;
REDUCE debtors figure by this year's provision.
Last year's provision:
    PROFIT AND LOSS ACCOUNT;
    REDUCE expense of bad debts by last year's provision.
    BALANCE SHEET;
    NO effect.

Depreciation

PROFIT AND LOSS ACCOUNT;
Show the depreciation for the current year only as an EXPENSE.
BALANCE SHEET;
Show the cost price of the asset

LESS any accumulated depreciation from previous years
AND less the depreciation for the current year.

5.6 Reminder of key points

1. Bad debts are an expense;

2. A provision for doubtful debts is an adjustment and it will affect both the Profit and Loss account and the Balance Sheet—see the summary at para 5.5 above on how to deal with it;

3. Depreciation records the fall in value of assets as an expense and will affect both the Profit and Loss account and the Balance Sheet—see the summary at para 5.5 above on how to deal with it;

4. Note on sale of assets an asset disposal account would be opened and the cost price and depreciation to date would be transferred to it; the balance on this account would give the current estimated value of the asset, known as the current book value. When the sale price is recorded this would show either a profit or a loss on the current book value of the asset.

online resource centre

Now try the self-test exercises at the end of this chapter and the online multiple choice questions available through your tutor via the Online Resource Centre that accompanies this book, then move on to partnership accounts in Chapter 6.

5.7 Exercises on adjustments and final accounts

1 Allow 10 to 15 minutes.

An extract from the Trial Balance of Lightfoot drawn up on 31 December 200— shows the following:

Name of account	DR	CR
Debtors	4,340	
Bad debts	625	

It is decided to make a provision for doubtful debts of £450 for the year. Show the figures for expenses on the Profit and Loss account for the year and the figures that would be shown on the Balance sheet as at 31 December 200—.

2 Allow about 10 minutes.

An extract from the Trial Balance of Davis drawn up on 31 March 200—shows the following:

Name of account	DR	CR
Cost price of cars	30,000	
Accumulated depreciation on cars		9,000

Depreciation for the year ending 31 March 200— is to be 15% of the cost price. Show the figure for expenses on the Profit and Loss account and the details in respect of cars on the Balance Sheet.

3 Allow 30 to 40 minutes.

The Trial Balance for Karsh on 30 September 200— is set out below:

Name of account	DR	CR
Capital		170,000
Profit costs		90,000
Drawings	32,000	
Office furniture	8,500	
Accumulated depreciation on office furniture		2,550
Premises cost price	160,000	
General and administrative expenses	46,000	
Cash at bank, office account	13,915	
Petty cash	165	
Creditors		1,980
Debtors	3,544	
Bad debts	406	
Cash at bank, client account	249,000	
Due to clients		249,000
	513,530	513,530

Depreciation for the year on office furniture is 10% of the cost price. The provision for doubtful debts for the year is £360 and Work in Progress at the end of the year is £6,200. Draw up the Profit and Loss account for the year ending 30 September and Balance Sheet as at that date.

4 Allow 40 to 50 minutes.

The Trial Balance of Chandra, prepared on 31 December 200—, is as follows:

Trial Balance as at 31 December 200—

Name of account	DR	CR
Drawings	19,000	
Fixtures and fittings	5,200	
Cars	20,600	
Accumulated depreciation (cars)		4,120
Accumulated depreciation (fixtures and fittings)		1,300
Premises	132,000	
Capital		140,000
Telephone/postage	1,300	
Council tax	2,950	
Light and heat	1,550	
Salaries	25,270	
Cash at bank:		
Office account	14,190	
Client account	315,000	
Petty cash	123	
Debtors	4,422	
Due to creditors		4,763
Due to clients		315,000
Profit costs		76,422
	541,605	541,605

In addition:

(a) Depreciation at 10% and 5% is to be charged against the cost price of cars and fixtures and fittings, respectively.

(b) At 31 December 200— electricity and telephone bills outstanding amount to £551 and £505, respectively.

(c) Included in the amount for debtors is £122 which is to be written off. A provision for doubtful debts of 5% of remaining debtors is to be made.

(d) Work in Progress at 31 December 200— is valued at £8,569.

Prepare final accounts for the year ended 31 December 200—.

5 Allow 50 minutes to 1 hour.

The following balances were taken from the accounts of C. Arnold, solicitor, on 31 December 200—.

Capital	223,059
Work in Progress at 1 January 200—	16,582
Petty cash	55
Bank overdraft on office account	4,552
Bank client account	450,000
Debtors	12,009
Creditors	9,235
Car: cost price	20,000
Accumulated depreciation: car	8,000
Drawings	20,459
Fixtures and fittings at cost	8,000
Accumulated depreciation: fixtures and fittings	1,200
Profit costs	78,021
Rent and rates	2,626
Salaries	30,226
General expenses	12,500
Interest on overdraft	735
Insurance commission received	369
Freehold premises	200,500
Bad debts	2,400
Provision for doubtful debts b/d (last year's)	1,656
Due to clients	450,000

C. Arnold provides the following additional information about the practice:

(a) Work in Progress was valued at £14,270 on 31 December 200—.

(b) Salaries outstanding on 31 December 200— were £426.

(c) Council tax paid in advance on 31 December 200— amounted to £500.

(d) This year's provision for doubtful debts is to be increased to £2,600.

(e) Depreciation is to be charged at 20% per annum on cost of cars and 5% per annum on cost of fixtures and fittings.

Prepare a Profit and Loss account and Balance Sheet for the year ended 31 December 200—.

5.8   Suggested answers to exercises on adjustments and final accounts

1 Lightfoot: Profit and Loss account for the year ending 31 December 200—

EXPENSES	
Bad debts	625
ADD this year's provision for doubtful debts	450
	1,075

Lightfoot: Profit and Loss account for the year ending 31 December 200—

CURRENT ASSETS	
Debtors	4,340
LESS provision for doubtful debts	450
	3,890

2 Davis: Profit and Loss account for the year ending 31 March 200—

EXPENSES	
Depreciation on cars	4,500
(15% of £30,000)	

Davis: Balance Sheet as at 31 March 200—

FIXED ASSETS	
Cost price of cars	30,000
LESS total accumulated depreciation	
(being 9,000 plus 4,500)	13,500
	16,500

3 Karsh: Profit and Loss account for the year ending 30 September 200—

INCOME		
Profit costs	90,000	
ADD		
Work in Progress at end of year	6,200	
VALUE OF WORK DONE	96,200	
ADDITIONAL INCOME	Nil	
TOTAL INCOME		96,200
LESS EXPENSES		
General and administrative expenses	46,000	
Depreciation on office furniture	850	
Bad debts	406	
Provision for doubtful debts	360	
Total expenses		47,616
NET PROFIT		48,584

Karsh: Balance Sheet as at 30 September 200—

FIXED ASSETS			
Premises cost price		160,000	
Office furniture cost price	8,500		
Less total depreciation			
(2,550 + 850)	3,400		
		5,100	
			165,100
CURRENT ASSETS			
Work in Progress		6,200	
Debtors (due from clients)	3,544		
LESS provision for doubtful			
debts	360		
		3,184	
Cash at bank, office account		13,915	
Petty cash		165	
		23,464	
LESS CURRENT LIABILITIES			
Creditors		1,980	
NET CURRENT ASSETS			21,484
			186,584
LESS LONG-TERM LIABILITIES			–
TOTAL NET ASSETS			186,584
Capital employed			
Capital	170,000		
ADD net profit	48,584		
		218,584	
LESS drawings		32,000	
TOTAL DUE TO OWNER			186,584
CLIENT ACCOUNT			
Cash at bank, client account			249,000
Amount due to clients			249,000

4 Chandra: Profit and Loss account for the year ended 31 December 200—

INCOME			
Profit costs		76,422	
ADD closing Work in Progress		8,569	84,991
LESS expenses			
Telephone and postage	1,300		
ADD provision	505	1,805	
Council tax		2,950	
Light and heat	1,550		
ADD provision	551	2,101	
Salaries		25,270	
Depreciation:			
Motor cars	2,060		

Fixtures and fittings	260	2,320
Bad debts and provision		337	34,783
(£122 + £215 provision)		
NET PROFIT		50,208

Chandra: Balance Sheet as at 31 December 200—

FIXED ASSETS			
Premises		132,000	
Fixtures and fittings at cost	5,200		
LESS accumulated depreciation	1,560		
		3,640	
Motor cars at cost	20,600		
LESS accumulated depreciation	6,180		
		14,420	
			150,060
CURRENT ASSETS			
Closing Work in Progress		8,569	
Debtors	4,300		
LESS provision	215		
		4,085	
Cash at bank, office account		14,190	
Petty cash		123	
		26,967	
LESS CURRENT LIABILITIES			
Creditors		4,763	
Outstanding expenses		1,056	
		5,819	
NET CURRENT ASSETS			21,148
			171,208
LESS LONG-TERM LIABILITIES			—
TOTAL NET ASSETS			171,208
CAPITAL EMPLOYED			
Capital at start		140,000	
ADD net profit		50,208	
		190,208	
LESS drawings		19,000	
TOTAL DUE TO OWNER			171,208
Client account			
Cash at bank, client account		315,000	
Due to clients		315,000	

5   **C. Arnold: Profit and Loss account for the year ended 31 December 200—**

INCOME		
Profit costs	78,021	
ADD closing Work in Progress	14,270	
	92,291	
LESS opening Work in Progress	16,582	75,709

Additional income

Insurance commission received		369
		76,078

LESS EXPENSES

Rent and rates	2,626		
LESS paid in advance	500	2,126	
Salaries	30,226		
PLUS outstanding	426	30,652	
General expenses		12,500	
Interest on overdraft		735	
Bad and doubtful debts		3,344 [see *Note* below]	
Depreciation: cars	4,000		
Fixtures and fittings	400	4,400	53,757
NET PROFIT			22,321

Note:

Bad debts	2,400
ADD this year's provision	2,600
	5,000
LESS last year's provision	1,656
	3,344

C. Arnold: Balance Sheet as at 31 December 200—

FIXED ASSETS

Freehold premises		200,500	
Fixtures and fittings at cost	8,000		
LESS accumulated depreciation	1,600		
		6,400	
Motor cars at cost	20,000		
LESS accumulated depreciation	12,000		
		8,000	
			214,900

CURRENT ASSETS

Closing Work in Progress		14,270	
Debtors	12,009		
LESS provision	2,600	9,409	
Petty cash		55	
Payment in advance			
Rates		500	
		24,234	

LESS CURRENT LIABILITIES

Creditors	9,235		
Office bank account overdraft	4,552		
Outstanding expenses: salaries	426		
		14,213	
NET CURRENT ASSETS			10,021
			224,921

LESS LONG-TERM LIABILITIES			—
TOTAL NET ASSETS			224,921
CAPITAL EMPLOYED			
Capital at start	223,059		
ADD net profit	22,321		
		245,380	
LESS drawings		20,459	
TOTAL DUE TO OWNER			224,921
CLIENT ACCOUNT			
Cash at bank, client account	450,000		
LESS due to clients	450,000		

Partnership accounts

6.1 Introduction

This chapter includes:

1. An overview of partnership accounts;
2. The Profit and Loss account/Appropriation account and Current accounts;
3. Drawings;
4. Capital and Current accounts;
5. The Balance Sheet—a summary;
6. Example of partners' final accounts;
7. Partnership changes;
8. Reminder of key points;
9. Exercises on partnership final accounts;
10. Test on partnership accounts.

> **❗ INTENDED OUTCOME**
>
> An understanding of the capital structure of a partnership and of the need for an appropriation of the net profit between the partners, together with an understanding of the need for separate Capital and Current accounts for the partners, evidenced by the ability to draw up a Profit and Loss and Appropriation account, and a Balance Sheet for a partnership, including the Schedule of movement on partners' current accounts.

6.2 The accounts kept by a partnership—overview

6.2.1 General

The accounts kept by a partnership are largely the same as those kept by a sole practitioner. The asset and income and expense accounts are the same and the client accounts are the same, as are the accounting procedures up to the preparation of final accounts. The main differences are as follows:

6.2.1.1 Profit and Loss account—Appropriation account

There is an extension to the Profit and Loss account, known as the Appropriation account, which will show how the profit is divided between the partners.

6.2.1.2 The Balance Sheet

In the Capital Employed section, the partners each have a separate Capital account and a separate Current account, which shows details of all the profit allocated to the partner, less drawings.

6.3 Profit and Loss account—Appropriation account

6.3.1 Profit and Loss account—Appropriation account

Up to the point of calculating the firm's net profit, the Profit and Loss account of a partnership is the same as that of a sole practitioner. In a partnership the Profit and Loss account is extended to show the allocation of the net profit amongst the partners in the profit-sharing ratio provided for in the partnership agreement, after such items as agreed salaries and interest on capital, also provided for in the partnership agreement, have been taken into account. The extension of the Profit and Loss account is called an Appropriation account. Note that partners' salaries used in this context are merely a fixed prior allocation of profit.

EXAMPLE

The firm has three partners A, B, and C. The Profit and Loss account records a net profit for the year of £120,000. The partnership agreement provides that A is to receive interest on capital of £2,000 and a salary of £8,000, C is to receive interest on capital of £1,000 and a salary of £2,000, and B is to receive a salary of £2,000. Profits are then shared in the ratio A2:B2:C1 (this could also be expressed as 2/5ths 2/5ths 1/5th or 40% 40% 20%). The Appropriation account for A, B, and C will appear as follows:

A, B, and C: Appropriation account for the year ending

NET PROFIT			120,000
SALARIES:			
A	8,000		
B	2,000		
C	2,000		
		12,000	
INTEREST ON CAPITAL:			
A	2,000		
C	1,000	3,000	
PROFIT SHARE:			
A: 2/5ths	42,000		
B: 2/5ths	42,000		
C: 1/5th	21,000	105,000	
			120,000

Note the following with regard to the Appropriation account:

(a) Net profit is carried down from the Profit and Loss account.

(b) Partners' entitlements to salary and interest on capital, for example, **must** be deducted first from the net profit.

(c) The resulting balance is shared amongst the partners in the profit-sharing ratio.

The salaries, interest on capital, and shares of profit will be transferred to the partners' current accounts, see para 6.5.2 below.

To continue the above example, the Current account for partner A would appear as follows:

Current account: A

Date	Details	DR	CR	Balance
	Appropriation: salary		8,000	8,000 CR
	Appropriation: interest on capital		2,000	10,000 CR
	Appropriation: profit share		42,000	52,000 CR

6.4 Drawings

A drawings account may be opened for each partner or alternatively drawings may be debited to the partners' current accounts when they are made.

6.4.1 Cash drawings

If a drawings account is used the following entries will be made to record the partners' cash drawings.

(a) DEBIT Drawings account.

(b) CREDIT Cash account.

EXAMPLE

On 31 March partner A draws £2,000, on 30 April A draws £2,000, and on 10 May the firm pays A's home gas bill, £150.

Drawings account: A

Date	Details	DR	CR	Balance
31 Mar	Cash	2,000		2,000 DR
30 Apr	Cash	2,000		4,000 DR
10 May	Cash: home gas bill	150		4,150 DR

If the firm does not use a drawings account for the partners but debits drawings into the partners' current accounts, when the drawings are made, the above entries would have been recorded in A's current account, see the example in para 6.5.2.

6.4.2 End of the financial year

At the end of the financial year the partners' drawings accounts will be closed and the balances on the accounts will be transferred to the partners' current accounts.

6.5   Capital accounts and current accounts

6.5.1   Capital accounts

In a partnership the capital is introduced by more than one person and therefore a separate capital account must be kept for each partner.

Note that the partners' profit entitlement and drawings will be shown separately on current accounts; see later.

EXAMPLE

A and B enter into partnership introducing £30,000 and £90,000 capital, respectively.

Capital account: A

Date	Details	DR	CR	Balance
	Balance			30,000 CR

Capital account: B

Date	Details	DR	CR	Balance
	Balance			90,000 CR

6.5.2   Current accounts

A current account is opened for each partner.

A partner's current account is credited with any sums which the partner is entitled to receive from the practice, for example, the profit share, interest on capital, and salary.

A partner's current account is debited with any sums which the partner has taken out of the practice or which are owed to the practice, for example drawings (transferred at the end of the financial year from the partner's drawings account).

If a partner's current account has a credit balance, then the firm owes money to the partner. If the current account has a debit balance, then the partner owes money to the firm, which is a current asset of the firm.

However, by convention, the balances on the partners' current accounts will always be shown on the Capital Employed section of the Balance Sheet.

EXAMPLE

In the example in para 6.5.1, assume that at the end of the first year of practice net profit is £86,000. Interest on capital is allowed at £1,500 for A and £4,500 for B. B is also given a salary of £5,000, before the remaining profit of £75,000 is split as to A £25,000 and B £50,000. During the year A has made drawings of £20,000 and B has made drawings of £30,000. The current accounts would look as follows:

Current account: A

Date	Details	DR	CR	Balance
200—				
30 June	Profit share		25,000	25,000 CR
	Interest on capital		1,500	26,500 CR
	Drawings	20,000		6,500 CR

Current account: B

Date	Details	DR	CR	Balance
200—				
30 June	Profit share		50,000	50,000 CR
	Salary		5,000	55,000 CR
	Interest on capital		4,500	59,500 CR
	Drawings	30,000		29,500 CR

Thus at the end of the year the firm owes A £6,500 and B £29,500.

6.6   The Balance Sheet summary

The Balance Sheet of a partnership is the same as that of a sole practitioner except:

(a) The capital accounts of the partners are shown separately. The capital accounts show capital at the start of the year.

(b) Net profit and drawings are *not* transferred to a partner's capital account and therefore are not shown as additions to and deductions from capital, respectively, as happens with a sole practitioner.

(c) The current accounts of the partners are shown on the liabilities section (Capital Employed) of the Balance Sheet. If there is a credit balance on the current accounts, this is added to the capital account balance. If there is a debit balance on the current accounts, this is deducted from the capital account balance.

(d) It is not usual to show the detailed movements on partners' current accounts on the Balance Sheet itself. A schedule showing the movements on the current accounts can be shown at the end of the Balance Sheet.

6.7   Abridged example on partners' Appropriation account and Balance Sheet

Das, Begum, and Ahmed are in partnership, sharing profits and losses in the ratio 2:2:1. Each partner is entitled to interest on capital at 10% per annum and to salaries of £10,000 to Das and £7,000 to Ahmed.

An abridged Trial Balance prepared from the partnership books shows the following position at 30 September 200—:

	DR	CR
Total assets	320,000	
Total liabilities		150,000
Profit for the year from the Profit and Loss account		140,000
Drawings		
Das	30,000	
Begum	25,000	
Ahmed	25,000	
Capital accounts		
Das		50,000
Begum		40,000
Ahmed		20,000
	400,000	400,000

The Profit and Loss Appropriation account for the year ended 30 September 200—, together with a Balance Sheet as at that date, based on the above information are set out below.

Profit and Loss Appropriation account for the year ended 30 September 200—

NET PROFIT		140,000
INTEREST ON CAPITAL:		
Das 10% on £50,000	5,000	
Begum 10% on £40,000	4,000	
Ahmed 10% on £20,000	2,000	11,000
		129,000
SALARIES:		
Das	10,000	
Ahmed	7,000	17,000
		112,000
SHARE OF PROFIT:		
Das: 2/5ths	44,800	
Begum: 2/5ths	44,800	
Ahmed: 1/5th	22,400	112,000

Das, Begum, and Ahmed: Balance Sheet as at 30 September 200—

ASSETS	320,000	
LESS liabilities	150,000	
TOTAL NET ASSETS		170,000
CAPITAL EMPLOYED		
Capital accounts:		
Das	50,000	
Begum	40,000	
Ahmed	20,000	
		110,000

Current accounts (see 'Movements on partners'
current accounts' below):

Das	29,800	
Begum	23,800	
Ahmed	6,400	
		60,000
TOTAL DUE TO PARTNERS		170,000

Schedule to Balance Sheet

Movements on partners' current accounts

	Das	Begum	Ahmed
Opening balance	—	—	—
Salary	10,000	—	7,000
Interest on capital	5,000	4,000	2,000
Profit share	44,800	44,800	22,400
	59,800	48,800	31,400
LESS drawings	30,000	25,000	25,000
	29,800 CR	23,800 CR	6,400 CR

6.8 Partnership changes—split the appropriation

The constitution of a partnership may change during the financial year as a result of a partner dying, retiring from the practice, a new partner joining the practice, or because the partners decide to vary their profit-sharing agreement.

When there is a partnership change during the year, the format of the Balance Sheet and the Profit and Loss account to the net profit stage will not change.

The format of the Appropriation account will change as there will be a split appropriation. This means that there will be one Appropriation account for the period before the change and one for the period after the change to the end of the financial year. Each Appropriation account will reflect the terms of the partnership agreement in force for the period to which the Appropriation account relates. Unless you are told the net profit for the period before and after the change you will have to apportion the net profit for each period on a time basis.

The net profit, interest on drawings, interest on capital, and salaries must be apportioned. For example, if there is a partnership change three months into the year, in the first Appropriation account, net profit, etc for the year will be divided by four to reflect the fact that the Appropriation account relates to only one quarter of the year.

If a sole practitioner takes in a partner part-way through the year, the profits for the time as a sole practitioner will belong wholly to the sole practitioner. There will be no salary, interest on capital, etc in the first part of the Appropriation account as these are relevant only where there is a partnership. It therefore follows that provision for salaries, etc in the partnership agreement can apply only to the second appropriation period.

EXAMPLE

A and B are in partnership. A's capital is £60,000 and B's is £40,000. They share the profits in the ratio 3:2. Their financial year runs from 1 January to 31 December. C joins the partnership on 1 July 200—. C is to receive a salary of £12,000 per annum and A and B interest on capital of 10% per annum. A, B, and C are to share the profits in the ratio of 2:2:1.

Net profit for the year ended 31 December 200— is £140,000.

A, B, and C: profit and loss account for the year ended 31 December 200—

NET PROFIT			140,000

Appropriation account 1 January to 30 June 200—

PROFIT SHARE:			
A: 3/5ths	42,000		
B: 2/5ths	28,000		70,000

1 July to 31 December 200—

INTEREST ON CAPITAL:			
A for half year on 60,000 at 10%	3,000		
B for half year on 40,000 at 10%	2,000	5,000	
SALARIES:			
C for half year at 12,000 per annum		6,000	
PROFIT SHARE:			
A: 2/5ths	23,600		
B: 2/5ths	23,600		
C: 1/5th	11,800	59,000	70,000
			140,000

6.9 Reminder of key points

1. There is an extension to the Profit and Loss account—the Appropriation Account—this shows the division of profit between the partners:
   (a) Partners may be given interest on capital and salaries as a prior allocation of profit before dividing the remaining profit in the agreed proportions;
   (b) The interest on capital, salaries, and profit shares allocated will then be transferred to the partners' current accounts;
   (c) Note that any drawings will be deducted from the partners' current accounts.
2. On the Balance Sheet the Capital Employed section will show a separate Capital account and Current account for each partner;
3. The full details of the partners' current accounts will be shown in a schedule to the Balance Sheet and only the resulting current account balances will be shown on the Balance Sheet itself.

Now try the self-test exercises at the end of this chapter and the online multiple choice questions available through your tutor via the Online Resource Centre that accompanies this book. Then move on to basic accounting concepts in Chapter 7.

6.10   Exercises on partnership final accounts

1   Allow 15 to 20 minutes.

Allan, Black, and Clark are in partnership sharing profits as to Allan 50%, Black 25%, and Clark 25%.

Each partner is entitled to interest on capital of 5% and Clark is entitled to a partnership salary of £5,000 a year. The net profit at the end of the year is £250,000 and the partners' Capital account balances are Allan £60,000, Black £40,000, and Clark £20,000.

Draw up the Appropriation account for the partners.

2   Allow about 30 minutes.

The Trial Balance of Javid and Khan at the end of the year 31 December 200— showed the following Capital and Current account balances:

Capital accounts	
Javid	40,000
Khan	20,000
Current accounts	
Javid	5,426 CR
Khan	3,040 CR

Net profit for the partnership at the end of the year was £110,000. Interest on capital is 6% a year. Khan has a salary of £2,000 a year and the profit share ratio is Javid 2: Khan 1. Drawings for the year were Javid £50,000 and Khan £35,000.

Draw up the Appropriation account, the movement on Current accounts, and the Capital Employed section of the Balance Sheet at the end of the year.

3   Allow 1 hour to 1 hour 20 minutes.

The bookkeeper of the firm Bertram, Crawford, and Norris, solicitors, draws up a trial balance in respect of the year ending 31 December 200—.

Trial balance at 31 December 200—

	DR	CR
Profit costs less Work in Progress at start of year		544,060
General and administrative expenses	372,900	
Due to clients		943,560
Bad debts	4,900	
Capital accounts		
Bertram		130,000
Crawford		100,000
Norris		80,000
Current accounts		

Bertram		5,000
Crawford		4,000
Norris		6,000
Sundry creditors		8,100
Interest received		6,420
Freehold premises	320,000	
Library furniture and equipment at cost	42,000	
Accumulated depreciation on library		
Furniture and equipment		12,600
Motor cars	45,000	
Accumulated depreciation on motor cars		18,000
Due from clients	51,820	
Overdraft office account		3,000
Cash at bank, client current account	493,560	
Cash at bank, client deposit account	450,000	
Petty cash	560	
Drawings		
Bertram	30,000	
Crawford	25,000	
Norris	25,000	
	1,860,740	1,860,740

The partnership agreement provides that Crawford has a partnership salary of £5,000 per annum, interest on capital for the partners is 5% per annum and profits and losses are shared equally.

Work in Progress as at 31 December 200— is £50,000. Payments in advance are £1,800 and outstanding expenses are £2,100. Provision for doubtful debts for the year to 31 December 200— is set at £1,200. Depreciation for the year on the library furniture and equipment is 10% of the cost price, and depreciation for the year on motor cars is 20% of the cost price.

Draw up the Profit and Loss and Appropriation accounts for the partners together with the Balance Sheet. Show full details of the movement on current accounts.

4 Allow 1 hour to 1 hour 20 minutes.

Ash and Rowland are in partnership as solicitors, sharing profits and losses as to Ash two thirds and Rowland one third. Each partner is entitled to interest on capital in the firm at the rate of 5% per annum. Rowland is also entitled to a salary of £10,000 per annum. The following Trial Balance was prepared from the firm's accounts for the year ended 31 December 200—.

Trial balance at 31 December 200—

	DR	CR
Capital accounts		
Ash		50,000
Rowland		25,000
Current accounts		
Ash		3,450
Rowland		1,620

Lease at cost price	15,000	
Motor cars	30,000	
Furniture, library, and equipment	22,000	
Partners' drawings		
Ash	23,500	
Rowland	28,000	
Administration and general expenses	118,520	
Profit costs		190,425
Interest received		2,900
Due to clients		425,380
Provision for doubtful debts b/d from previous year		560
Creditors		18,375
Cash at bank, client account:		
Deposit account	350,000	
Current account	75,380	
Petty cash	270	
Cash at bank, office account	12,840	
Opening Work in Progress (1 January 200—)	34,200	
Due from clients (debtors)	24,000	
Loan account: bank		10,000
Rent received		6,000
	733,710	733,710

Work in Progress at 31 December 200— is valued at £38,000. This year's provision for doubtful debts is £800.

Depreciation on motor cars for the year ending 31 December 200— is £6,000. Depreciation on furniture, library, and equipment is £4,800.

From the above information prepare a Profit and Loss and Appropriation account for the year ended 31 December 200— together with a Balance Sheet as at that date.

5   Allow 50 minutes to 1 hour.

Beth and Amy are in partnership as solicitors sharing profits and losses in the ratio 3:2. Each partner is entitled, under the partnership agreement, to interest on capital at the rate of 10% per annum and Amy is entitled, in addition, to a partnership salary of £12,000 per annum.

On 1 July 200—, Jo is admitted into the partnership, contributing £10,000 as her share of the capital in the firm. The new partnership agreement provides that, as from 1 July 200—, profits and losses will be shared between Beth, Amy, and Jo in the ratio 2:2:1 respectively. Furthermore, partnership salaries of £20,000, £15,000, and £10,000 per annum will be allowed to Beth, Amy, and Jo respectively. No interest is to be allowed on capital, and no interest is to be charged on partners' drawings.

An abridged trial balance, prepared from the partnership books, shows the following position as at 31 December 200—.

NET PROFIT for the year, before charging
interest on capital, and other appropriations | | 120,000

Partners' drawings:

Beth	30,700	
Amy	28,400	
Jo	11,000	

Partners' Capital accounts:

Beth		70,000
Amy		50,000
Jo		10,000
Sundry assets	194,700	
Sundry liabilities		14,800
	264,800	264,800
Amounts due to clients		894,568
Cash at bank, clients	894,568	
	1,159,368	1,159,368

From the above information, prepare the Profit and Loss and Appropriation account for the year ended 31 December 200—, together with a Balance Sheet as at that date. The allocation of profits between the partners is to be determined on a time basis. (Calculations to be made in months.) Detailed movements on partners' current accounts should also be shown.

6 Allow 1 hour to 1 hour 20 minutes.

Hale and Owen are in partnership as solicitors. Hale and Owen receive interest on capital of 5% per annum and Owen receives a salary of £2,000 per annum. The remaining profits are shared equally. Their financial year ends on 31 December. On 31 December 200— the Trial Balance is:

	DR	CR
Freehold premises	145,000	
Fixtures and fittings	15,000	
Accumulated depreciation on fixtures and fittings		3,000
Library	2,000	
Accumulated depreciation on library		500
Capital accounts:		
Hale		80,000
Owen		75,000
Current accounts:		
Hale		2,500
Owen		2,000
Drawings:		
Hale	24,000	
Owen	24,500	
Profit		
Profit costs		78,000

Insurance commission received		600
Salaries	20,000	
Insurance paid	1,500	
Council tax	1,620	
Light and heat	1,400	
Stationery	900	
Travelling	400	
Creditors		820
Debtors	3,000	
Office bank account	3,000	
Petty cash	100	
Client bank account	465,000	
Client ledger account		465,000
	707,420	707,420

At 31 December 200— Work in Progress amounts to £5,000; there is a stock of stationery valued at £300. Depreciation is charged on fixtures and fittings and library at 10% on the cost price. There is an amount outstanding for electricity of £100.

Prepare final accounts for Hale and Owen for the year ended 31 December 200—.

6.11   Suggested answers to exercises on partnership final accounts

1   **Allan, Black, and Clark: Appropriation account for the year ending—**

NET PROFIT			250,000
LESS			
Salary Clark			5,000
			245,000
INTEREST ON CAPITAL			
Allan 5% on 60,000		3,000	
Black 5% on 40,000		2,000	
Clark 5% on 20,000		1,000	
			6,000
			239,000
PROFIT SHARE			
Allan 50%	119,500		
Black 25%	59,750		
Clark 25%	59,750		
			239,000

2 **Javid and Khan: Appropriation account for the year ending 31 December 200—**

NET PROFIT			110,000
INTEREST ON CAPITAL			
Javid 6% on 40,000		2,400	
Khan 6% on 20,000		1,200	
			3,600
			106,400
SALARY Khan			2,000
			104,400
PROFIT SHARE			
Javid	69,600		
Khan	34,800		
			104,400

Javid and Khan: Balance Sheet as at 31 December 200—

CAPITAL EMPLOYED			
Capital accounts			
Javid	40,000		
Khan	20,000		
			60,000
Current accounts (see 'Movements on partners' current accounts')			
Javid	27,426		
Khan	6,040		
			33,466
TOTAL DUE TO PARTNERS			93,466

Schedule to Balance Sheet

Movements on partners' current accounts

	Javid	Khan
Opening balance	5,426	3,040
Interest on capital	2,400	1,200
Salary		2,000
Profit share	69,600	34,800
Total	77,426	41,040
LESS drawings	50,000	35,000
Balance	27,426	6,040

3 **Bertram, Crawford, and Norris: Profit and Loss and Appropriation account for the year ending 31 December 200—**

INCOME			
Profit costs		544,060	
ADD Work in Progress at end of year		50,000	
Value of work done			594,060
ADDITIONAL INCOME			
ADD interest received		6,420	600,480

LESS EXPENSES

General and administrative Expenses	372,900	
Bad debts	4,900	
Provision for doubtful debts	1,200	
Depreciation on cars	9,000	
Depreciation on furniture, etc	4,200	
ADD outstanding expenses	2,100	
	394,300	
LESS payments in advance	1,800	392,500
NET PROFIT		207,980
APPROPRIATION ACCOUNT		
Profit available		207,980
SALARY		
Crawford		5,000
INTEREST ON CAPITAL		
Bertram	6,500	
Crawford	5,000	
Norris	4,000	15,500
PROFIT SHARE		
Bertram	62,494	
Crawford	62,493	
Norris	62,493	187,480

Bertram, Crawford, and Norris: Balance Sheet as at 31 December 200—

FIXED ASSETS			
Freehold premises		320,000	
Library, etc cost price	42,000		
LESS depreciation	16,800		
		25,200	
Motor cars cost price	45,000		
LESS depreciation	27,000		
		18,000	
			363,200
CURRENT ASSETS			
Work in Progress		50,000	
Debtors (due from clients)	51,820		
LESS provision	1,200		
		50,620	
Petty cash		560	
Payments in advance		1,800	
		102,980	
LESS CURRENT LIABILITIES			
Sundry creditors		8,100	
Overdraft office account		3,000	

Outstanding expenses		2,100	
			13,200
NET CURRENT ASSETS			89,780
			452,980
LESS LONG-TERM LIABILITIES			—
TOTAL NET ASSETS			452,980
CAPITAL EMPLOYED			
Capital accounts:			
Bertram	130,000		
Crawford	100,000		
Norris	80,000		
		310,000	
Current accounts (see 'Movements on partners' current accounts')			
Bertram	43,994		
Crawford	51,493		
Norris	47,493		
		142,980	
TOTAL DUE TO PARTNERS			452,980
CLIENT ACCOUNT			
Due to clients		943,560	
Cash at bank, client			
current account	493,560		
Cash at bank, client			
deposit account	450,000		
		943,560	

Schedule to Balance Sheet

Movements on partners' current accounts

	Bertram	Crawford	Norris
Opening Balance	5,000	4,000	6,000
Salary	—	5,000	—
Interest on capital	6,500	5,000	4,000
Profit share	62,494	62,493	62,493
	73,994	76,493	72,493
LESS drawings	30,000	25,000	25,000
	43,994	51,493	47,493

4 **Ash and Rowland: Profit and Loss and Appropriation account for the year ending 31 December 200—**

Profit costs	190,425
ADD closing Work in Progress	38,000
	228,425
LESS opening Work in Progress	34,200
Value of work done	194,225

ADDITIONAL INCOME			
Interest received	2,900		
Rent received	6,000		
		8,900	
			203,125
LESS: EXPENSES			
Administrative and general expenses		118,520	
Provision for doubtful debts			
This year's provision	800		
LESS last year's provision	560	240	
Depreciation:			
Cars	6,000		
Furniture, etc	4,800	10,800	129,560
NET PROFIT			73,565
APPROPRIATION			73,565
SALARIES:			
Rowland		10,000	
INTEREST ON CAPITAL:			
Ash	2,500		
Rowland	1,250	3,750	
PROFIT SHARE:			
Ash: 2/3rds		39,877	
Rowland: 1/3rd		19,938	

(round up or down to nearest pound to balance)

Note that last year's provision for doubtful debts brought down will reduce the expense this year.

Ash and Rowland: Balance Sheet as at 31 December 200—

FIXED ASSETS			
Leasehold premises		15,000	
Furniture, library, and equipment at cost	22,000		
LESS depreciation	4,800		
		17,200	
Motor cars	30,000		
LESS depreciation	6,000		
		24,000	
			56,200
CURRENT ASSETS			
Closing Work in Progress		38,000	
Debtors (due from clients)	24,000		
LESS provision	800		
		23,200	
Cash at bank, office account		12,840	
Petty cash		270	
		74,310	
LESS CURRENT LIABILITIES			
Creditors		18,375	

NET CURRENT ASSETS		55,935
		112,135
LESS LONG-TERM LIABILITIES		
Bank loan		10,000
TOTAL NET ASSETS		102,135
CAPITAL EMPLOYED		
Capital accounts:		
Ash	50,000	
Rowland	25,000	75,000
Current accounts:		
(see 'Movements on partners' current accounts')		
Ash	22,327	
Rowland	4,808	27,135
TOTAL DUE TO PARTNERS		102,135
CLIENT ACCOUNT		
Bank balance:		
Deposit account	350,000	
Current account	75,380	
	425,380	
Due to clients	425,380	

Schedule to Balance Sheet

Movement on partners' current accounts

	Ash	Rowland
Balance	3,450 CR	1,620 CR
Salary	—	10,000
Interest on capital	2,500	1,250
Profit share	39,877	19,938
	45,827	32,808
LESS drawings	23,500	28,000
	22,327 CR	4,808 CR

5 **Beth, Amy, and Jo: Profit and Loss and Appropriation account for period 1 January 200— to 30 June 200—**

NET PROFIT (for 6 months)		60,000
SALARY (for 6 months):		
Amy	6,000	
INTEREST ON CAPITAL (for 6 months):		
Beth	3,500	
Amy	2,500	
		12,000
PROFIT SHARE:		
Beth: 3/5ths	28,800	
Amy: 2/5ths	19,200	48,000

Profit and Loss and Appropriation account for period 1 July to 31 December 200—

NET PROFIT (for 6 months)		60,000

SALARIES (for 6 months):

Beth	10,000	
Amy	7,500	
Jo	5,000	
		22,500

PROFIT SHARE:

Beth: 2/5ths	15,000	
Amy: 2/5ths	15,000	
Jo: 1/5th	7,500	37,500

Beth, Amy and Jo: Balance Sheet as at 31 December 200—

ASSETS		194,700	
LESS LIABILITIES		14,800	
TOTAL NET ASSETS			179,900
CAPITAL EMPLOYED			
Capital accounts:			
Beth	70,000		
Amy	50,000		
Jo	10,000		
			130,000
Current accounts:			
Beth	26,600 CR		
Amy	21,800 CR		
Jo	1,500 CR		
			49,900
TOTAL DUE TO PARTNERS			179,900
CLIENT ACCOUNT			
Client bank balance		894,568	
Due to clients		894,568	

Schedule to Balance Sheet

Movement on partners' current accounts

	Beth	Amy	Jo
Salary	10,000	13,500	5,000
Interest on capital	3,500	2,500	—
Profit share	43,800	34,200	7,500
	57,300	50,200	12,500
Less drawings	30,700	28,400	11,000
Balance	26,600 CR	21,800 CR	1,500 CR

6 **Hale and Owen: Profit and Loss and Appropriation account for the year ending 31 December 200—**

INCOME		
Profit costs	78,000	
ADD closing Work in Progress	5,000	
Value of work done		83,000
ADD insurance commission received	600	
		83,600

LESS EXPENSES

Salaries		20,000	
Insurance paid		1,500	
Council tax		1,620	
Light and heat	1,400		
Plus outstanding expense	100	1,500	
Stationery	900		
LESS closing stock	300	600	
Travel expenses		400	
Depreciation:			
Fixtures and fittings	1,500		
Library	200	1,700	27,320
NET PROFIT			56,280

APPROPRIATION ACCOUNT

Salary:			
Owen		2,000	
Interest on capital:			
Hale	4,000		
Owen	3,750	7,750	
Profit share:			
Hale: ½	23,265		
Owen: ½	23,265	46,530	
		56,280	

Hale and Owen: Balance Sheet as at 31 December 200—

FIXED ASSETS			
Premises		145,000	
Fixtures and fittings	15,000		
LESS accumulated depreciation	4,500		
		10,500	
Library	2,000		
LESS accumulated depreciation	700		
		1,300	
			156,800
CURRENT ASSETS			
Closing Work in Progress	5,000		
Debtors	3,000		
Office bank account	3,000		
Petty cash	100		
Stock of stationery	300		
		11,400	
LESS CURRENT LIABILITIES			
Creditors	820		
Outstanding expenses	100		
		920	
NET CURRENT ASSETS			10,480
			167,280
LESS LONG-TERM LIABILITIES			—
TOTAL NET ASSETS			167,280

CAPITAL EMPLOYED

Capital accounts:

Hale	80,000	
Owen	75,000	
		155,000

Current accounts: see 'Movement on
  partners' current accounts'

Hale	5,765	
Owen	6,515	
		12,280
TOTAL DUE TO PARTNERS		167,280

CLIENT ACCOUNT

Client bank balance	465,000	
Due to clients	465,000	

Schedule to Balance Sheet

Movement on partners' current accounts

	Hale	Owen
Opening balance	2,500	2,000
Salary		2,000
Interest on capital	4,000	3,750
Profit share	23,265	23,265
	29,765	31,015
LESS drawings	24,000	24,500
	5,765	6,515

6.12   Test on partnership final accounts

Allow 1 hour to 1 hour 20 minutes to complete this test.

From the Trial Balance of Shaw, Lewis, and Walsh set out below draw up a Profit and
Loss account and Appropriation account for the year ended 31 December 200—, together
with a Balance Sheet as at that date.

	DR	CR
Current accounts:		
Shaw		2,771
Lewis		3,055
Walsh	760	
Capital accounts:		
Shaw		160,000
Lewis		120,000
Walsh		80,000
Drawings:		
Shaw	25,000	
Lewis	25,000	
Walsh	25,000	
Creditors		5,923

Premises—cost price	300,000	
Office equipment—cost price	25,000	
Office furniture—cost price	30,000	
Motor cars—cost price	45,000	
Accumulated depreciation on office equipment		5,000
Accumulated depreciation on office furniture		6,000
Accumulated depreciation on motor cars		9,000
General expenses	415,000	
Cash at bank, office account	7,543	
Petty cash	96	
Profit costs		539,700
Interest received		7,150
Work in Progress as at 1 January 200—	35,000	
Cash at bank, client account		
current account	176,000	
deposit account	490,000	
Amount due to clients		666,000
Due from clients	5,200	
	1,604,599	1,604,599

Expenses due and not yet paid during the year amount to £895; expenses prepaid amount to £625. A bad debt has to be written off in the sum of £600, and provision for bad and doubtful debts amounts to £530. Work in Progress as at 31 December 200— amounts to £38,800. Depreciation on office equipment and on office furniture is 10% per annum on the cost price and depreciation on cars is 20% per annum on the cost price. Shaw has a partnership salary of £5,000, and the partners allow interest on capital at 5% per annum. The profits are then shared equally between the partners.

6.13 Suggested answer to test on partnership final accounts

Shaw, Lewis, and Walsh: Profit and Loss and Appropriation account for the year ending 31 December 200—

INCOME		
Profit costs	539,700	
ADD Work in Progress at the end of the year		
31 December 200—	38,800	
	578,500	
LESS Work in Progress at the start of the year		
1 January 200—	35,000	
Value of work done	543,500	
ADD ADDITIONAL INCOME		
Interest received	7,150	
		550,650
LESS EXPENSES		
Administrative And general expenses	415,000	
Outstanding expenses	895	
Bad debt written off	600	

Provision for doubtful debts		530	
		417,025	
LESS prepaid expenses		625	
		416,400	
Depreciation:			
Office equipment		2,500	
Office furniture		3,000	
Motor cars		9,000	
			14,500
			430,900
NET PROFIT			119,750
APPROPRIATION ACCOUNT			
Profit available for distribution			119,750
SALARY			
Shaw			5,000
INTEREST ON CAPITAL			
Shaw		8,000	
Lewis		6,000	
Walsh		4,000	
			18,000
Profit share			
Shaw		32,250	
Lewis		32,250	
Walsh		32,250	
			96,750

Shaw, Lewis, and Walsh: Balance Sheet as at 31 December 200—

FIXED ASSETS			
Premises cost price		300,000	
Office equipment cost price	25,000		
LESS total depreciation	7,500	17,500	
Office furniture cost price	30,000		
LESS total depreciation	9,000		
		21,000	
Motor cars cost price	45,000		
LESS total depreciation	18,000		
		27,000	
			365,500
CURRENT ASSETS			
Work in Progress		38,800	
Debtors (5,200–600)	4,600		
LESS provision	530		
		4,070	
Cash at bank, office account		7,543	
Petty cash		96	
Prepaid		625	
		51,134	

LESS CURRENT LIABILITIES			
Creditors	5,923		
Outstanding expenses	895		
		6,818	
NET CURRENT ASSETS			44,316
			409,816
LESS LONG-TERM LIABILITIES			—
TOTAL			409,816
CAPITAL EMPLOYED			
CAPITAL ACCOUNTS			
Shaw	160,000		
Lewis	120,000		
Walsh	80,000		
			360,000
CURRENT ACCOUNTS			
(see 'Movement on partners' current accounts')			
Shaw	23,021		
Lewis	16,305		
Walsh	10,490		
			49,816
TOTAL			409,816

Schedule to Balance Sheet

Movements on partners' current accounts

	Shaw	Lewis	Walsh
Opening balance	2,771	3,055	760 (DR)
Salary	5,000	—	—
Interest on capital	8,000	6,000	4,000
Profit share	32,250	32,250	32,250
	48,021	41,305	35,490
LESS drawings	25,000	25,000	25,000
	23,021	16,305	10,490

7

Basic accounting concepts and trading accounts

7.1 Introduction

This chapter includes:

1. An explanation of financial accounting concepts;
2. Accounting bases and policies;
3. Trading and Profit and Loss accounts;
4. Reminder of key points;
5. Practice exercises.

! **INTENDED OUTCOME**

An understanding of:

1. Basic accounting concepts and their use;
2. Accounting bases and policies;
3. The entries in a Trading and Profit and Loss account, evidenced by the ability to draw up a simple Trading and Profit and Loss account.

7.2 Financial accounting concepts

Accounting has certain rules, known as accounting concepts, which are applied in drawing up accounts and making adjustments. There are detailed accounting standards set out for accountants, earlier these were known as Statements of Standard Accounting Practice (SSAPs), later standards are known as Financial Reporting Standards (FRSs).

Any accounting methods used are supposed to give a true and fair view of a business, of its profit and loss and its value.

Fundamental accounting concepts are the assumptions on which accounts of businesses are drawn up. They include the following:

7.2.1 The business entity concept

This means that for accounting purposes a business is treated as a separate entity from its owner or owners, even though in law this may not be the case for a sole trader or a partnership. Thus when an owner puts money into the business this is recorded as the business having received the money and that the business owes that money to the owner (see paras 1.5.2 and 1.5.2.1).

7.2.2 The money measurement concept

Accounts give information about a business, but only in money terms. They do not, for example, give information about the motivation of the workforce or how competent the managing director is.

7.2.3 The cost concept

This means that assets would be valued at cost price rather than by estimating their current value.

7.2.4 The going-concern concept

This is the assumption that the business will continue to operate in the future. Thus the Profit and Loss account and the Balance Sheet will be drawn up on the assumption that the business will continue at the same level and not be sold. For example, if a business ceases to operate, its assets may be worth considerably less on a closing down sale than if the business continues.

7.2.5 The accruals concept

This is the assumption that income and expenses should be matched and actually recorded in the period in which they are earned or incurred, rather than the period in which they are actually received or paid, for example adjustments for work in progress, payments in advance, outstanding expenses, etc that we have seen previously (see Chapters 4 and 5). Thus if work has been carried out within a particular accounting period, then the amount earned in respect of that work should be shown as income. Or if a payment is made in advance it should not be treated as an expense of the period in which it has been paid, but should be shown as an expense in the next period.

7.2.6 The consistency concept

This means that there should be consistency in the accounting methods used for similar items, in the same accounting period and in later periods. If a firm changes the basis on which it values stock or work in progress, then the profit figure may be different from the figure that would be obtained had stock or work in progress been valued in the same way. Thus if businesses wish to change the basis on which they value stock, or value assets, then they must mention the effect on the profit of the change in accounting method.

7.2.7 The concept of prudence

This is the principle that profit should not be overstated. Thus income should not be anticipated and should be recorded in the Profit and Loss account only when received in cash, or as assets (for example debtors) which can be converted readily into cash. However, provision should be made for all possible known or expected future losses.

7.2.8   The concept of materiality

This means that there is no need to make detailed accounting records of items which are regarded as not material. For example, small items purchased, such as biros used in the office, will be treated as part of the expenses in the period in which they are purchased, and there will be no need to record on the Balance Sheet at the end of the year that the firm has six biros. Firms will decide individually whether an item is material, for example for a large firm items costing less than £500 may be treated as not material, if the firm is smaller then it may treat items costing less than £50 as not material. All such items will be treated as expenses and any remaining items will not be shown on the Balance Sheet, ie there is no need to make adjustments for small amounts.

7.3   Accounting bases and policies

Accounting bases are methods which have been developed for applying the accounting concepts to accounting transactions and items. These will vary according to the type of business and business transaction. They can be used, for example, to decide the accounting periods in which income and expenses should be recognised in the Profit and Loss account, and to decide the amounts at which items are considered material for inclusion in the Balance Sheet.

Accounting policies are particular accounting bases which are considered by individual businesses to be most appropriate to their particular circumstances for the purpose of giving a true and fair view. Accounting policies used by a business should be disclosed by way of a note to the accounts, for example how depreciation is treated, or how work in progress or stock is valued.

7.4   Trading accounts

7.4.1   Introduction

We have previously looked at the accounts of solicitors, who derive their income from services, or work done (see Chapters 1–6). With a trader, goods will be purchased for resale, thus there will be an account to record the value of all purchases and a separate account to record the value of all sales.

7.4.2   Trading account

When the trader draws up his final accounts, a trading account will be drawn up, showing the sales less purchases, to give the gross profit. This will be followed by the Profit and Loss account, showing all income, being the gross profit and any other income not derived from trading, for example interest receivable, less other expenses, being administrative expenses, financial expenses, etc. For example:

Trading account

Sales	£80,000
Less purchases	£25,000
Gross profit	£55,000

This is a simple form of trading account. Additional items to be taken into account might include sales returns; for example, where goods have been returned to the business, the sales returns account would be debited and then the cash book or the customer's personal ledger card would be credited. The debit balance on the sales returns account will be deducted from the sales figure, to give net sales. For example:

Sales	£700,000
Less sales returns	£10,000
	£690,000

The purchases figure will also have to be adjusted, to take account of any stock held by the trader at the start of the year, and any stock left at the end of the year, to give the actual cost of the goods sold.

EXAMPLE

A trader starts the year with £60,000 worth of goods (opening stock). During the year a further £300,000 worth of goods is purchased, and at the end of the year there is £40,000 worth of goods remaining.

The cost of goods sold is therefore:

Opening stock	60,000	
Plus purchases	300,000	
		360,000
Less closing stock		40,000
Cost of goods sold		320,000

The adjustment for stock will be shown on the Purchases account.

Purchases account

Date	Details	DR	CR	Balance
	Opening stock brought down from previous period	60,000		60,000 DR
	Purchases during the year	300,000		360,000 DR
	Closing stock		40,000	320,000 DR
	Transfer to Profit and Loss		320,000	—
	Opening stock b/d	40,000		40,000 DR

Assuming the Sales figure is £700,000, sales returns are £10,000, and expenses are £100,000, then the Trading and Profit and Loss account would appear as set out below:

Trading and Profit and Loss account for the year ending 31 December 200—

Sales	700,000	
Less returns	10,000	
		690,000
Less		

Cost of goods sold		
Opening stock	60,000	
Plus purchases	300,000	
	360,000	
Less closing stock	40,000	
Cost of goods sold		320,000
GROSS PROFIT		370,000
Less expenses		100,000
NET PROFIT		270,000

7.5 Reminder of key points

1. Accounting concepts are basic assumptions on which accounts of businesses are drawn up. They include:

   (a) the business entity concept—the business is treated as separate to its owner(s);

   (b) the money measurement concept—accounts only give information about a business in money terms;

   (c) the cost concept—that assets are valued at the cost price not the current value;

   (d) the going-concern concept—the assumption that the business will continue to operate;

   (e) the accruals concept—that income and expenses should be shown in the year when actually earned or incurred;

   (f) the consistency concept—that accounting methods used by a business are consistent;

   (g) the concept of prudence—income is not anticipated but provision should be made for known or expected future losses;

   (h) the concept of materiality—for example, no need to adjust for non-material (ie small) items.

2. Accounting bases and policies—bases are methods of applying accounting concepts; policies are the accounting bases used as most appropriate for a business.

3. Trading and Profit and Loss accounts—a Trading account will show first net sales less the cost of the goods sold to give gross profit, then the Profit and Loss account will show any further income and deduct any other expenses to give the net profit.

 online resource centre You may find it helpful to try the self-test exercises at the end of this chapter and also the online multiple choice questions available through your tutor via the Online Resource Centre that accompanies this book before moving on to company accounts in Chapter 8.

7.6 Practice exercises

1 Allow 10 to 15 minutes.

From the following figures extracted from the Trial Balance of Dell on 31 December 2009, draw up a Trading account for the period.

	DR	CR
Purchases	250,000	
Sales		600,000
Sales returns	30,500	
Stock on 1 January 2009	18,600	

Stock on 31 December 2009 is £10,400.

2 Allow 15 to 20 minutes.

Figures extracted from the Trial Balance of Kirk are shown below. From these draw up a Trading and Profit and Loss account for Kirk for the period.

Kirk: Trial Balance 31 December 200—

	DR	CR
Purchases	35,000	
Sales		99,850
Salaries	22,000	
Stock on 1 January	3,945	
General expenses	5,680	
Sales returns	4,500	
Light and heat	1,900	
Rent paid	10,000	

Stock on 31 December 200— is £5,625.

3 Allow 50 minutes to 1 hour.

The Trial Balance for Zaidi drawn up on 31 December 2009 is shown below:

	DR	CR
Loan		40,000
Drawings	55,000	
Capital		200,000
Stock on 1 January 2009	20,800	
Purchases	95,000	
General expenses	12,560	
Administrative expenses	5,490	
Sales		215,280
Sales returns	10,450	
Car cost price	24,000	
Freehold premises cost price	190,000	
Fixtures and fittings cost price	12,300	
Cash at bank	3,240	
Petty cash	520	
Salaries	30,000	
Debtors	8,900	
Creditors		12,980
	468,260	468,260

Closing stock on 31 December 2009 is £11,000. Depreciation of cars is 15% and on fixtures and fittings 10%. Draw up the Trading and Profit and Loss account and the Balance Sheet for Zaidi.

7.7 Suggested answers to practice exercises

1 **Dell: Trading account for the year ending 31 December 2009**

Sales		600,000
LESS returns		30,500
		569,500
LESS cost of goods sold		
Opening stock	18,600	
Plus purchases	250,000	
	268,600	
LESS closing stock	10,400	
		258,200
Net profit		311,300

2 **Kirk: Trading and Profit and Loss account for the year ending 31 December 200—**

Sales		99,850
LESS returns		4,500
		95,350
Less cost of goods sold		
Opening stock	3,945	
Plus purchases	35,000	
	38,945	
LESS closing stock	5,625	
		33,320
GROSS PROFIT		62,030
LESS EXPENSES		
Salaries	22,000	
General expenses	5,680	
Light and heat	1,900	
Rent paid	10,000	
		39,580
NET PROFIT		22,450

3   **Zaidi: Trading and Profit and Loss account for the year ending 31 December 2009**

Sales			215,280
LESS returns			10,450
			204,830
LESS COST OF GOODS SOLD			
Opening stock	20,800		
Plus purchases	95,000		
		115,800	
LESS closing stock		11,000	
			104,800
GROSS PROFIT			100,030
LESS EXPENSES			
General expenses	12,560		
Administrative expenses	5,490		
Salaries	30,000		
Depreciation on car	3,600		
Depreciation on fixtures and fittings	1,230		52,880
NET PROFIT			47,150

Zaidi: Balance Sheet as at 31 December 2009

Fixed assets			
Freehold premises cost price		190,000	
Car cost price	24,000		
LESS depreciation	3,600		
		20,400	
Fixtures and fittings	12,300		
LESS depreciation	1,230		
		11,070	
			221,470
CURRENT ASSETS			
Closing stock	11,000		
Debtors	8,900		
Cash at bank	3,240		
Petty cash	520		
		23,660	
LESS CURRENT LIABILITIES			
Creditors		12,980	
NET CURRENT ASSETS			10,680
Total			232,150
LESS LONG-TERM LIABILITY			40,000
TOTAL NET ASSETS			192,150
CAPITAL EMPLOYED			
Capital	200,000		
ADD net profit	47,150		
		247,150	
LESS drawings		55,000	
TOTAL DUE TO OWNER			192,150

8

Company accounts

8.1 Introduction

This chapter includes:

1. Entries on accounts of limited companies in respect of the issue of share capital and debentures;

2. Company Profit and Loss accounts—example and treatment of taxation, dividends, retained profit and reserves, provisions reserves, and liabilities compared;

3. An example of a company Balance Sheet;

4. Reminder of key points;

5. Practice exercises.

You may find the following websites useful:
<http://www.companieshouse.gov.uk>;
<http://www.berr.gov.uk>;
<http://www.hrmc.gov.uk>.

! INTENDED OUTCOME

An understanding of:

1. Entries required on accounts of limited companies in respect of share capital and debentures;

2. The structure of a company Profit and Loss account, including the treatment of taxation and dividends, retained profit and reserves, evidenced by the ability to draw up a company Trading and Profit and Loss Account;

3. The structure of a company Balance Sheet, evidenced by the ability to draw up a company Balance Sheet.

8.2 Accounts of limited companies

Different types of companies may be incorporated, note that the relevant provisions in the Companies Act 2006 will be brought into force on 1 October 2009.

In this chapter we will just look at companies limited by shares, where a member's liability is limited to any part of the issued price of the member's shares not yet paid to the company.

8.2.1 Share capital

The capital of a limited company is divided into shares which will have a nominal value, for example £1 each, or £5 or £10. When the company issues shares for cash, the entries are the same as the entries made when a sole proprietor or a partner introduces capital. The capital account will be known as the Share Capital account.

EXAMPLE

A company issues 60,000 £1 ordinary shares for £60,000 cash.

DEBIT the Cash Book.
CREDIT the Share Capital account.

Cash Book

Date	Details	DR	CR	Balance
	Share capital	60,000		60,000 DR

Share Capital account
£1 ordinary shares

Date	Details	DR	CR	Balance
	Cash		60,000	60,000 CR

A company may issue the shares at par, ie sell the shares at their nominal value. Thus if the company above issued 60,000 shares at a nominal value of £1 for £1 each, then the entries would be as above.

The Balance Sheet would show:

FIXED ASSETS	XX
CURRENT ASSETS	
Cash	60,000
CAPITAL EMPLOYED	
Share capital £1 ordinary shares	60,000

8.2.2 Issuing shares at a premium

A company may, however, set a price which is higher than the nominal value, when it will issue the shares at a premium. For example, the company issues 60,000 £1 shares at £1.20 each, giving total cash of £72,000. The Cash Book will be debited with the total amount received, broken down into the nominal value of £60,000 and the premium of £12,000. The Share Capital account will be credited with the £60,000 and the Share Premium account will be credited with the £12,000.

Cash Book

Date	Details	DR	CR	Balance
	Share capital	60,000		60,000 DR
	Share premium	12,000		72,000 DR

Share Capital account

Date	Details	DR	CR	Balance
	Cash		60,000	60,000 CR

Share Premium account

Date	Details	DR	CR	Balance
	Cash		12,000	12,000 CR

The Balance Sheet would show:

FIXED ASSETS		XX
CURRENT ASSETS		
Cash		72,000
CAPITAL EMPLOYED		
Share capital £1 ordinary shares	60,000	
Share premium	12,000	
		72,000

Note that a company may not issue all the shares which it is authorised to sell. The shares that are sold are called the issued capital.

Different types of shares may be offered, for example ordinary, preference, or deferred shares. There may also be voting and non-voting shares.

8.2.3 Preference shares

These will get an agreed percentage rate of dividend before the ordinary shareholders, ie they have priority. There may be different classes of preference shares, for example:

8.2.3.1 Non-cumulative preference shares

These receive the dividend before the ordinary shareholders up to an agreed percentage. However, if the amount paid in a year is less than the maximum agreed percentage, the shareholder cannot claim the shortage in the next year or years.

8.2.3.2 Cumulative preference shares

In this case, if a full dividend is not received in a year, the arrears of dividend can be carried forward and paid together with the dividend due in the next year before the ordinary shareholders are entitled to receive any dividend.

8.2.3.3 Participating preference shares

In this case the shareholders may also have the right to participate in any remaining profits after the ordinary shareholders have received their dividend.

8.2.3.4 Redeemable preference shares

In such a case the shares will be repaid by the company at some time in the future.

This may sound complicated, but the accounting entries for the issue of all types of preference shares will be the same. A separate Share Capital account for each type of shares will be opened.

EXAMPLE

A company issues 50,000 ordinary shares at £1 each, and 10,000 7% preference shares at £1 each.

DEBIT the Cash Book for each.
CREDIT the relevant share account for each.

Cash Book

Date	Details	DR	CR	Balance
	Ordinary shares	50,000		50,000 DR
	7% preference shares	10,000		60,000 DR

Ordinary Share Capital account

Date	Details	DR	CR	Balance
	Cash		50,000	50,000 CR

7% Preference Share Capital account

Date	Details	DR	CR	Balance
	Cash		10,000	10,000 DR

Note: the cash received from the share issue will be used in the business, for example to purchase assets.

8.2.4 Debentures

A debenture is a bond which acknowledges a loan to a company and which bears a fixed rate of interest. As this is really a type of loan to the company, the debenture holder is not a member of the company like a shareholder and the interest will be paid whether the company makes a profit or not. A debenture may be redeemable, ie repayable at or before a specified date, or irredeemable and thus only repayable when the company is liquidated.

When debentures are issued, then the entries will be similar to those shown on the issue of share capital.

EXAMPLE

A company issues debentures of £60,000 at fixed interest of 10%.

DEBIT the Cash Book.
CREDIT the Debenture stock account.

Cash Book

Date	Details	DR	CR	Balance
	10% debentures	60,000		60,000 DR

10% Debenture stock

Date	Details	DR	CR	Balance
	Cash		60,000	60,000 CR

8.2.5 Issuing debentures at a discount

EXAMPLE

A company issues 12% (interest) debentures at a discount of 10%. The debentures have a nominal value of £40,000. With the discount of 10%, ie £4,000, the cash received will be £36,000. The 12% Debenture account will be credited with £40,000, broken down into the cash received and the amount of the discount. The Cash Book will be debited with the cash received, and a Debenture discount account will be debited with the discount.

12% Debenture account

Date	Details	DR	CR	Balance
	Cash		36,000	36,000 CR
	Discount		4,000	40,000 CR

Cash Book

Date	Details	DR	CR	Balance
	12% debenture	36,000		36,000 DR

Debenture discount account

Date	Details	DR	CR	Balance
	12% debenture	4,000		4,000 DR

When the company redeems the debentures, it will repay them at the full price, ie £40,000. This is shown by the credit balance on the Debenture account, ie the company owes £40,000. The debit balance on the Debenture discount account shows the loss in issuing the debenture. If, for example, the ordinary share capital of the company was £100,000 the Balance Sheet would show:

LONG-TERM LIABILITY	
12% debenture	40,000
CAPITAL EMPLOYED	
Ordinary share capital	100,000

The debit balance on the Debenture discount account will be shown as a deduction in the Capital Employed section until it has been written off.

LONG-TERM LIABILITY		
12% debenture		40,000
CAPITAL EMPLOYED		
Ordinary share capital		100,000
Reserves, say (see para 8.3.6)	80,000	
LESS debenture discount	4,000	
		76,000
		176,000

8.3   Limited companies' Profit and Loss accounts

A company may draw up its own final accounts for internal use in any way it considers most suitable. However, when the accounts are sent to the Registrar of Companies or to a shareholder, the Companies Act 2006, Pt 15 dictates the information that must be shown, and also how it should be shown, in line with European Community requirements.

A company's Profit and Loss account is similar to that of a sole trader or partnership. However, there are some differences.

Salaries paid to directors will be shown as an expense of the company (like wages of employees). Contrast this with a salary paid to a partner, which was shown as an allocation of profit in the Appropriation account. The Appropriation account shows how the net profit will be used. After the net profit has been calculated, tax will have to be considered, and provided for. Once this has been done then dividends should be provided for, and then any surplus profit may be retained or transferred to reserves.

Set out below is a simple form of Company Trading and Profit and Loss account.

Company name

Trading and Profit and Loss account for the year ending—

Sales/Turnover			680,000
LESS cost of goods sold			
Opening stock	60,000		
Add purchases	220,000		
	280,000		
LESS closing stock		40,000	
			240,000
Gross profit			440,000
LESS EXPENSES			
Wages		120,000	
Directors' remuneration		80,000	
General expenses		23,000	
Debenture interest payable		5,000	
Depreciation on equipment		4,000	
Depreciation on cars		8,000	
Total expenses			240,000
Profit before taxation			200,000
LESS provision for taxation, say			42,000
Profit after taxation			158,000
LESS Ordinary share dividend			
Interim paid	10,000		
Final dividend	30,000		
			40,000
RETAINED PROFIT			118,000

8.3.1 Appropriation of profit—taxation

Corporation tax is NOT an expense of the company but is regarded as an appropriation of profit.

The rate of corporation tax is currently 21% for small companies as from April 2008, rising to 22% in April 2010. There is a marginal relief rate for medium-sized companies, and the rate for large companies is 28% as from 2008/2009. Small companies are those with taxable profits up to £300,000 a year. Medium-sized companies are those with taxable profits between £300,000 and £1.5 million a year. Large companies are those with taxable profits over £1.5 million a year.

To provide for taxation, the Appropriation account will be debited (remember that this forms part of the double-entry system) and a Taxation account will be credited.

EXAMPLE

The net profit of a company is £200,000. Assuming the rate of corporation tax to be 21%, the tax would be £42,000.

DEBIT the Profit and Loss Appropriation account.
CREDIT the Taxation Account.

Profit and Loss account

Net profit	200,000
Less corporation tax (debit)	42,000
	158,000

Taxation account

Date	Details	DR	CR	Balance
	Profit and Loss account		42,000	42,000 CR

These entries do not involve any payment or transfer of cash. The net profit is merely appropriated, and the credit balance on the taxation account shows that £42,000 is due to HMRC. Until the tax is paid this will be shown as a current liability on the Balance Sheet. When the tax is actually paid, the Cash Book will be credited, and the Taxation account debited. Continuing the above example:

Cash Book

Date	Details	DR	CR	Balance
	Balance, say			150,000 DR
	Taxation—HMRC		42,000	108,000 DR

Taxation account

Date	Details	DR	CR	Balance
	Balance			42,000 CR
	Cash	42,000		Nil

8.3.2   Dividends

The directors of a company will propose that part of the net profit be distributed to the shareholders, usually expressed as a percentage of the nominal value of the shares.

8.3.2.1   Appropriation of dividend

DEBIT the Appropriation account.
CREDIT the Dividend account.

EXAMPLE

A company declares a dividend of 10% in respect of ordinary shares with a nominal value of £100,000, being £10,000. Net profit after tax is £94,800. The directors will not allocate all the profit remaining after taxation, as:

(a) Profit will need to be retained to run the business, or for expansion;
(b) Net profit will not necessarily be represented by cash at the bank.

Profit and Loss account

Net profit	120,000
Less corporation tax (debit)	25,200
	94,800
Less dividend	10,000
	84,800

Dividend account

Date	Details	DR	CR	Balance
	Profit and Loss account		10,000	10,000 CR

The amount shown on the dividend account shows the amount due for the dividend. This will be shown as a current liability on the Balance Sheet. The size of the dividend will be agreed at the annual general meeting of the company, when the accounts are agreed. The dividend can then be paid. Continuing the above example:

8.3.2.2   Payment of dividend

CREDIT the Cash Book.
DEBIT the Dividend account.

Cash Book

Date	Details	DR	CR	Balance
	Balance, say			25,000 DR
	Dividend		10,000	15,000 DR

Dividend account

Date	Details	DR	CR	Balance
	Balance			10,000 CR
	Cash	10,000		Nil

8.3.2.3 Payment of interim dividend

If the company has paid an interim dividend before the end of the year, the entries to record the payment of the interim dividend will be the same as the payment of the dividend above. The interim dividend will be shown in the Appropriation section of the Profit and Loss account, in the same way that the end of year dividend was shown.

EXAMPLE

During the year a company pays an interim dividend of £10,000. At the end of the year the net profit after taxation is £80,000. A final dividend of £15,000 is recommended by the directors.

1. Payment of the interim dividend during the year.

   CREDIT Cash Book.
   DEBIT Dividend account.

Cash Book

Date	Details	DR	CR	Balance
	Balance, say			48,000 DR
	Interim dividend		10,000	38,000 DR

Dividend account

Date	Details	DR	CR	Balance
	Cash—interim dividend	10,000		10,000 DR

2. Final dividend at the end of the year.

Profit and Loss account

Net profit after taxation			80,000
Less dividend			
Interim	10,000		
Final	15,000		
			25,000
			55,000

Dividend account

Date	Details	DR	CR	Balance
	Balance (interim dividend)			10,000 DR
	Profit and Loss account			
	Interim dividend		10,000	Nil
	Final dividend		15,000	15,000 CR

The £15,000 credit balance on the dividend account will be shown on the Balance Sheet as a current liability, being the amount due to the shareholders. When the final dividend is paid, the entries will be as shown previously.

8.3.3 Appropriation—retained profit and reserves

After providing for taxation and dividends, the balance of the net profit is retained on the Appropriation account, or it may be transferred to a reserve account. Either way it will be shown as a reserve on the Balance Sheet, in the Capital Employed section (like the net profit due to a sole proprietor).

Net profit is not necessarily represented by cash—it is represented by an increase in recorded net assets. Thus 'retention of profit' or 'reserves' is merely retaining in the business the assets which are attributable to profit.

The balance of net profit will be transferred to a reserve account if it is to be retained for a specific purpose, for example replacement of fixed assets or redemption (repayment) of debentures. The entries to record a transfer to a reserve account are:

DEBIT the Appropriation account.
CREDIT the Reserve account.

EXAMPLE

Net profit after taxation is £40,000. A dividend of £10,000 is declared. Of the remaining £30,000, £16,000 is transferred to a reserve account.

Net profit after taxation	£40,000
Less dividend	£10,000
	£30,000
Transferred to reserve	£16,000
	£14,000

Note: both the balance of £14,000 and the reserve of £16,000 will be shown on the Balance Sheet as part of the capital employed.

CAPITAL EMPLOYED		
Share capital		100,000 (say)
Reserves		
Special reserve	16,000	
Profit and Loss	14,000	
		30,000
		130,000

As mentioned in para 3.5.1.3, this is the same principle as in the Balance Sheet of a sole proprietor, where the net profit would be shown added to their capital.

The share capital and reserves shown above are known as the shareholders' equity or the ordinary shareholders' funds. These will be represented by the assets of the company, shown in the Capital Employed section of the Balance Sheet.

In the event of the company being wound up the shareholders would be entitled to the return of their capital, plus a share in the surplus assets of the company, represented by the reserves.

8.3.4 Provisions, reserves, and liabilities

A provision, as we have seen in para 5.2.3, may be debited to the Profit and Loss account, or it may be debited to the Appropriation account of a company. A provision may be created in respect of a known liability which exists at the date of the Balance Sheet where the amount cannot be determined with substantial accuracy. The provision may, for example, be for (estimated) doubtful debts, or depreciation, which would be debited to the Profit and Loss section. Provision may also be made for estimated taxation, or a dividend, which would be debited to the Appropriation section.

Provisions are in contrast to liabilities, which are amounts owed and which can be determined with substantial accuracy, for example rent due. Provisions may also be contrasted with reserves, which can only be debited to the Appropriation section, and which do not relate to any liability or loss which is known to exist at the time of the Balance Sheet.

Definitions of these are contained in the Companies Act 2006.

8.3.5   Capital and revenue reserves

8.3.5.1   Revenue reserves

These are reserves transferred from the Profit and Loss appropriation account (ie retained profit) which can be general, or for some particular purpose, for example a foreign exchange reserve account, to meet any possible losses through devaluation of a foreign currency. General revenue reserve accounts may be used in future years, should profit be insufficient for dividends, when the reserve may be used for the payment of dividends, provided that cash is available. (If this was done, then the revenue reserve account would be debited and the Profit and Loss Appropriation account would be credited.)

General reserve accounts may also be used to increase the capital required with inflation as the amount of working capital required by the company will increase. When we looked at final accounts in Chapter 2, we saw on the Balance Sheet a figure for net current assets, or working capital—this means the portion of capital invested in the business which is left to run the business after providing the fixed assets.

8.3.5.2   Capital reserves

These are not available for distribution by way of dividend under the Companies Act.

Capital reserves which cannot be used for the declaration of dividends payable in cash are:

(a) capital redemption reserves;

(b) a share premium account;

(c) a revaluation reserve.

Capital redemption reserves include a preference shares redemption reserve, which can be used to redeem redeemable preference shares or, for example, a debenture redemption reserve, which can be used to redeem debentures on the date specified. A company may transfer a certain amount of net profit each year to a redemption reserve account.

A share premium account is needed when the company issues shares at a premium—the additional amount over the nominal value of the shares is shown in the share premium account.

A revaluation reserve is used when a company revalues its assets. If the value of the assets is increased, then there must be a corresponding increase in the Capital Employed section of the Balance Sheet. The asset account is debited and the revaluation reserve account is credited. Note that this cannot be used to pay a dividend as it merely represents the increase in value of the assets.

8.3.6   Capitalisation of reserves: bonus issue of shares

Although reserves may not be available for distribution by way of dividend, they may be capitalised by issuing bonus or free shares to shareholders.

EXAMPLE

A company has an issued share capital of 40,000,000 £1 ordinary shares and general reserves of £15,000,000. It makes a bonus issue of one share for every four shares held. The bonus issue will therefore be £10,000,000.

Before the bonus issue the Balance Sheet would show:

	'000
CAPITAL EMPLOYED	
Share capital	40,000
General reserves	15,000
	55,000

After the bonus issue the Balance Sheet will show:

	'000
CAPITAL EMPLOYED	
Share capital	50,000
General reserves	5,000
	55,000

The entries on the accounts would be:

Share Capital account

Date	Details	DR	CR	Balance
		'000	'000	'000
	Balance			40,000 CR
	General reserve		10,000	50,000 CR

General reserve account

Date	Details	DR	CR	Balance
		'000	'000	'000
	Balance			15,000 CR
	Share capital	10,000		5,000 CR

Although each shareholder will own more shares, these will be worth less individually, as the shares are still represented by the same amount of assets. Any dividend payable in respect of the shares may be at a lower percentage, as the same net profit will have to be apportioned between the shares.

8.3.7 Sinking funds

As mentioned in para 8.3.3, retained net profit is not equivalent to cash, it merely represents an increase in assets. If cash is required, then it will be necessary, at the same time as profit is transferred to a reserve, to transfer the required amount of cash, or easily realisable assets, to a sinking fund (or reserve fund) which can then be used when needed.

EXAMPLE

A company transfers £200,000 to the debenture redemption reserve from net profit after taxation and dividends of £500,000. It also transfers £200,000 from the cash at the bank to a deposit account, to be used as a reserve fund for debenture redemption.

Profit and Loss Appropriation account

Net profit after tax and dividend	£500,000
Transfer to debenture redemption reserve	£200,000
	£300,000

Debenture redemption reserve account

Date	Details	DR	CR	Balance
	Profit and Loss		200,000	200,000 CR

Cash Book

Date	Details	DR	CR	Balance
	Balance, say			350,000 DR
	Debenture redemption reserve (sinking) fund		200,000	150,000 DR

Debenture redemption reserve (sinking) fund account

Date	Details	DR	CR	Balance
	Cash	200,000		200,000 DR

The Balance Sheet would show:

FIXED ASSETS
Debenture redemption reserve (sinking fund)   200,000
NET CURRENT ASSETS
CAPITAL EMPLOYED
Share capital   XX
Debenture redemption reserve   200,000

8.4 The form of the Balance Sheet

Again the Companies Act 2006 specifies the information that must be shown and how it should be shown. A simple example of a company Balance Sheet is set out below.

8.4.1 Example Balance Sheet

Balance Sheet as at—

	'000	'000	'000
FIXED ASSETS			
Intangible assets			
Goodwill		10,000	
Tangible assets			
Premises	200,000		
Machinery	80,000		
Motor cars	40,000		
		320,000	
			330,000

CURRENT ASSETS			
Stock	30,000		
Debtors	26,000		
Cash at bank	20,000		
		76,000	
LESS CREDITORS			
Amounts falling due within one year			
Proposed dividend	10,000		
Creditors	18,000		
Corporation tax due	9,000		
		37,000	
			39,000
TOTAL ASSETS LESS CURRENT LIABILITIES			369,000
CREDITORS			
Amounts falling due after more than one year			90,000
TOTAL			279,000
CAPITAL AND RESERVES			
Authorised and issued fully paid ordinary £1 shares		240,000	
Share premium account		13,000	
General reserve		15,000	
Profit and Loss account retained profit		11,000	
TOTAL			279,000

8.5 Reminder of key points

1. Entries required in respect of the issue of share capital and debentures: on issue of shares the Cash Book will be debited with the receipt of cash and the Share Capital account credited, showing the amount due to the shareholders, on issue of debentures (which are effectively loans to a company); the Cash Book will be debited with the receipt of the cash; and the Debenture account will show the amount due to the debenture holder. Note also that interest will be paid to the debenture holder;

2. The form of a company Trading and Profit and Loss account; note that salaries to directors are an expense for the company;

3. Appropriation of profit—taxation and dividends: on appropriation any provision for tax due will also be shown, then any provision for dividends payable to the shareholders, then surplus profit may be retained or transferred to reserves;

4. Retained profit and reserves on the Balance Sheet; these will be shown in the Capital Employed section;

5. Note the simple form of a company Balance Sheet in para 8.4.

Now try the self-test exercises at the end of this chapter and the online multiple choice questions available through your tutor via the Online Resource Centre that accompanies this book, and then move on to Chapter 9 on group companies and consolidated accounts.

8.6 Practice exercises

The following exercises will aid your understanding of company accounts.

1 Allow 5 to 10 minutes.

Explain what would be shown on a company's Balance Sheet after it has issued for cash 100,000 £1 ordinary shares at a price of £3 per share.

2 Allow 5 to 10 minutes.

A company estimates its taxation liability at the end of the year to be £40,000. Explain where this would be recorded on the company's final accounts.

3 Allow 10 minutes.

Look at the following abbreviated company's Balance Sheet. Would the directors be able to authorise payment of a cash dividend to shareholders totalling £30,000?

Fixed assets			800,000
Current assets			
Stock	45,000		
Debtors	32,000		
Cash at bank	15,000		
		92,000	
Current liabilities			
Taxation	12,000		
Creditors	26,000		
		38,000	
Net current assets			54,000
			854,000
Capital employed			
Share capital	700,000		
Reserves	154,000		
			£854,000

4 Allow about 1 hour for this exercise.

From the following trial balance of Randall Ltd drawn up on 31 March 200—, draw up the Trading and Profit and Loss account and the Balance Sheet for the year ending 31 March 200—.

Trial Balance	DR	CR
Ordinary share capital		120,000
10% preference share capital		25,000
Debentures		20,000
Buildings	150,000	
Equipment	45,000	
Motor cars	20,000	
Accumulated depreciation: equipment		5,000
Accumulated depreciation: motor cars		10,000
Stock at start of year	19,000	

Sales		375,000
Purchases	149,000	
Wages	40,000	
Directors' remuneration	70,000	
Motor expenses	6,000	
Rates insurance	4,000	
General expenses	19,000	
Debenture interest payable	2,000	
Debtors	29,000	
Creditors		19,000
Cash at bank	26,000	
Interim ordinary dividend paid	10,000	
General reserve		15,000
	588,000	588,000

Additional information required to complete the accounts:

stock at the end of the year is £21,000;

depreciation on equipment is £2,000, and on motor cars is £5,000;

taxation is estimated at £16,800;

the preference share dividend is £2,500; and

the final dividend for the ordinary shareholders is £2,000.

5 Allow about 1 hour for this exercise.

From the Trial Balance of Downey Ltd shown below, draw up a Trading and Profit and Loss account and a Balance Sheet in the format required under the Companies Act.

Trial Balance as at 31 December 2009

	DR	CR
	'000	'000
Ordinary share capital £1 shares fully paid		160,000
12% debentures		40,000
Goodwill at cost	20,000	
Buildings	150,000	
Fixtures and fittings	40,000	
Motor cars	25,000	
Accumulated depreciation: fixtures and fittings		8,000
Accumulated depreciation: motor cars		10,000
Stock as at 1 January 2009	23,000	
Sales		179,000
Purchases	70,000	
Salaries/wages	33,000	
Directors' fees	39,000	
Motor expenses	2,500	
Council tax	2,300	
General expenses	11,400	
Debenture interest	6,000	
Debtors	26,500	
Creditors		19,900
Cash at bank	13,200	

General reserve		15,000
Share premium account		16,000
Interim ordinary dividend paid	3,000	
Profit and Loss account as at 1 January 2009		17,000
	464,900	464,900

The following should be taken into account:

	'000
stock at the end of the year	26,000
depreciation on cars for the year	5,000
depreciation on fixtures	4,000
proposed final dividend	2,000
provision for corporation tax due	2,460

8.7 Suggested answers to practice exercises

1 The Balance Sheet would show a current asset of cash of £300,000 and in the Capital Employed section share capital of £1 ordinary shares at £100,000 and share premium at £200,000.

2 The taxation would be shown as a deduction from net profit in the Appropriation section. It would also be shown as a liability in current liabilities on the Balance Sheet.

3 Although the company has net current assets of £54,000 it only has £15,000 cash, it is likely this will be needed to pay creditors, etc. If stock could be sold and debtors paid then the company may be able to consider a cash distribution. Note that reserves in the Capital Employed section are not cash, nor are they necessarily represented by cash. Reserves show the total due to shareholders, and only reflect any increase in assets.

4 **Randall Ltd: Trading and Profit and Loss account for the year ending 31 March 200—**

Sales			375,000
LESS cost of goods sold			
Opening stock	19,000		
ADD purchases	149,000		
	168,000		
LESS closing stock	21,000		
			147,000
Gross profit			228,000
LESS expenses			
Wages	40,000		
Motor expenses	6,000		
Directors' remuneration	70,000		
Rates and insurance	4,000		
General expenses	19,000		
Debenture interest payable	2,000		
Depreciation on equipment	2,000		
Depreciation on cars	5,000		
			148,000

Profit before taxation			80,000
Taxation			16,800
Profit after taxation			63,200
LESS appropriation			
Preference share dividend		2,500	
Ordinary share dividend			
Interim paid	10,000		
Final dividend	2,000		
		12,000	
			14,500
Reserves (retained profit)			48,700

Randall Ltd: Balance Sheet as at 31 March 200—

FIXED ASSETS			
Buildings		150,000	
Equipment	45,000		
LESS depreciation	7,000		
		38,000	
Motor cars	20,000		
LESS depreciation	15,000		
		5,000	
			193,000
CURRENT ASSETS			
Stock	21,000		
Debtors	29,000		
Cash at bank	26,000		
		76,000	
LESS CURRENT LIABILITIES			
Creditors	19,000		
Preference share dividend	2,500		
Final dividend	2,000		
Taxation	16,800		
		40,300	
NET CURRENT ASSETS			35,700
TOTAL ASSETS LESS CURRENT LIABILITIES			228,700
LESS debentures			20,000
			208,700
CAPITAL AND RESERVES			
Ordinary share capital		120,000	
Preference shares		25,000	
		145,000	
Reserves	15,000		
This year	48,700		
		63,700	
			208, 700

5 **Downey Ltd: Trading and Profit and Loss account for the year ending 31 December 2009**

	'000	'000	'000
Sales			179,000
LESS cost of goods sold			
Opening stock	23,000		
ADD purchases	70,000		
	93,000		
LESS closing stock	26,000		
			67,000
Gross profit			112,000
LESS expenses			
Salaries	33,000		
Directors' fees	39,000		
Motor expenses	2,500		
Council tax	2,300		
General expenses	11,400		
Debenture interest	6,000		
Depreciation on fixtures	4,000		
Depreciation on cars	5,000		
			103,200
Profit for the year			8,800
LESS provision for corporation tax			2,460
Profit after tax			6,340
ADD retained profit from last year			17,000
			23,340
LESS dividends			
Interim dividend paid	3,000		
Final dividend proposed	2,000		
			5,000
Retained profit carried forward to next year			18,340

Downey Ltd: Balance Sheet as at 31 December 2009

	'000	'000	'000
FIXED ASSETS			
Intangible assets			
Goodwill			20,000
Tangible assets			
Premises		150,000	
Fixtures costs	40,000		
LESS depreciation	12,000		
		28,000	
Cars cost	25,000		
LESS depreciation	15,000		
		10,000	
			188,000
			208,000

CURRENT ASSETS:

Stock		26,000	
Debtors		26,500	
Cash at bank		13,200	
		65,700	
Creditors: amounts falling due within one year			
Creditors	19,900		
Proposed dividend	2,000		
Taxation due	2,460		
		24,360	
NET CURRENT ASSETS			41,340
Total assets less current liabilities			249,340
LESS LONG-TERM LIABILITIES			
Debentures			40,000
TOTAL			209,340
CAPITAL AND RESERVES			
Share capital £1 ordinary shares		160,000	
Share premium		16,000	
General reserve		15,000	
Profit and Loss account		18,340	
TOTAL			209,340

9

Group companies and consolidated accounts

9.1 Introduction

This chapter includes:

1. Group companies and the requirement for consolidated accounts—parent and subsidiary undertakings;
2. Definition of parent and subsidiary undertakings;
3. The consolidated Balance Sheet;
4. Acquisition of shares for more or less than the book value of the assets of the company;
5. The consolidated Profit and Loss account;
6. Consolidated accounts where a company holds a majority interest in the subsidiary;
7. Reminder of key points;
8. Practice exercise.

! **INTENDED OUTCOME**

An understanding of:

1. The circumstances in which consolidated final accounts are required;
2. The structure of a consolidated Balance Sheet and Profit and Loss account.

9.2 Companies and their subsidiaries

Separate companies operating independently will have separate accounting records and financial statements. Where one company controls another, this is regarded as a group, with a controlling, or parent, company which is called the parent undertaking, and the subsidiary company, called the subsidiary undertaking. Although the companies are still separate legal entities with separate financial records, the idea is that the shareholders of the parent company should be given some information about the subsidiary company. This information is provided by consolidated accounts for the group, being a consolidated Profit and Loss account and a consolidated Balance Sheet. These are created by aggregating the separate Profit and Loss accounts and Balance Sheets of the parent and subsidiary undertaking and are produced *in addition* to the separate final accounts for each company.

9.2.1   What is a parent undertaking? Companies Act 2006, s 1162

An undertaking is a parent undertaking in relation to another undertaking, a subsidiary undertaking, if:

(a) it holds a majority of the voting rights in the undertaking; or

(b) it is a member of the undertaking and has the right to appoint or remove a majority of its board of directors; or

(c) it has the right to exercise a dominant influence over the undertaking;

   (i)   by virtue of provisions contained in the undertaking's articles; or

   (ii) by virtue of a control contract; or

(d) it is a member of the undertaking and controls alone, pursuant to an agreement with other shareholders or members, a majority of the voting rights in the undertaking.

An undertaking is also a parent undertaking in relation to another undertaking, a subsidiary undertaking, if it has the power to exercise, or actually exercises, dominant influence or control over it, or it and the subsidiary undertaking are managed on a unified basis.

The above is really based on a company's ability to exercise control over another company. A group will thus exist whenever legal entities which are independent of each other are under central management, regardless of the share ownership. This legislation implements the EC Seventh Directive on consolidated accounts (Directive 83/349/EEC).

9.3   The consolidated Balance Sheet

9.3.1   Merging the Balance Sheets

The Balance Sheets of each company will be merged. The issued capital shown will be that of the parent company only, which is represented by the assets of the two companies. Merging does not mean that the two Balance Sheets are just added together: the inter-company shares should be cancelled out first, and then the assets of the two companies will be added together. Inter-company shares mean those shares in the subsidiary company owned by the parent company shown in its Balance Sheet, and the subsidiary company's capital and reserves which represent those shares shown in the subsidiary company's Balance Sheet.

EXAMPLE

Company P Ltd owns the whole share capital of company S Ltd and the two separate Balance Sheets show:

	P Ltd	(parent company)
	'000	
Fixed assets	25,000	
Shares in B Ltd (at cost)	15,000	inter-company shares (investment in subsidiary)
Net current assets	10,000	
Total	50,000	
Share capital	50,000	

	S Ltd	(subsidiary company)
	'000	
Fixed assets	10,000	
Net current assets	5,000	
	15,000	
Share capital	15,000	(representing the above)

The inter-company shares are cancelled out, ie the shares held in S Ltd by P Ltd are taken out from P Ltd's Balance Sheet and the share capital representing this must be taken out from S Ltd's Balance Sheet.

Then, the assets of S Ltd must be added into P Ltd's Balance Sheet to make the consolidated account for P Ltd and S Ltd.

Thus the consolidated Balance Sheet would be as follows:

P Ltd and S Ltd: Consolidated Group Balance Sheet

	'000	'000
Fixed assets: P Ltd		25,000
S Ltd		10,000
		35,000
Net current assets: P Ltd	10,000	
S Ltd	5,000	
		15,000
Total		50,000
Share capital		50,000

Reserves

If the subsidiary company has reserves, then both the share capital and the reserves (shareholders' funds) in the subsidiary company will be excluded.

9.3.2   Acquiring shares for more or less than the Balance Sheet value of the assets

If a company pays more than the Balance Sheet value, then the excess is known as goodwill, which will be included on the consolidated Balance Sheet. If a company pays less than the Balance Sheet value, then the company has made a 'profit' which is due to the shareholders, but cannot be distributed to them. A capital reserve account will be opened in respect of the 'profit' and will be shown on the consolidated Balance Sheet.

9.4 The consolidated Profit and Loss account

9.4.1 Merging the Profit and Loss accounts

These can be fairly complicated. The sales, cost of sales, and expenses will be merged and the net profits, taxation, and transfers to reserves will be merged, but the dividend payable to the parent undertaking (inter-company dividend) will be excluded. In order to keep things simple, the following example will just show the net profit onwards.

EXAMPLE

The Profit and Loss accounts of P Ltd and S Ltd are as follows:

P Ltd (parent)

	'000	'000
Net profit		50,000
Add dividend from S Ltd		10,000
		60,000
Taxation, say		15,000
Profit after tax		45,000
Dividend (to P Ltd's shareholders)		15,000
Retained profit (reserves)		30,000

S Ltd (subsidiary)

	'000	'000
Net profit		40,000
Taxation		12,000
Profit after tax		28,000
Dividend to P Ltd		10,000
Retained profit (reserves)		18,000

P Ltd and S Ltd: consolidated Profit and Loss account

	'000	'000
Net profit: P Ltd	50,000	
S Ltd	40,000	
		90,000
Taxation: P Ltd	15,000	
S Ltd	12,000	
		27,000
		63,000
Dividend		15,000
Reserves: P Ltd	30,000	
S Ltd	18,000	
		48,000

9.5   Where a company holds a majority interest in the subsidiary

In these circumstances consolidated final accounts will still be required.

9.5.1   The Balance Sheet

This will show the whole of the subsidiary's assets and liabilities. The minority shareholders' interest will be shown as liabilities.

EXAMPLE

Company P Ltd has acquired 80% of the issued share capital of S Ltd
      The consolidated Balance Sheet will show:

Fixed assets: P Ltd	200,000	
S Ltd	60,000	
		260,000
Net current assets: P Ltd	70,000	
S Ltd	40,000	
		110,000
Total assets less current liabilities		370,000
Less interest of minority shareholders		
in S Ltd capital	16,000	
reserves	4,000	20,000
		350,000
Share capital	300,000	
Reserves	50,000	
		350,000

9.5.2   The Profit and Loss account

That part of the subsidiary's net profit after tax which belongs to the minority shareholders in respect of dividend and reserves will be deducted first, before appropriations are made for dividend and reserves.

EXAMPLE

Company P Ltd holds 80% of the share capital of S Ltd.

Consolidated Profit and Loss account for P Ltd and S Ltd

	'000	'000
Net profit: P Ltd	90,000	
S Ltd	40,000	
		130,000
Taxation: P Ltd	27,000	
S Ltd	12,000	
		39,000
		91,000

Less minority interest		
Dividend	2,000	
Reserve	3,600	
		5,600
		85,400
Dividend		20,000
Reserves: P Ltd	51,000	
S Ltd	14,400	
		65,400

9.6 Reminder of key points

1. The requirement for consolidated accounts for group companies, which are in addition to the separate final accounts for each company; the separate Profit and Loss accounts and Balance Sheets of the parent and subsidiary companies are aggregated;

2. The definition of parent and subsidiary undertakings in the Companies Act 2006, s 1162 requires a majority of voting rights, or a right to appoint or remove a majority of the board of directors, or some sort of dominant influence or control;

3. The structure of the consolidated Balance Sheet; inter-company shares and the capital and reserves representing those shares are cancelled out;

4. The structure of the consolidated Profit and Loss account: the Profit and Loss accounts are merged, but the dividend payable to the parent company (inter-company dividend) will be excluded;

5. Consolidated final accounts will still be required where a company holds a majority interest in the subsidiary.

online resource centre

There is a self-test exercise on a consolidated Profit and Loss account and Balance Sheet at the end of this chapter which may help you understand the structure of each, and there are the online multiple choice questions for this chapter available through your tutor via the Online Resource Centre that accompanies this book. After this the next chapter deals with interpretation of accounts.

9.7 Practice exercise

Bond Ltd owns all the shares in Delta Ltd. The summarised Profit and Loss accounts and Balance Sheets for Bond and Delta drawn up on 30 September 200— are shown below. The Balance Sheets take into account retained profit (reserves) shown on the Profit and Loss account. Draw up the consolidated Profit and Loss account and the consolidated Balance Sheet for Bond Limited and Delta Limited.

Bond Ltd: Profit and Loss account for the year ending 30 September 200—

	'000	'000
Net profit	100,000	
ADD dividend from Delta Ltd	12,000	
	112,000	
LESS taxation, say	30,000	
Profit after tax	82,000	
Dividend to Bond Ltd's shareholders	20,000	
Reserves	62,000	

Delta Ltd: Profit and Loss account for the year ending 30 September 200—

	'000	'000
Net profit	44,000	
LESS taxation	13,200	
Profit after tax	30,800	
Dividend to Bond Ltd	12,000	
Reserves	18,800	

Bond Ltd: Balance Sheet as at 30 September 200—

	'000	'000
Fixed assets		300,000
Shares in Delta Ltd at cost		89,000
Net current assets		192,000
TOTAL		581,000
Share capital		500,000
Reserves	19,000	
This year's	62,000	
		81,000
TOTAL		581,000

Delta Ltd: Balance Sheet as at 30 September 200—

	'000	'000
Fixed assets		65,000
Net current assets		42,800
TOTAL		107,800
Share capital		80,000
Reserves	9,000	
This year's	18,800	
		27,800
TOTAL		107,800

9.8 Suggested answer to practice exercise

Bond Ltd

Consolidated Profit and Loss account for Bond Ltd and Delta Ltd for the year ending 30 September 200—

Net profit: Bond Ltd	100,000	
Delta Ltd	44,000	
		144,000
LESS taxation: Bond Ltd	30,000	
Delta Ltd	13,200	
		43,200
		100,800
Dividend to Bond Ltd shareholders		20,000
Reserves: Bond Ltd	62,000	
Delta Ltd	18,800	80,800

Consolidated Balance Sheet for Bond Ltd and Delta Ltd as at 30 September 200—

Fixed assets: Bond Ltd	300,000	
Delta Ltd	65,000	
		365,000
Net current assets: Bond Ltd	192,000	
Delta Ltd	42,800	
		234,800
		599,800
Share capital		500,000
Reserves: Bond Ltd	19,000	
plus this year's	62,000	
	81,000	
Delta increase in reserve	18,800	
		99,800
TOTAL		599,800

Interpretation of accounts and accounting ratios

10.1 Introduction

This chapter includes:

1. Use of accounts;

2. Checking factors outside the accounts;

3. General areas to look at;

4. Trends;

5. Ratios;

6. Example of application of ratios to a company's final accounts over two years;

7. Reminder of key points;

8. Exercise.

! INTENDED OUTCOME

An understanding of:

1. The need for interpretation of accounts;

2. Factors to be taken into account outside the accounts;

3. Ratios used to analyse accounts.

10.2 Use of accounts

Accounts may be used by many different people; for example, by the management of a business, by employees, by investors in the business, by shareholders, by long-term lenders or trade creditors, or by the Government for taxation and statistics. Each of these may be looking for different things in the accounts. A creditor, for example, would want to make sure that the debt could be repaid, whereas a shareholder in the business may be looking for increasing profit, so that dividends will be higher, or may be looking for capital appreciation.

The interpretation of accounts can help to assess how a business is performing at present and can also enable inferences to be made about its future performance. The current level of profit may be compared with other similar businesses to see if it is satisfactory, and whether it can be improved. By looking at the accounts of a business over a number of years trends may be seen. A business may have sufficient assets to cover liabilities, but if these are tied up in fixed assets, stock which is not selling, work in progress, or debtors who are unlikely to pay, it may not be able to pay its current liabilities.

You may wonder whether you need to know about interpretation of accounts at all. Why not leave it to the accountants? One good reason is that, as a sole practitioner or as a partner, the accounts will explain the profit due to you. It is not a good idea to leave the understanding of accounts to your accountants or to one or two of the other partners. You will not be able to make informed decisions about the business where necessary, for example, whether to retain staff, or take on more staff, or change the type of work done by the firm. Understanding accounts will also be necessary where you are dealing with commercial work; even where accountants are involved, you should have at least some idea of the advice given. You may be asked to give advice on proposed investments suggested by a stockbroker for a client or, for example, a trust in which you are a trustee. Note that there may be financial services implications here. There are few areas of work today where an understanding of accounts will not be needed.

10.3 Checking factors outside the accounts

To interpret accounts, ratio analysis may be used, as ratios can be used to compare performances from year to year and to compare different companies. Take care, however, as reading the accounts and looking at ratios on their own will not provide sufficient information about a company; other information should be sought as well. A company may have been doing very well, but may have just lost its managing director or industrial action may be threatened by its workforce. The business may possibly have been involved in an area which has now expanded to saturation point, and the market may no longer be there. A business should be compared with others of a similar type, ie dealing with the same services or products and of a similar size. If profits are disappointing there may be a recession generally. Are the markets for the business still there? Is there increased competition, for example from abroad?

10.4 General areas to look at

When accounts are looked at, absolute changes may be found; for example, is this year's profit more than last year's, have the expenses of the business gone up? Relative changes should also be found, for example what are the expenses of the business as a percentage of the turnover or sales? What is the profit as a percentage of the sales? How much profit has been generated from the capital employed (ie total assets less current liabilities)? The business may have invested heavily in fixed assets, but profit may have gone up by only a modest amount.

10.4.1 Accounts for past years

In interpreting accounts, the accounts for the last few years should be looked at, as these should establish general trends. Note that the figures shown on the accounts may not always be accurate. The business may be overstating the value of its assets. Examples may include stock or work in progress. If stock is valued at cost price, rather than its sale price, this may sound reasonable but the stock may not have been sold for some time, and it may be necessary to sell the stock at a lower price than that shown on the Balance Sheet. How work in progress is valued should be checked—is this based on an accurate time-recording system, or does it involve some guesswork? Other assets shown may be falling in value, for example office furniture or equipment, and it is important that sufficient provision for depreciation has been made. On the other hand, if the business has freehold premises shown at cost price, then the present value should be checked as it may be much higher.

The figure for debtors (an asset) may be high, but if this is in respect of one or two debtors who are in trouble themselves, the debts may not be paid. Check that sufficient provision has been made for bad debts and doubtful debts.

There may also be changes in circumstances. A company may have just employed a new managing director who has a reputation as a troubleshooter, able to improve companies with poor performance. Thus in future years profit may go up dramatically.

It is also always worth reading the information supplied by a company and the notes attached to the accounts.

There are two main areas that will be looked at in any analysis:

(a) the solvency or liquidity of the business;

(b) the profitability of the business.

10.5 Trends

Figures over the years may be compared, for example the profit over the last five years may show a general trend up, even though there may be the odd year when profit has fallen. Has the turnover increased? Have expenses increased?

10.6 Ratios

These will be calculated from a set of accounts for a year, but can then be compared with other years.

10.6.1 Liquidity ratios

Liquidity means the ability of a business to pay its short-term debts. This is not the same as solvency, which means the ability of the business to pay all its liabilities. A firm may have sufficient assets to pay all its liabilities, but will still not be able to pay off short-term liabilities because it has insufficient cash or easily realisable assets.

10.6.1.1 The current assets ratio

$$\frac{\text{Current assets}}{\text{Current liabilities}}$$

This compares current assets with current liabilities. There should normally be enough current assets to cover current liabilities. The comparison is between assets which should be converted into cash in approximately 12 months; with liabilities which will be due for payment within the same 12 months. What is a satisfactory figure will vary with the type of business or with the reputation of the business. For example:

'000

$$\frac{\text{Current assets}}{\text{Current liabilities}} \qquad \frac{40,000}{20,000} = 2:1$$

This would be a satisfactory ratio.
For example:

$$\frac{\text{Current assets}}{\text{Current liabilities}} \qquad \frac{30,000}{20,000} = 1.5:1$$

Again this may be an acceptable ratio.

A very high figure may not mean that the business is safe and it is essential to look behind the figures. The company may have overvalued its current assets, for example the stock (or work in progress). Generally, if the ratio is less than 1:1, there may be a problem.

Where, however, the company has a bank overdraft and the bank is prepared to allow the overdraft to continue long term, this may then be treated as a long-term liability instead of a short-term liability and thus can be left out of the ratio. This will clearly improve the ratio.

10.6.1.2   The acid test

This ratio uses only cash or assets which can be converted quickly into cash, thus stock or work in progress will be excluded from the figure for current assets.

$$\frac{\text{Current assets less stock (or work in progress)}}{\text{Current liabilities}}$$

If this is 1:1 or better then the company will have sufficient liquid assets to meet its current liabilities: this is provided that the creditors are paid and debtors pay at approximately the same time. Sometimes an even stricter test is used, that of measuring cash as against current liabilities. If debtors have been included in the ratio then, to check how fast debts will be paid, another ratio can be used; see para 10.6.2 below.

10.6.2   The average collection period—trade debtors to sales ratio

To find the length of time in days that debtors will pay debts, the following formula is used:

$$\frac{\text{Trade debtors}}{\text{Sales}} \times 365 \qquad \text{or for solicitors' use} \qquad \frac{\text{Debtors}}{\text{Profit costs}} \times 365$$

EXAMPLE

Sales are £200,000 for the year and trade debtors are £10,000.

$$\frac{£10,000}{£200,000} \times 365 = 18.25 \text{ days}$$

If, for example, sales are £200,000 for the year and trade debtors are £40,000:

$$\frac{£40,000}{£200,000} \times 365 = 73 \text{ days}$$

The ratio may not accurately reflect the length of time allowed to debtors. If, for example, sales had been strong just before the Balance Sheet was drawn up, this may give a high debtors figure, which would distort the ratio, making it appear that the length of credit given was much longer, as in the second example.

If the length of time allowed for debtors to pay is too long, then steps should be taken to tighten up debt collection. It is usual for a business to allow a specified length of time for debtors to pay the amount due before action is taken by the business. This time should be compared with the actual time which the debtors are taking. Whether the time has increased from previous years will need to be checked, as will the times for other similar businesses. It may also be advisable to check the individual debts to see how long each one has been outstanding. Some of them may be irrecoverable.

To check how quickly the business pays its creditors, a similar ratio is used; see para 10.6.3 below.

10.6.3   The average payment period—trade creditors to purchases ratio

$$\frac{\text{Trade creditors}}{\text{Purchases}} \times 365$$

If purchases for the year are £90,000 and trade creditors are £20,000:

$$\frac{\pounds20,000}{\pounds90,000} \times 365 = 81.1 \text{ days}$$

Again this should be compared with previous years, with similar businesses, and the length of time that creditors allow for payment. Note that a business may deliberately delay payment of creditors for as long as reasonably possible. Large companies in particular may do this as they have stronger bargaining power than their smaller creditors. If the period has dramatically increased, it may be that the business is having difficulty in paying its bills. However, a large figure for creditors may just be due to an increase in purchases just before the date of the Balance Sheet, and this may have been in anticipation of increased sales, or to buy in before prices are increased.

10.6.4   Shortage of working capital

Working capital or net current assets is that portion of capital left to run the business after providing for fixed assets. A business needs to pay out money to run the business, for example paying salaries and other expenses, or buying goods or services, before receiving payment itself for the goods or services it provides. How much will be needed will vary. It may be that credit is given on purchases: if this is a longer period than the time in which the business collects its own debts, then not as much working capital will be required. The amount of working capital will need to increase if there is inflation, as expenses will increase. If the business wishes to expand then again more working capital will be required. Reserve funds based on retained profit (see para 8.3.7) can be used to finance the increased requirement. If this is not possible then the business will have to raise funds by issuing more shares or borrowing.

If a business runs short of working capital, then it will have insufficient funds to meet its short-term liabilities, and may not be able to take advantage of, for example, discounts for prompt payment. It may also have to offer discounts itself to customers for prompt payment.

Indications of a shortage of working capital may be found from using the following ratios:

10.6.4.1   The working capital ratio

$$\frac{\text{Net current assets (working captial)}}{\text{Sales (or use profit costs for solicitors)}}$$

EXAMPLE

A company has net current assets of £20,000 and sales are £200,000. The working capital ratio is:

$$\frac{20,000}{200,000} = 0.1{:}1$$

If net current assets were still £20,000 and sales were £400,000, then the ratio would be 0.05:1, clearly a lower ratio.

10.6.4.2   The ratio between debtors and creditors

$$\frac{\text{Debtors}}{\text{Creditors}}$$

If this ratio falls, then again it may be a sign of overtrading. There may also be a shortage of cash. If the company is unable to find more capital to finance working capital, through borrowing or from the shareholders, then it may have to sell fixed assets, and lease instead, although there may be disadvantages in doing this.

Alternatively the business may be able to reduce the requirement for working capital, by ensuring that stock or work in progress is kept to a minimum and that debtors pay quickly, thereby releasing cash to use in the business.

If the company has over-expanded, ie sales have increased too fast, it may be necessary to halt the expansion.

10.6.5   Profitability ratios

10.6.5.1   Return on capital employed

This is the most important ratio in relation to profitability: for those who invest in the business it shows the rate of return on the capital used in the business. If net assets of the business are £2,000,000 and the profit is £20,000 then the return is only 1%, which is too low; as an investment the money would be better used elsewhere.

The ratio is:

$$\frac{\text{Operational profit (before interest and tax)}}{\text{Captial employed (total assets less current liabilities)}} \times 100\%$$

$$\frac{20,000}{2,000,000} \times 100\% = 1\%$$

The figure taken for profit is before tax and interest. If the figure was taken after interest on debentures, loans, and overdrafts, the return on assets would be understated. Any interest received should also be excluded from the calculation, to ensure that the profit shown is that made by operations.

A problem with this particular ratio is that the capital employed is measured at the date of the Balance Sheet. This may be misleading if, for example, the company has recently increased its capital to fund expansion, by purchasing fixed assets, which have not yet created any increased profit. The figure for capital employed could be taken from the Balance Sheet at the end of the year, or at the start of the year, or an average of the figure at the start of the year and the figure at the end of the year.

Even if the return is satisfactory, it should be looked at with caution. The true value of the assets on the balance sheet should be checked. They may have been undervalued, for example premises may have been shown at cost price.

The ratio may also be adjusted in respect of a bank overdraft. If this is effectively long-term lending, it should be included in the figure for capital employed, ie added back.

$$\frac{\text{Operating profit (before taxation and interest)}}{\text{Total assets less current liabilities + overdraft}} \times 100\%$$

10.6.5.2   The gross profit percentage

$$\frac{\text{Gross profit}}{\text{Sales}} \times 100\%$$

This shows the profitability of the sales. Even if sales have increased, this does not necessarily mean that the gross profit has increased.

EXAMPLE

Year 1

$$\frac{30,000}{125,000} \times 100\% = 24\%$$

EXAMPLE

Year 2

$$\frac{40,000}{200,000} \times 100\% = 20\%$$

Although the sales and the gross profit have increased in year 2, it should be noted that the gross profit percentage is lower. If the gross profit percentage has fallen this may be because:

(a) the cost of goods sold has increased, but selling prices have not been increased by an equivalent amount;

(b) sale prices have been reduced in order to sell more goods;

(c) if different types of goods have been sold, profit margins on some goods may be greater than on other goods.

10.6.5.3   Net profit percentage

$$\frac{\text{Operating or trading before interest and tax}}{\text{Sales}} \times 100\%$$

$$\text{or for solicitors' use } \frac{\text{Net profit}}{\text{Profit costs}} \times 100\%$$

Both this ratio and the ratio in para **10.6.5.2** above will vary, depending on the type of business being carried out. As with all ratios they should be compared with similar businesses. Some businesses operate with a very low profit margin, relying on a large turnover.

If the gross profit ratio has remained the same, but the net profit ratio has fallen, then the expenses must have increased.

Each type of expense can be compared with the sales figure, for the current year and previous years, to find whether the increase is general or limited to a particular area.

EXAMPLE

$$\frac{\text{Marketing costs}}{\text{Sales}} \times 100\%$$

$$\frac{\text{Administrative expenses}}{\text{Sales}} \times 100\%$$

10.6.6 Efficiency ratio—rate of stock turnover

The faster stock is turned over, or sold, the more profit will be made, provided the gross profit percentage stays the same. There are two ratios which may be used to find stock turnover:

(a) either divide stocks by sales:

$$\frac{\text{Stocks}}{\text{Sales}} \text{ (based on the selling price)}$$

EXAMPLE

If stock was £80,000 and sales were £700,000 the ratio would be:

$$\frac{80,000}{700,000} = 0.114 \text{ or every 41.7 days}$$

(b) or probably the better ratio, divide cost of goods sold by average stock:

$$\frac{\text{Cost of goods sold (sales at cost price)}}{\text{Average stock (at cost)}}$$

As you will not have the detailed accounts of the business to find average stock, use the average of the opening and closing stock:

EXAMPLE

If opening stock was £50,000 and closing stock was £80,000 then the average would be:

$$\frac{50,000 + 80,000}{2} = 65,000$$

If the cost of goods sold was £450,000 then the stock turnover would be:

$$\frac{450,000}{65,000} = 6.92 \text{ times per year, ie stock is turned over 6.92 times per year, or every 52.75 days}$$

The rate of stock turnover will vary, depending on the type of stock being carried. Although a fast rate of stock turnover should lead to increased profit, the business must be careful to have enough stock at any given time to meet demand.

If the rate of stock turnover has fallen then the business should check whether it is carrying too much stock, or whether sales have decreased generally.

After analysing the profitability of the business, it may be that profitability is satisfactory, or it may be considered that there is room for improvement. The business may attempt to reduce expenses, or increase prices or sales, to improve profitability. Increasing prices may not be the best solution, as customers may decide to go somewhere cheaper. If sales are to be increased, the business will have to work more efficiently or expect its workforce to work harder. It may be that the business decides to reduce its workforce, but expects the remaining employees to retain the same level of sales. Increased sales will be possible only if the market for those goods is there.

10.6.7 Capital gearing ratios

Gearing relates to the capital structure of the company, the relationship between the capital provided by shareholders and the capital provided by borrowing. A high-geared company is one which has a high proportion of borrowing. A company with low gearing has most of its funds provided by the ordinary shareholder. The ratios used may be calculated in different ways.

10.6.7.1 A commonly used ratio

$$\frac{\text{Preference shares} + \text{long-term loans}}{\text{All shareholders funds} + \text{long-term loans}} \times 100\%$$

EXAMPLE

A company has share capital and long-term borrowings as follows:

Ordinary share capital	100
Reserves	50
7% preference shares	10
12% debentures	30
	190

$$\frac{10 + 30}{190} \times 100 = 21.05\%$$

EXAMPLE

A company has share capital and long-term borrowings as follows:

Ordinary share capital	80
Reserves	20
Preference shares	10
Debentures	40
	150

$$\frac{10 + 40}{150} \times 100 = 33.33\%$$

The second company is a higher geared company than the first company.

If a company is highly geared, then any change in the profits will affect the shareholders more than in a low-geared company, as the interest on the borrowing will have to be paid before any dividend is available to the ordinary shareholders. The company will be susceptible to changes in interest rates, for example if these increase substantially. The borrowing will also have to be repaid at some stage. If the company requires additional capital to expand the business it may be better to do this through increasing the share capital.

10.6.7.2 An alternative ratio

Another ratio is the ratio of borrowings to shareholders' funds.

EXAMPLE

If borrowing is £200,000 and shareholders' funds are £500,000 then the ratio will be:

Borrowing	200,000
Shareholders' funds	500,000
Gearing	2:5

10.6.8 Investment ratios

An investor will be concerned with the profitability of a business, and whether the investment will give a good return.

10.6.8.1 The return on capital employed ratio

This ratio, shown previously, can be used.

$$\frac{\text{Net profit (before interest and tax)}}{\text{Capital employed}} \times 100\%$$

10.6.8.2   Return on ordinary shareholders' interest

The return on capital employed shows only the return before tax and interest. An ordinary shareholder will want to know what the return is after payment of interest and tax, and after payment of any preference shares dividends.

$$\frac{\text{Net profit after interest, tax, and preference share dividend}}{\text{Ordinary shareholders' interest (ordinary share capital plus}} \times 100\%$$
$$\text{any reserves attributable to them)}$$

10.6.8.3   Earnings per share

This will show the return per single share, in money.

$$\frac{\text{Net profit after interest, tax, and preference share dividend}}{\text{Number of ordinary shares}}$$

This is an important ratio and FRS14 requires limited companies to show the earnings per share in the published accounts.

However, this figure will not be the amount that the shareholder receives per share—the amount received will be the dividend declared by the directors. As we have seen in para 8.3.5, part of the profit will often be transferred to reserves and, although these belong to the shareholders, they may not be available for distribution.

10.6.8.4   Dividend yield

This is the annual return by way of dividend based on an investment of £100 in the shares at the current price. If, for example, the shares cost £2 each, then 50 shares could be purchased for £100. If the dividend was 10p per share, then the total would be £5.00, giving a dividend yield of 5%.

10.6.8.5   Dividend cover

$$\frac{\text{Earnings per share}}{\text{Dividend per share}}$$

This shows the proportion of earnings distributed against the proportion retained by way of reserves.

EXAMPLE

If net profit after tax and any preference share dividend was £8,000,000 and the number of ordinary shares was 4,000,000, then the earnings per share would be £2. If the dividend was £2,000,000, then the dividend per share would be 50p.

$$\frac{2.00}{.50} = 4 \text{ times}$$

An alternative way of showing this would be:

$$\frac{\text{Net profit after tax and preference share dividend}}{\text{Dividend to ordinary shareholders}}$$

Continuing the above example:

$$\frac{8,000,000}{2,000,000} = 4 \text{ times}$$

This shows that the dividend is covered four times by the profit earned, after tax and the preference share dividend. The higher this is, the more the company is reinvesting its profits in the business.

The amount retained will not only increase the underlying value of the shares but ensure that dividends can be paid if in any future year there is insufficient net profit available.

10.6.8.6   Price earnings ratio (PE ratio)

Once the earnings per share has been calculated, the actual earnings based on the present market price of the share (where applicable), rather than the value at which the share was issued, can be calculated.

$$\frac{\text{Marketing price per share}}{\text{Earnings per share}}$$

$$\text{eg}\ \frac{2.00}{.20} = 10$$

This means that the investor has to pay £2 to get the benefit of earnings of 20p per annum—10 times the year's earnings have been paid, or 10 years' purchase of earnings.

When the market is convinced that the future earnings of a company are going to increase, the market price of the shares may go up. The PE ratio will therefore be higher. If the market is convinced that future earnings are not going to be as good, then the price of the shares may go down, and the PE ratio will be lower. However, PE ratios will vary depending on the type of business being carried out.

If a takeover bid is rumoured in respect of the company, then the value of the shares may well go up, which will lead to a high PE ratio.

If a PE ratio for a company is higher than other companies in a similar business, it may be that the company is highly regarded, or possibly that the shares are overvalued. A lower PE ratio may mean that the company is not highly regarded, or possibly that the shares are undervalued.

10.7   Example

Goodwin Ltd: Profit and Loss accounts for the year ending 31 December

	2008	2009
	'000	'000
Sales	800,000	1,200,000
LESS cost of sales	500,000	700,000
Gross profit	300,000	500,000
LESS expenses	132,000	240,000
Loan interest	8,000	40,000
Profit before tax	160,000	220,000
Taxation, say	40,000	55,000
Profit after tax	120,000	165,000
Dividends	30,000	40,000
Retained profit	90,000	125,000

Goodwin Ltd: Balance Sheet as at 31 December

	2008	2009
Fixed assets		
	'000	'000
Tangible assets	810,000	960,000

Current assets		
Stock	80,000	175,000
Debtors	50,000	110,000
Cash	10,000	5,000
	140,000	290,000
Creditors:		
Amounts falling due within one year	80,000	80,000
Net current assets	60,000	210,000
Total assets less current liabilities	870,000	1,170,000
Creditors:		
Amounts falling due after more than one year		
Loans and other borrowings	50,000	225,000
	820,000	945,000
Capital and reserves		
Called up share capital		
Ordinary £1 shares	600,000	600,000
Profit and loss account		
Retained profit	220,000	345,000
	820,000	945,000

Ratios

	2008	2009
Liquidity		
Current ratio	'000	'000

$$\frac{\text{Current assets}}{\text{Current liabilities}} \qquad \frac{140,000}{80,000} \qquad \frac{290,000}{80,000}$$

$$= 1.75 \text{ to } 1 \qquad\qquad = 3.625 \text{ to } 1$$

The liquidity ratio or the acid test

$$\frac{\text{Current assets less stock}}{\text{Current liabilities}} \qquad \frac{60,000}{80,000} \qquad \frac{115,000}{80,000}$$

$$= 0.75 \text{ to } 1 \qquad\qquad = 1.438 \text{ to } 1$$

The average collection period—debtors to sales ratio

$$\frac{\text{Debtors}}{\text{Sales}} \times 365 \qquad \frac{50,000}{800,000} \times 365 \qquad \frac{110,000}{1,200,000} \times 365$$

$$= 22.8 \text{ days} \qquad = 33.46 \text{ days}$$

The average payment period—creditors to purchases ratio

$$\frac{\text{Creditors}}{\text{Purchases}} \times 365 \qquad \frac{80,000}{500,000} \times 365 \qquad \frac{80,000}{700,000} \times 365$$

Note: no purchases figure shown

Cost of sales taken as an

approximation $\qquad\qquad = 58.4 \text{ days} \qquad\qquad = 41.7 \text{ days}$

The working capital ratio

$$\frac{\text{Net current assets (working capital)}}{\text{Sales}} \qquad \frac{60,000}{800,000} \qquad \frac{210,000}{1,200,000}$$

$$= 0.075 \text{ to } 1 \qquad\qquad = 0.175 \text{ to } 1$$

The ratio between debtors and creditors

$$\frac{\text{Debtors}}{\text{Creditors}} \qquad \frac{50,000}{80,000} \qquad \frac{110,000}{80,000}$$

$$= 0.625 \text{ to } 1 \qquad\qquad = 1.375 \text{ to } 1$$

Return on capital employed

$$\frac{\text{Operating profit (before tax and interest)}}{\text{Capital employed (total assets less current liabilities)}} \times 100\%$$

$$\frac{168,000}{870,000} \times 100\% \qquad \frac{260,000}{1,170,000} \times 100\%$$

$$= 19.31\% \qquad\qquad = 22.22\%$$

The gross profit percentage

$$\frac{\text{Gross profit}}{\text{Sales}} \qquad \frac{300,000}{800,000} \times 100\% \qquad \frac{500,000}{1,200,000} \times 100\%$$

$$= 37.5\% \qquad\qquad = 41.67\%$$

The net profit percentage

$$\frac{\text{Operating or trading profit before interest and tax}}{\text{Sales}} \times 100\%$$

$$\frac{168,000}{800,000} \times 100\% \qquad \frac{260,000}{1,200,000} \times 100\%$$

$$= 21\% \qquad\qquad = 21.67\%$$

Rate of stock turnover

$$\frac{\text{Stocks}}{\text{Sales}} \qquad \frac{80,000}{800,000} \qquad \frac{175,000}{1,200,000}$$

$$0.1 \ (36.5 \text{ days}) \qquad 0.146 \ (53.29 \text{ days})$$

Capital gearing

$$\frac{\text{Preference shares + long-term liabilities}}{\text{Capital employed}} \times 100\%$$

$$\frac{50,000}{870,000} \times 100\% \qquad \frac{225,000}{1,170,000} \times 100\%$$

$$= 0.057 \text{ to } 1 \qquad\qquad = 0.192 \text{ to } 1$$

or $\qquad\qquad\qquad\qquad\qquad\qquad 5.7\% \qquad\qquad\qquad\qquad 19.2\%$

Return on ordinary shareholders' interest

$$\frac{\text{Net profit after interest, tax, and preference share dividend}}{\text{Ordinary shareholders' interest}} \times 100\%$$

$$\frac{120,000}{820,000} \times 100\% \qquad \frac{165,000}{945,000} \times 100\%$$

$$= 14.63\% \qquad\qquad = 17.46\%$$

Earnings per share

$$\frac{\text{Net profit after interest, tax, and preference share dividend}}{\text{Number of ordinary shares}}$$

$$\frac{120,000}{600,000} \qquad \frac{165,000}{600,000}$$

$$= 20\text{ p} \qquad\qquad = 27.5\text{ p}$$

Dividend cover

$$\frac{\text{Net profit after tax, etc.}}{\text{Dividend to ordinary shareholders}} \qquad \frac{120,000}{30,000} \times 100\% \qquad \frac{165,000}{40,000} \times 100\%$$

$$= 4 \text{ times} \qquad\qquad = 4.125 \text{ times}$$

Comment

Liquidity: the current ratio was acceptable in 2008 at 1.75 to 1. In 2009 it increased to 3.625 to 1 as current assets, particularly stock and debtors, have increased dramatically, but creditors have remained the same. Clearly sales have increased, but the rate of stock turnover has reduced from 36.5 days to 53.29 days. This should be checked; also debtors should be checked to make sure that these will pay. Funding has come from increased long-term borrowing, now £225,000,000 instead of £50,000,000. Presumably the company has decided to increase turnover. The liquidity or acid test again shows an improvement from a rather weak 0.75 to 1 to an acceptable 1.438 to 1.

Given the high debtors figure, the average collection period has increased from 22.8 days to 33.46 days. This should be looked at with care and possibly steps taken to ensure that debtors pay within a set time.

The average payment period shown is an approximation; seemingly this has improved from 58.4 days to 41.7 days.

The working capital ratio has again improved, showing more working capital as mentioned above. The ratio of debtors to creditors has increased.

Return on capital employed has improved from 19.31% to 22.22%. There is also an improvement in the gross profit percentage. However, the net profit percentage has not improved much, ie from 21% to 21.67%. Expenses have increased, in particular the loan interest on the increased borrowing.

As mentioned previously, the rate of stock turnover has slowed and this should be looked at.

Given the increased long-term borrowing the gearing is now higher at 19.2% instead of the very low 5.7%. However, this is still not a high-geared company.

The return on ordinary shareholders' interest has improved as have earnings per share. Dividend cover remains approximately the same.

Clearly a decision was made to increase borrowing to invest in the company. Perhaps a further year is needed to consolidate.

10.8 Reminder of key points

1. Use of accounts;
2. Checking factors outside the accounts;
3. General areas to look at;
4. Trends;
5. Ratios and their application to accounts.

online resource centre

There is a self-test exercise at the end of this chapter on accounting ratios and their analysis based on a set of final accounts which will consolidate your understanding, and there are the online multiple choice questions available through your tutor via the Online Resource Centre that accompanies this book.

This chapter now completes the section on business accounts.

10.9 Exercise

When you have completed this exercise, you will have covered the entire business accounts section.

Allow about 45 minutes for this exercise.

Below are shown the accounts of Price and Murray for the year ending 30 November 200—

Price and Murray: Profit and Loss account for the year ending 30 November 200—

Income			
Profit costs		300,000	
ADD Work in Progress at 30 Nov 200—		50,000	
		350,000	
LESS Work in Progress at start of year		40,000	
Work done			310,000
Interest received			4,000
			314,000
LESS expenses			
General and administrative expenses,			
including staff wages		210,000	
ADD outstanding expenses		920	
		210,920	
LESS payments in advance		1,040	
		209,880	
Travelling expenses		1,000	
Depreciation: library, furniture,			
and equipment		7,000	
			217,880
Net profit			96,120
Appropriation account			
Interest on capital at 5%	Price	8,500	
	Murray	6,000	
		14,500	
Profit share	Price	40,810	
	Murray	40,810	
		81,620	
			96,120

Price and Murray: Balance Sheet as at 30 November 200—

FIXED ASSETS			
Freehold premises		240,000	
Library furniture and equipment	35,000		
Less depreciation	14,000		
		21,000	
			261,000
CURRENT ASSETS			
Work in Progress	50,000		
Debtors	60,000		
Petty cash	360		
Payments in advance	1,040		
		111,400	
LESS CURRENT LIABILITIES			
Creditors	10,000		
Outstanding expenses	920		
Bank overdraft	35,000		
		45,920	
NET CURRENT ASSETS			65,480
			326,480

LESS LONG-TERM LIABILITIES		—
		326,480

CAPITAL EMPLOYED

Capital accounts:

Price	170,000	
Murray	120,000	
		290,000

Current accounts (see 'Movement on current accounts'):

Price	22,310	
Murray	14,170	
		36,480
		326,480

Client account

Cash at the bank client account

Current account	190,510	
Deposit account	266,380	
		456,890
Amount due to clients		456,890

Schedule to Balance Sheet

Movement on current accounts

	Price	Murray
Interest on capital	8,500	6,000
Profit share	40,810	40,810
	49,310	46,810
LESS drawings	27,000	32,640
	22,310	14,170

From these calculate:

(a) the current ratio;

(b) the acid test;

(c) the net profit percentage;

(d) the average collection period;

(e) the return on capital employed.

Comment on these ratios and on the accounts themselves. How relevant is the return on capital employed ratio? What suggestions would you have for the partners, who are concerned at the overdraft and would like to draw out more cash if possible? What further information would you ask for?

10.10 Suggested answer to exercise

The current ratio

$$\frac{\text{Current assets}}{\text{Current liabilities}} \qquad \frac{111,400}{45,920} = 2.43 \text{ to } 1$$

The acid test

$$\frac{\text{Current assets less work in progress}}{\text{Current liabilities}} \qquad \frac{61,400}{45,920} = 1.34 \text{ to } 1$$

The net profit percentage

$$\frac{\text{Net profit}}{\text{Profit costs}} \qquad \frac{96,120}{300,000} \times 100 = 32.04\%$$

The average collection period

$$\frac{\text{Debtors}}{\text{Profit costs}} \qquad \frac{60,000}{300,000} \times 365 = 73 \text{ days}$$

The return on capital employed

$$\frac{\text{Net profit}}{\text{Capital employed}} \times 100 \qquad \frac{96,120}{326,480} \times 100 = 29.44\%$$

The current ratio measures the short-term financial position of the firm. Here clearly there are sufficient current assets to cover current liabilities, a ratio of 2.43 to 1 is good. The acid test is also satisfactory at 1.34 to 1. However, the figures for work in progress and debtors are high; there is no cash at the bank. The value of work in progress should be checked, and bills should be sent out. Debtors should also be checked. There may be some debts that have been outstanding for a long time, some of these may be irrecoverable, and provision for doubtful debts should be checked. Debtors should be chased, and much tighter control exerted over the length of time that they are taking to pay—see the average collection period of 73 days. However, if a large number of bills were sent out just before the Balance Sheet was drawn up this would distort the period calculated.

The net profit percentage at 32.04% may be reasonable, but previous years should be checked, and comparison made, if possible, with similar firms.

The return on capital employed is not very useful in a partnership, as account must be taken of the partners' work—notional salaries could be taken to give a more accurate ratio. The partners have provided for interest on capital as part of the appropriation of profit.

Note that the profit is not cash, and the partners must solve the cash flow problem. Provided that the Work in Progress figure is realistic, and that the bulk of the debtors are able to pay, this should be possible—see above. It is also possible that the bank is happy to continue financing the firm by way of an overdraft, when the overdraft could be treated as long-term lending. However, given the Work in Progress and debtors, this would not seem to be necessary, and the firm will save interest charges, etc if it manages to convert these assets into cash.

As mentioned above, previous years' accounts would be helpful to establish any trends. Is the firm checking bad debts, provision, etc? What are other similar firms doing? The value of the premises should be checked—is this the correct value, or has it increased or decreased? Should the partners consider sale/leaseback or do they regard this as investment for the future? Any new partner coming in would have to fund this, if, for example, one of the existing partners left. How old are the partners? Possibly check expenses; can these be reduced?

Basic solicitors' accounts

11.1 Introduction

Before continuing with this chapter it is essential that you either have read, or now read, Chapter 1, which gives an introduction to accounts and basic entries on the accounts. You should also have completed the exercises on double-entry bookkeeping at the end of Chapter 1. You will need your copy of the Solicitors' Accounts Rules 1998 as amended when working on solicitors' accounts.

This chapter includes:

1. Using the Solicitors' Accounts Rules 1998 (SAR) and the consequences of failing to comply with the rules;

2. Basic principles underpinning the SAR;

3. Keeping client money and office money separate with the definitions of client money and office money, receipts of client money, including treatment of receipt of mixed office/client money, payments out of client money and receipts and payments of office money;

4. Basic entries on solicitors' accounts in respect of receipt and payment of office money (including petty cash) and client money;

5. Profit costs and VAT—entries on delivering a bill to the client;

6. Treatment of the receipt of agreed fees;

7. Record-keeping requirements and powers of the Solicitors Regulation Authority to secure compliance;

8. Reminder of key points;

9. Self-test exercises.

! **INTENDED OUTCOME**

An understanding of:

1. The basic principles of the SAR and the consequences of non-compliance with the rules;

2. What constitutes office money and client money;

3. Entries required on receipt and payment of office and client money;

4. Entries required on delivery of a bill to the client;

5. Treatment of the receipt of agreed fees.

The above evidenced by the ability to draw up the relevant accounts.

11.2 Solicitors' Accounts Rules 1998 (SAR)

11.2.1 Using the rules

It is essential that you become familiar with the rules and refer to them when working on exercises. As the notes form part of the rules and are mandatory these are as important as the rules themselves.

11.2.2 Consequences of failure to comply with the rules

Solicitors may be referred to the Solicitors Disciplinary Tribunal (<http://www.solicitorstribunal.org.uk>) by the Solicitors Regulation Authority (<http://www.sra.org.uk>), which is the independent body set up by the Law Society to regulate solicitors in England and Wales. The tribunal has power to strike a solicitor off the roll, to suspend a solicitor, and to fine a solicitor. In the last reports of the tribunal available at the time of writing, for the year to 30 April 2008, 234 applications, involving 356 practising solicitors, were made, not all applications were dealt with in the year, but of those that were 61 solicitors were struck off, 47 were suspended, 110 were fined, and 37 were reprimanded. 28% of the applications related to breaches of the SAR, and a further 4% related to improper utilisation or misappropriation of clients' money.

An example of a solicitor struck off for unbefitting conduct showed that he failed to ensure compliance with the SAR, breached rule 6, failed to remedy a shortage of money in client account in breach of rule 7(1), improperly withdrew client money from designated client account in breach of rule 22(1), improperly made payments of client money from designated client account in excess of funds held in breach of rule 22(5), failed to reconcile the bank statements with client accounts in breach of rule 32(7), and failed to keep proper accounting records under rule 32(1). In addition to all these breaches of the SAR, he also failed to avoid conflict of interest in property transactions and related services, failing to act in the best interest of the client. Have a look at recent copies of the Law Society's *Gazette*, where you will find details of recent Solicitors Disciplinary Tribunal cases.

11.2.3 Basic principles: SAR rule 1

This rule gives the principles which underpin the SAR.

Solicitors must comply with the requirements of rule 1 of the Solicitors' Code of Conduct 2007 and in particluar;

(a) keep other people's money separate from office money belonging to the solicitor or the practice;

(b) keep other people's money safely in a bank or building society account identifiable as a client account (except where the rules specifically provide otherwise);

(c) use each client's money for that client's matters only;

(d) use money held as trustee of a trust for the purposes of that trust only;

(e) establish and maintain proper accounting systems, and proper internal controls over those systems, to ensure compliance with the rules;

(f) keep proper accounting records to show accurately the position with regard to the money held for each client and trust;

(g) account for interest on other people's money in accordance with the rules;

(h) co-operate with the Solicitors Regulation Authority in checking compliance with the rules; and

(i) deliver annual accountant's reports as required by the rules.

11.2.4 Keeping client and office money separate

Solicitors must keep money belonging to clients (client money) separate from their own money (office money). This means having at least two separate accounts at the bank or building society: the Client bank account and the Office bank account.

A Client account must be in the name of the solicitor, the practice name, or solicitors company name, or LLP (limited liability partnership) name, or name of recognised body or trustee and must contain the word 'Client' (SAR rule 14).

The solicitor must therefore have two cash accounts in the ledger system: the Office cash account and the Client cash account. For convenience the Office account and the Client account are shown side by side, as follows:

Cash account

Date	Details	Office account			Client account		
		DR	CR	Balance	DR	CR	Balance

Each client ledger card will also show that there are two accounts:

Smith: re conveyancing

Date	Details	Office account			Client account		
		DR	CR	Balance	DR	CR	Balance

Although the money for all clients will, as a general rule, be kept in one bank account, the solicitor must record separately in respect of each client the money which is being held for that client. This means that the solicitor must not use money belonging to one client for the purposes of another client, nor may the solicitor transfer the money of one client from that client's ledger account to the ledger account of another client except as provided for in the rules.

11.2.5 The definition of client money (SAR rule 13)

Whenever a solicitor receives or pays money on behalf of a client, the solicitor must decide whether it is client or office money. The rules define 'client money' as money held or received by a solicitor for a client or as a trustee. This also includes money held as agent, bailee, stakeholder, or as the donee of a power of attorney, or as a liquidator, trustee in bankruptcy, Court of Protection deputy or trustee of an occupational pension scheme.

11.2.5.1 Solicitors not to operate banking facilities

Note that the Solicitors Disciplinary Tribunal stated in the case of Wood and Burdett 2004 that it is not a proper part of a solicitor's everyday business or practice to operate a banking facility for third parties, whether they are clients of the firm or not.

Solicitors should also bear in mind that there are criminal sanctions against assisting money launderers. See SAR rule 15, note (ix).

11.2.6   Payments into client account

Where a solicitor receives client money, the solicitor must normally pay it into a client bank account without delay. This means on the day the money is received or, if not possible, on the next working day (SAR rules 2(2)(z) and 15).

11.2.6.1   Money received from client on account of costs and disbursements (SAR rules 13 and 19)

Money paid generally on account of costs and disbursements is client money and must be paid into the client account (SAR rule 13, note (i)(d)).

11.2.6.2   Money which may be paid into client account (SAR rule 15(2))

The following money may be paid into a client account:

    (a) the solicitor's own money required to open or maintain the account;

    (b) an advance from the solicitor to fund a payment needed on behalf of a client or trust in excess of funds held for that client or trust. Note that the sum becomes client money or trust money on payment into the account;

    (c) money to replace that withdrawn in breach of the rules;

    (d) a sum in lieu of interest paid into client account, to comply with SAR rule 24;

    (e) cheques which the solicitor would be entitled to 'split' but does not (ie mixed office/client money) (SAR rule 20(2)(b)).

11.2.6.3   Receipt of mixed office/client money (SAR rules 19 and 20)

Where money is received which is part office and part client money, this can be:

    (a) split, part paid into office account, and part into client account;

    (b) all paid into client account and then the office money transferred to office account within 14 days;

    (c) if the mixed money consists of office money and unpaid professional disbursements only (for example unpaid counsel's fees) then the money can be paid into the office account, and within two working days the unpaid disbursement must either be paid or the unpaid amount transferred to client account.

There are also special rules relating to the treatment of moneys received from the Legal Services Commission and payments from a third party in respect of legal aid work (see para 11.2.7 below).

11.2.6.4   Money which can be withheld from client account (SAR rule 16)

    (a) Money should not be paid into a client account if the client has asked for it not to be paid into a client account. It can be held, for example, in the solicitor's safe in the form of cash or in an account in the solicitor's name, such as an account outside England and Wales, or paid into a bank, building society, or other financial institution account in the name of the client or a person designated by the client. (Such a request from the client should be in writing or confirmed in writing by the solicitor.)

    (b) Where a solicitor agrees to hold a cheque 'to the order' of a third party, the cheque should not be paid into a client account until it is released by the third party, as until that point it does not become the client's money.

11.2.6.5   Money which may be withheld from client account (SAR rule 17)

A solicitor need not pay client money into client account if received:

(a) in cash, which is, without delay, paid in cash, in the ordinary course of business, to the client or on the client's behalf, to a third party, or paid in cash in the execution of a trust to a beneficiary or third party; or

(b) as a cheque or banker's draft which is endorsed over in the ordinary course of business to the client or, on the client's behalf, to a third party, or without delay endorsed over in execution of a trust to a beneficiary or third party.

Note: if a solicitor negotiates cash or endorses a cheque made out to him, then the solicitor has handled client money and must make entries in the account to show the receipt and payment of client money. However, most cheques are now non-endorsable.

If a solicitor receives a cheque made out to a third party which the solicitor passes on to that third party, then the solicitor has not handled client money and should not record a receipt and payment of client money in the accounts. It is, however, advisable to record the fact that the cheque has been received and passed on. This can be done by a file note and/or an entry on the client's ledger account by way of memorandum.

11.2.7   Receipts from the Legal Services Commission (SAR rule 21)

An advance payment from the Legal Services Commission (LSC) in anticipation of work to be carried out, although client money, may be placed in office account provided the LSC instructs in writing that this may be done.

A payment for costs, interim or final, may be paid into office account, even though it may include client money re advance payments for fees of disbursements or money for unpaid professional disbursements, provided all money for payment of disbursements is transferred to client account or the disbursements paid within 14 days of receipt.

Regular payments from the LSC are office money and must be paid into office account. Within 28 days of submitting a report to the LSC notifying completion a solicitor must either:

(a) pay any unpaid professional disbursements; or

(b) transfer to a client account a sum equivalent to the amount of the unpaid professional disbursements.

11.2.8   Withdrawals from a client account (SAR rule 22)

The following, in particular, should be noted with regard to the withdrawal of money from a client account:

(a) Client or trust money can be used to make payments only if enough money is held in client account for the particular client or trust on whose behalf it is desired to make the payment (SAR rule 22(5)).

(b) If insufficient money is held in client account for the particular client the solicitor may either:

(i) pay the disbursement out of office account (the solicitor may then transfer the balance held on client account to office account); or

(ii) draw two cheques, one on client account for the balance held and one on office account for the remainder.

Note also that the solicitor may advance money to fund a payment on behalf of a client in excess of funds held for that client.

(c) **Client money** can be withdrawn if:

    (i)   properly required for a payment to or on behalf of the client or in the execution of a trust;

    (ii)   properly required for payment of a disbursement on behalf of the client or trust;

    (iii) properly required in full or partial reimbursement of money spent by the solicitor on behalf of the client or trust. Money is spent by the solicitor at the time when the solicitor dispatches a cheque unless the cheque is to be held to the solicitor's order. Money is also spent by the use of a credit account, for example search fees or taxi fares.

    (iv) transferred to another client account;

    (v)   withdrawn on the client's instructions provided the instructions are for the client's convenience and are given in writing or confirmed by the solicitor in writing;

    (vi) transferred to an account other than a client account (such as an account outside England and Wales) or retained in cash, by a trustee in the proper performance of his or her duties;

    (vii) a refund to the solicitor of an advance no longer required to fund a payment on behalf of a client;

    (viii) money which has been paid into the account in breach of the rules (for example money paid into the wrong separate designated client account or interest wrongly credited to a general client account);

    (ix) money withdrawn from the account on the written authorisation of the SRA.

(d) **Office money** can be withdrawn from client account if it is:

    (i)   money which had properly been paid in to open or maintain the account;

    (ii)   money properly required for payment of the solicitors' costs, where a bill of costs or other written notification of the costs incurred has been given to the client. Once the solicitor has done this the money must be transferred out of client account within 14 days;

    (iii) the whole or part of payment re legal aid payment paid in;

    (iv) part of a mixed office/client payment previously paid in.

Note also that it is possible to draw against an uncleared cheque under the SAR.

However, a solicitor should use discretion in drawing against an uncleared cheque. If the cheque is not met then other client money will have been used to make the payment in breach of the rules and the breach must be remedied. A solicitor may be able to avoid a breach of the rules by instructing the bank or building society to charge all unpaid credits to the solicitor's office or personal account.

11.2.9   Surplus client money and left over balances

The Solicitors' Accounts (Residual Client Account Balances) Amendment rules 2008 amended the Solicitors' Accounts Rules 1998 with effect from 14 July 2008.

11.2.9.1 Returning surplus client money

The new rule 15(3) imposes a specific obligation to return client money promptly as soon as there is no longer any proper reason to retain the funds. 'Promptly' is not defined but should be given its natural meaning in the particular circumstances (note (x) to rule 15). Rule 15(3) does not apply to the return of surplus funds whilst a matter is ongoing (note (xi) to rule 15).

11.2.9.2 Reporting to clients

New rule 15(4) requires a solicitor to inform a client promptly of the amount of any funds retained at the end of a matter, and the reason for that retention. There is also an obligation to report in writing to the client on at least an annual basis if funds continue to be retained, with an explanation for the ongoing retention.

11.2.9.3 Left over balances on client account

Rule 22 has been amended so that solicitors have the option to withdraw from client account left over balances of £50 or less without prior SRA authorisation, subject to paying the balances to a charity and complying with the other safeguards set out in the new rule 22(2A). Prior SRA authorisation will still be required for amounts exceeding £50, or for amounts not to be paid to a charity because, for example they represent costs—notes (viii) and (viiia) to rule 22.

Solicitors should have set up appropriate procedures and systems to ensure compliance with the new provisions of Rule 22.

11.2.10 Note also the following under the SAR

Liquidators, trustees in bankruptcy, and Court of Protection receivers and deputies are included in the rules, limited to record-keeping requirements, and subject to monitoring and inspection by the Law Society and reporting accountants, to protect the clients and the profession from claims on the Solicitors' Indemnity and Compensation Funds.

Solicitors operating a client account, for example under a power of attorney, should receive all statements and passbooks and retain these, as they will be subject to monitoring and inspection by the Law Society and reporting accountants.

11.2.11 The definition of office money (SAR rule 13(xi))

This is money that belongs to the solicitor or to the practice. It includes:

(a) money held or received in connection with running the practice, for example PAYE or VAT on the firm's fees;

(b) interest on general client accounts

(c) payments received in respect of:

  (i) fees due to the practice re bills or written notification of costs incurred;

  (ii) disbursements already paid by the practice;

  (iii) disbursements incurred but not yet paid by the practice, but excluding unpaid professional disbursements.

  (iv) money paid for or towards an agreed fee;

    (d) money held in a client account and earmarked for transfer of costs under rule 19(3);

    (e) money held or received from the Legal Services Commission as a regular payment under rule 21(2).

11.2.11.1 Partners' money is office money (SAR rule 13(xii))

Money belonging to a principal solicitor or one of his partners cannot be treated as client money and must always be paid into office account. For example, if the firm acts for one of the partners in the purchase of a house in his sole name, free of mortgage, and the partner hands a cheque for the deposit to the firm's cashier, the cheque must be paid into office account. Note the following, however:

    (a) If the firm is acting for a partner and that partner's spouse (who is not a partner), any moneys received will be held on their joint behalf and must be treated as client money.

    (b) If the firm is acting for a partner in the purchase of a property with the aid of a mortgage, the mortgage advance held or received on behalf of the lender is client money.

    (c) If the firm is acting for an assistant solicitor, a consultant, or a non-solicitor employee, or in the case of a company, a director, or a limited liability partnership, if a member, then they will be regarded as clients even if dealing with the matter personally.

11.3 Basic entries

You should refer back to Chapter 1 for basic double-entry bookkeeping and entries on accounts. For solicitors, the office and client accounts are totally separate. An entry in the client column of one account must have its corresponding double entry in the client column of another account. The same obviously applies also to office account entries.

Note again that the ledger accounts for each client and the Cash Book will show the office account and the client account side by side.

11.3.1 Receipt of office moneys

The firm must pay money owed to it into office account. The entries to record this are:

    (a) CREDIT client's ledger account—office column;

    (b) DEBIT Cash account—office column.

EXAMPLE

On 1 February the solicitor receives £100 from her client Blake in respect of payments already made (called disbursements) out of office account.

Blake

Date	Details	Office account			Client account		
		DR	CR	Balance	DR	CR	Balance
	Balance— due from you			100 DR			
	Cash: you		100	—			

Cash account

Date	Details	Office account			Client account		
		DR	CR	Balance	DR	CR	Balance
	Balance, say			4,000 DR			
1 Feb	Blake	100		4,100 DR			

11.3.2 Payments of office money

The firm must pay disbursements out of office account if there is insufficient money in client account for that particular client, unless the solicitor decides to transfer office money to client account (see para 11.2.6.2 above). The entries to record a payment of office moneys are:

(a) DEBIT client's ledger account—office column;

(b) CREDIT Cash account—office column.

EXAMPLE

Brown's solicitors are acting on his behalf with regard to a personal injury claim. They are not holding any money on Brown's behalf and pay £400 to counsel for an opinion on liability on 1 March.

Brown: re personal injury action

Date	Details	Office account			Client account		
		DR	CR	Balance	DR	CR	Balance
1 Mar	Cash: counsel	400		400 DR			

Cash account

Date	Details	Office account			Client account		
		DR	CR	Balance	DR	CR	Balance
	Balance, say			3,000 DR			
1 Mar	Brown—counsel		400	2,600 DR			

The client's ledger account should generally show a debit balance or a nil balance on office account. A credit balance may indicate a breach of the SAR. Exceptions to this include receipt of agreed fees (see para 11.2.11 above), mixed moneys, including unpaid professional disbursements, and interest (see Chapter 15, para 15.2.2).

If there is money held in client account but not enough to pay the particular disbursements, so that the whole payment is made out of office account, the solicitor may transfer the money held in client account to office account once the disbursement has been paid. As an alternative, two cheques could be drawn to pay the disbursement, one on client account for the amount held and the remainder on office account. In practice this is rarely done.

11.3.3   Receipt of client money

Once it has been decided that money received is client money it must be paid into client account promptly. The entries are:

(a)   CREDIT client's ledger account—client column;

(b)   DEBIT Cash account—client column.

EXAMPLE

On 1 April the firm receives a cheque for £10,000 from the Winchester Building Society to be used as a deposit on the purchase of 10 Willow Way by the firm's client, Ward.

Ward: re purchase of 10 Willow Way

Date	Details	Office account			Client account		
		DR	CR	Balance	DR	CR	Balance
1 Apr	Cash: Winchester Building Society					10,000	10,000 CR

Cash account

Date	Details	Office account			Client account		
		DR	CR	Balance	DR	CR	Balance
1 Apr	Ward: Winchester Building Society				10,000		10,000 CR

If money is received from a third party on behalf of a client, as in the preceding example, the receipt is recorded in the ledger account of the client on whose behalf the money is received. An account is not opened for the third party.

Remember the solicitor must NOT pay the following into client account:

(a)   the solicitor's own or a partner's money (except as allowed by the rules);

(b)   money received to pay profit costs after a bill has been delivered;

(c)   the money the client asks him or her not to pay into client account.

Solicitors may receive cash on behalf of a client and are permitted to pay this over to the client. However, they must still record the receipt and payment out of client money on the accounts. Also take care that there is no criminal activity involved.

11.3.4   Payment out of client money

Before making a payment out of client account, the solicitor should check that:

(a)   sufficient money is held in client account for the client on whose behalf the payment is being made;

(b)   the payment is permissible within the SAR.

The bookkeeping entries are:

(a) DEBIT the client's ledger account—client column.

(b) CREDIT the Cash account—client column.

Continuing the example:

EXAMPLE

On 7 April the firm pays the £10,000 deposit received from the Winchester Building Society for Ward to Farrells, the seller's solicitors.

Ward: re purchase of 10 Willow Way

Date	Details	Office account			Client account		
		DR	CR	Balance	DR	CR	Balance
1 Apr	Cash: Winchester Building Society					10,000	10,000 CR
7 Apr	Cash: Farrells re deposit				10,000		—

Cash account

Date	Details	Office account			Client account		
		DR	CR	Balance	DR	CR	Balance
1 Apr	Cash: Winchester Building Society				10,000		10,000 DR
7 Apr	Cash: Farrells re deposit					10,000	—

11.3.5 Cheques made payable to third parties

You may be required to show that you appreciate that when you hand over to a third party a cheque made payable to the third party, you have not handled client money. You can do this by making no entry at all in the accounts. Alternatively, you can make what is known as a memorandum entry. If you do this, remember: no entry is made in the cash account at all, no balance column entry is made in the client's ledger account, and the details column should show clearly that the entry is by way of memorandum only.

EXAMPLE

You act for Carr to recover a debt owed to him by Jones. On 1 February Jones sends you a cheque for £250 made payable to Carr.

Carr: re debt collection

Date	Details	Office account			Client account		
		DR	CR	Balance	DR	CR	Balance
1 Feb	Cheque received from Jones payable to Carr memorandum entry only				[250	250]	

11.4   Payments out of petty cash—office account

Small disbursements paid on behalf of clients, such as commissioners on oath fees, may be paid in cash rather than by cheque.

The solicitor maintains a petty cash float by drawing money out of office account at the bank. Any petty cash payments must therefore ALWAYS be made from the office account.

To record dealings with petty cash, a petty cash account is used, or a petty cash book if the ledger system is operated.

To record the transfer of money from the office bank account as a float to the petty cash account the following entries are made:

(a) CREDIT the Cash account in the office column;

(b) DEBIT the Petty Cash account (office account).

EXAMPLE

On 10 January a solicitor draws £500 out of office account for petty cash.

Cash account

Date	Details	Office account			Client account		
		DR	CR	Balance	DR	CR	Balance
	Balance, say			2,000 DR			
10 Jan	Petty cash		500	1,500 DR			

Only office money can be held in petty cash, therefore only office account columns are necessary.

Petty cash account (office account only)

Date	Details	DR	CR	Balance
10 Jan	Cash float	500		500 DR

As payments made out of petty cash are always office account payments, even if there is money in client account, a petty cash payment must always be recorded as coming out of office account.

To record the payment of a petty cash disbursement on a client's behalf the following entries are made in the accounts:

(a) DEBIT the client's ledger account in the office column;

(b) CREDIT the Petty Cash account (office).

Continuing the example:

EXAMPLE

On 15 January the firm pays £40 out of petty cash for local advertisements in the administration of Kasim's estate.

Kasim deceased: administration of estate

Date	Details	Office account			Client account		
		DR	CR	Balance	DR	CR	Balance
15 Jan	Petty cash: local advertisements	40		40 DR			

Petty cash account (office account)

Date	Details	DR	CR	Balance
10 Jan	Cash float	500		500 DR
15 Jan	Kasim deceased		40	460 DR

11.5 Profit costs and VAT

11.5.1 Delivery of bills of costs

When a solicitor delivers a bill of costs to the client, a central record or file of copies of bills must be kept. This is in addition to the entries shown below. (see SAR rule 32(8)).

When a bill of costs is delivered to a client the following entries are made in the accounts:

(a) DEBIT the Client ledger account office column with profit costs and VAT (on separate lines)—charging the client;

(b) CREDIT the Profit Costs account with profit costs;

(c) CREDIT the HM Revenue & Customs (HMRC) account (a personal account) with VAT.

Note that the Profit Costs account and HMRC account only record dealings with office money and therefore only have office columns. For more on VAT, see Chapter 13.

EXAMPLE

On 15 June 2008 the firm delivers a bill of costs to Bradley, for whom it has acted in divorce proceedings, for £600 plus £105 VAT.

Bradley: re divorce

Date	Details	Office account			Client account		
		DR	CR	Balance	DR	CR	Balance
15 June	Profit costs	600					
	VAT	105		705 DR			

Profit Costs account

Date	Details	Office account		
		DR	CR	Balance
15 June	Bradley		600	600 CR

HMRC account VAT

Date	Details	Office account		
		DR	CR	Balance
15 June	Bradley		105	105 CR

Note the credit balance on the HMRC account re VAT shows that the firm owes HMRC the VAT. See Chapter 13 for further details.

Note also that entries are made to record the delivery of the bill of costs on the date of delivery regardless of the date of payment. When payment of the bill is made entries are made in the accounts to record a receipt of office money.

EXAMPLE

Bradley pays her bill on 1 July

Date	Details	Office account			Client account		
		DR	CR	Balance	DR	CR	Balance
15 June	Profit costs	600		600 DR			
	VAT	105		705 DR			
1 July	Cash: you		705	—			

Note: also DEBIT the Cash account—office column with the receipt of £705.

11.5.2 Agreed fees (SAR rule 19(5))

A solicitor and client may agree a fee for work which the solicitor has done or is to do on the client's behalf. An agreed fee is one which is fixed and evidenced in writing. When the solicitor receives the agreed fee it must be paid into office account even though a bill of costs is not delivered until a later date. It is not necessary to draw a bill when a fee is agreed, but it is advisable as the date the agreed fee is received is the tax point for VAT purposes.

EXAMPLE

On 10 July the firm receives £94 from Jackman in respect of a fee agreed at the beginning of the month for work done by the firm on Jackman's behalf in connection with a tenancy dispute. A bill is delivered on receipt of the fee.

Jackman: re housing

Date	Details	Office account			Client account		
		DR	CR	Balance	DR	CR	Balance
10 July	Cash: you—agreed fee		94	94 CR			
	Profit costs—agreed fee						
		80		14 CR			
	VAT	14		—			

Note:

(a) It would be a breach of the SAR to pay money, expressly paid in respect of an agreed fee, into client account.

(b) The tax point for VAT arises when the fee is received, not when a bill is subsequently delivered (see Chapter 13, para 13.4.1).

(c) Contrast money received from a client on general account of costs which is client money.

11.6   Record keeping and compliance

11.6.1   Solicitors' duty to keep accounts

A solicitor has a duty to keep accounts to record transactions involving client money. The accounts and all bank statements must be preserved for a minimum period of six years (SAR rule 32(9)). Where a computerised system is used the solicitor must ensure that a hard copy can be produced reasonably quickly and that it remains capable of reproduction for at least six years.

In addition, all paid cheques and copies of authorities for withdrawal of money from a client account must be retained for at least two years. To avoid the practical problems associated with storage, there is provision in the rules for the solicitor to obtain written confirmation from the bank that it will retain cheques for the required two-year period.

Under SAR rule 35, solicitors who hold client money or trust money during an accounting period must have their client accounts inspected by an accountant 'qualified' within the meaning of the rules, and must submit an accountant's report to the SRA for that accounting period within six months of the end of the accounting period.

The SRA has the power to appoint an accountant to investigate a solicitor's practice.

11.6.2   Powers of the SRA to secure compliance

As stated above, solicitors must deliver an annual accountant's report to the SRA. If solicitors fail to deliver such a report or fail to comply with the SAR, a complaint may be made to the Solicitors Disciplinary Tribunal by the SRA.

Under SAR rule 34, solicitors must produce to any person appointed by the SRA records necessary to enable preparation of a report on compliance with the rules.

Any report made by the person appointed may be sent to the Crown Prosecution Service or the Serious Fraud Office and/or used in proceedings before the Solicitors Disciplinary Tribunal.

11.7 Reminder of key points

1. Using the Solicitors' Accounts Rules 1998 (SAR)—you should become familiar with them and have them with you when working on exercises;

2. The consequences of failing to comply with the rules; solicitors could be referred to the Solicitors Disciplinary Tribunal, where they may be struck off, suspended, or fined;

3. The basic principles of the SAR—solicitors should comply with the Solicitors' Code of Conduct, keep office and client money separately, usually keep client money safely in a bank or building society account, use each client's money for that client only, maintain proper accounting systems, records, and controls, co-operate with the Solicitors Regulation Authority in checking compliance with the rules, account for interest on money held for clients where appropriate, and deliver annual reports;

4. Details of the requirement to keep client money and office money separate and the definitions of client money and office money;

5. Receipts of client money, including receipt of mixed office/client money, payments out of client money and receipts and payments of office money;

6. Basic entries on solicitors' accounts in respect of receipt and payment of office money (including petty cash) and client money;

7. Profit costs and VAT—the entries on delivering a bill to the client;

8. Treatment of the receipt of agreed fees;

9. Record-keeping requirements and powers of the SRA to secure compliance.

 online resource centre Now try the self-test exercises at the end of this chapter and the online multiple choice questions available through your tutor via the Online Resource Centre that accompanies this book before moving on to transfers and mixed money in Chapter 12.

11.8 Practice exercises

Treat each of the first six questions separately, and assume in each example the cash account starts with nil balances on office and client account.

Allow 5 minutes each for exercises 1 to 3.

1 On 1 January the firm receives an agreed fee of £470 from its client Abraham. Show the entries that would be made on the client ledger account for Abraham and on the firm's cash book.

2 On 2 February the firm receives a cheque for £270,000 in respect of the sale of a property on behalf of a partner, Quasim. Show the entries required on the relevant accounts for the receipt.

3 On 3 March the firm pays out £40, being a court fee on behalf of its client Silver. Silver has not yet made any payment on account of costs and disbursements. Show the relevant entries.

Allow 5 to 10 minutes each for exercises 4 and 5.

4 On 4 April the firm receives a cheque for £300 on general account of costs and disbursements from its client Manikai in respect of property transactions. The firm then pays a search fee of £120 on behalf of the client. Show the relevant entries on the accounts.

5 On 5 May the firm pays an expert £500 from office account on behalf of its client Humbert. On 10 May Humbert pays the firm £500 in respect of the disbursement paid. Show the relevant entries on the accounts.

6 Allow 10 to 15 minutes.

On 6 June the firm pays out an expert's fee of £200 on behalf of its client Campbell from office account. On 9 June the firm sends a bill to Campbell for £160 plus VAT. On 15 June Campbell pays the total due to the firm. Show the relevant entries on the accounts.

11.9 Answers to practice exercises

1 Abraham—general matters

Date	Details	Office account			Client account		
		DR	CR	Bal	DR	CR	Bal
1 Jan	Cash: you—agreed fee		470	470 CR			

Cash account

Date	Details	Office account			Client account		
		DR	CR	Bal	DR	CR	Bal
1 Jan	Abraham—agreed fee	470		470 DR			

Note that as the date of receipt of the agreed fee is the tax point for VAT purposes then it would be advisable to send out a VAT invoice and record the fee and VAT on the account (see para 11.5.2 above and Chapter 13 on VAT).

2 Quasim—sale of property

Date	Details	Office account			Client account		
		DR	CR	Bal	DR	CR	Bal
2 Feb	Cash—sale proceeds		270,000	270,000 CR			

Cash account

Date	Details	Office account			Client account		
		DR	CR	Bal	DR	CR	Bal
2 Feb	Quasim—sale proceeds	270,000		270,000 DR			

Note that this money must be paid into office account as the partner is solely entitled to the money. See SAR rule 13, note (xii).

3 Silver—litigation

Date	Details	Office account			Client account		
		DR	CR	Bal	DR	CR	Bal
3 Mar	Cash—court fee	40		40 DR			

Cash account

Date	Details	Office account			Client account		
		DR	CR	Bal	DR	CR	Bal
3 Mar	Silver—court fee		40	40 CR			

4 Manikai—property sale and purchase

Date	Details	Office account			Client account		
		DR	CR	Bal	DR	CR	Bal
4 Apr	Cash: you—on account of costs and disbursements					300	300 CR
	Cash—search fee				120		180 CR

Cash account

Date	Details	Office account			Client account		
		DR	CR	Bal	DR	CR	Bal
4 Apr	Manikai—on account of costs				300		300 DR
	Manikai—search fee					120	180 DR

5 Humbert—general matters

Date	Details	Office account			Client account		
		DR	CR	Bal	DR	CR	Bal
5 May	Cash—expert	500		500 DR			
10 May	Cash: you—payment of disbursement		500	—			

Cash account

Date	Details	Office account			Client account		
		DR	CR	Bal	DR	CR	Bal
5 May	Humbert—expert		500	500 CR			
10 May	Humbert—payment of disbursement	500		—			

6 Campbell—general matters

Date	Details	Office account			Client account		
		DR	CR	Bal	DR	CR	Bal
6 June	Cash—expert	200		200 DR			
9 June	Profit costs—bill	160		360 DR			
	HM Revenue & Customs VAT	28		388 DR			
15 June	Cash: you—balance due		388	—			

Cash account

Date	Details	Office account			Client account		
		DR	CR	Bal	DR	CR	Bal
6 June	Campbell—expert		200	200 CR			
9 June	Campbell—balance due	388		188 DR			

Profit Costs account

Date	Details	Office account		
		DR	CR	Bal
9 June	Campbell—bill		160	160 CR

HM Revenue & Customs VAT account

Date	Details	Office account		
		DR	CR	Bal
9 June	Campbell—bill		28	28 CR

Note: the balances at the end of each account at the end of the transaction. Campbell's account is clear; he no longer owes the firm any money. The firm is holding £188 on the Cash Book, which represents £160 for the firm's profit costs and £28 due to HM Revenue & Customs. It has been repaid the £200 it paid out.

Transfers and mixed money

12.1 Introduction

This chapter includes:

1. When transfers from client account to office account are permitted under the Solicitors' Account Rules 1998 (SAR) and the bookkeeping entries required to record a transfer from client account to office account;

2. When transfers are required from office account to client account, ie for breach of the SAR, and the bookkeeping entries required to record a transfer from office account to client account;

3. When transfers are permitted between client accounts and the bookkeeping entries required to record a transfer from one client account to another;

4. Alternatives for dealing with the receipt of mixed office/client money, split cheque or transfers;

5. Reminder of key points;

6. Self-test exercises.

! **INTENDED OUTCOME**

An understanding of:

1. When transfers from client account to office account are permitted, and the entries required to record the transfer from client account to office account;

2. When transfers from office account to client account are required to correct a breach of the SAR and the bookkeeping entries required to record the transfer from office account to client account;

3. The alternatives available for dealing with the receipt of mixed office/client money.

The above evidenced by the ability to draw up the relevant accounts.

12.2 Transfers

12.2.1 Transfers from client account to office account

A transfer may be made from client to office account if the SAR allow a withdrawal of money from client account (SAR rule 22) (see para 11.2.8).

A solicitor may wish to transfer money from client to office account if:

(a) disbursements have been paid out of office account on the client's behalf;

(b) a bill of costs has been delivered to the client and the solicitor needs to obtain payment of costs by transferring money held in client account;

(c) a cheque for mixed office/client money has been paid into client account.

The bookkeeping entries to record a transfer from client to office account are:

(1) the entries to record a payment out of clients' money (see para 11.3.4);

(2) the entries to record a receipt of office money (see para 11.3.1).

EXAMPLE

On 2 September the firm delivered a bill of costs to its client Gibson, showing profit costs of £200 and VAT of £35. The firm is holding £500 in client account for Gibson. On 5 September the firm transfers £235 from client to office account.

Gibson

Date	Details	Office account			Client account		
		DR	CR	Balance	DR	CR	Balance
	Balance						500 CR
2 Sept	Profit costs	200					
	VAT	35		235 DR			
5 Sept	Cash: transfer		235[2] IN	—	235[1] OUT		265 CR

Cash account

Date	Details	Office account			Client account		
		DR	CR	Balance	DR	CR	Balance
	Gibson				500		500 DR
5 Sept	Cash: transfer	235[2] IN		235 DR		235[1] OUT	265 DR

Note:
(1) Payment of client money.
(2) Receipt of office money.

12.2.2   Transfer from office account to client account

A solicitor must make an immediate transfer from office account to client account if he or she has breached the SAR by overdrawing on client account, for example, by drawing against an uncleared cheque which is later dishonoured (SAR rule 7).

The bookkeeping entries to record a transfer of money from office account to client account are as follows:

(1) entries to record a payment of office money (see para 11.3.2);

(2) entries to record a receipt of client money (see para 11.3.3).

EXAMPLE

Bamford has a credit balance on client account of £50. On 20 October her solicitor inadvertently pays counsel's fee of £70 out of client account. She makes an immediate transfer from office to client account to correct the breach, as she has taken £20 of other clients' money.

Bamford

Date	Details	Office account			Client account		
		DR	CR	Balance	DR	CR	Balance
	Balance						50 CR
20 Oct	Cash: counsel				70		20 DR
	Cash: transfer	20[1]		20 DR		20[2]	—
		OUT				IN	

Cash account

Date	Details	Office account			Client account		
		DR	CR	Balance	DR	CR	Balance
	Balance, say				150		150 DR
20 Oct	Cash: counsel:						
	Bamford					70	80 DR
	Cash: transfer:						
	Bamford		20[1]	20 CR	20[2]		100 DR
			OUT		IN		

Note:

(1) Entries to record payment of office money.

(2) Entries to record receipt of client money.

Also note that on the cash book the £150 client account balance represents £50 for Bamford and £100 for other clients, after the incorrect payment out of £70 on client account the transfer in of £20 brings the balance to £100.

12.2.3   Transfers between client accounts (SAR rule 22(1)(d))

Money is not moved from one bank account to another and therefore NO entries are made in the Cash account.

A transfer can be made from one client ledger account to another client ledger account if:

(a) it is permissible within the rules to withdraw money from the account of client A;

(b) it is permissible within the rules to pay money into the account of client B.

When a transfer is made from one client ledger account to another, a separate record must be made. This may be, for example, in a journal if a ledger system is used, or on a transfer sheet if another system is used (SAR rule 32(2)).

The bookkeeping entries to record transfers between client accounts are as follows:

(a) DEBIT the ledger account of the client from whose account the transfer is being made (make a separate record on the journal or transfer sheet);

(b) CREDIT the ledger account of the client to whose account the transfer is being made (make a separate record on the journal or transfer sheet).

EXAMPLE

The firm is holding £10,000 in client account for its client Burns. The firm also acts for Burns's son-in-law, Reed, with regard to his house purchase. Burns is making a gift to Reed of the deposit of £8,000 and asks the firm to pay Reed's deposit on 7 April out of the money held for him.

Burns

Date	Details	Office account			Client account		
		DR	CR	Balance	DR	CR	Balance
	Balance						10,000 CR
7 Apr	Reed: transfer sheet				8,000		2,000 CR

Reed

Date	Details	Office account			Client account		
		DR	CR	Balance	DR	CR	Balance
7 Apr	Burns: transfer sheet					8,000	8,000 CR
	Cash: deposit paid				8,000		—

Note: a transfer may be made from the client account of one client to the office account of another or vice versa. For example, if one client has agreed to money being taken from his or her client account to discharge another client's liability for costs. If this is done, then the entries used to make a transfer from client to office account or vice versa must be shown (see paras 12.2.1 and 12.2.2 above).

EXAMPLE

The firm acts for the executors of Ashley. It also acts for O'Brien, Ashley's daughter and the sole beneficiary. There is a balance of £12,000 on Ashley's account. The firm has acted for O'Brien in her divorce proceedings and a bill has been delivered to O'Brien for £1,000 plus VAT. The executors agree to this being paid out of the estate. A double entry will be made showing (1) a payment out of Ashley deceased account client account and then (2) showing a receipt into O'Brien office account.

Executors of Ashley deceased

Date	Details	Office account			Client account		
		DR	CR	Balance	DR	CR	Balance
	Balance						12,000 CR
	Cash transfer— O'Brien				1,175		10,825 CR
					OUT (1)		

O'Brien: re divorce

Date	Details	Office account			Client account		
		DR	CR	Balance	DR	CR	Balance
	Profit costs	1,000					
	VAT	175		1,175 DR			
	Cash—Ashley		1,175	—			
			IN (2)				

Cash account

Date	Details	Office account			Client account		
		DR	CR	Balance	DR	CR	Balance
	Balance						12,000 DR
	Ashley—						
	transfer to O'Brien	1,175		1,175 DR		1,175	10,825 DR
		IN(2)				OUT(1)	

Note that the SAR restrict inter-client transfers in respect of private loans. Rule 30(2) states that no sum in respect of a private loan shall be paid out of funds held on account of the lender, either:

(a) directly to the borrower; or

(b) by means of a payment from one client account to another or by a paper transfer from the ledger of the lender to that of the borrower

without the prior written authority of **both** clients.

A private loan on standard terms is defined as meaning a loan other than one provided by an institution which provides loans in the normal course of its activities. The solicitor should also keep a register of the authorities for transactions of this type.

12.3 Mixed office/client money

When a solicitor receives mixed office/client money the alternatives are stated in SAR rule 20:

(a) pay the cheque into client account and then make a transfer from client to office account of the office money within 14 days of receipt; or

(b) split the cheque by paying the client's money into client account and the office money into office account.

(c) If the payment consists of office money and client money in the form of unpaid professional disbursements, the entire sum may be paid into office account and by the end of the second working day following receipt either the unpaid professional disbursement should be paid or the relevant sum transferred to client account. (See SAR rule 19(1)(b).)

There are also special rules relating to the treatment of moneys received from the Legal Services Commission and payment from a third party in respect of legal aid work (see SAR rule 21).

EXAMPLE

Price sends a cheque for £250 to his solicitor on 1 March. The cheque represents £200 owed by Price to a creditor and £50 costs owed to the solicitor in respect of which a bill was delivered to Price on 1 February.

(a) If the cheque is not split, the entries in Price's account will be:

Price account

Date	Details	Office account			Client account		
		DR	CR	Balance	DR	CR	Balance
	Balance			50 DR			
	Cash: you—mixed money					250	250 CR

The Cash account would be debited with £250. When the £50 in respect of costs is transferred to office account, entries will be made in Price's account and the cash account to record a transfer from client to office account leaving £200 in client account (see para 12.2.1 above).

(b) If the cheque is split the entries in Price's account will be:

Price account

Date	Details	Office account			Client account		
		DR	CR	Balance	DR	CR	Balance
	Balance			50 DR			
1 Mar	Cash: you— split cheque		50	—		200	200 CR

Cash account

Date	Details	Office account			Client account		
		DR	CR	Balance	DR	CR	Balance
1 Mar	Price—split cheque	50		50 DR	200		200 DR

12.4 Reminder of key points

1. When transfers from client account to office account are permitted under SAR rule 22, for example to pay the solicitor for a delivered bill of costs and VAT or to pay for disbursements paid out of office account;

2. The bookkeeping entries required to record a transfer from client account to office account—a double entry will be required showing the payment out of client account and a double entry for the receipt into office account;

3. When transfers from office account to client account are required to correct a breach of the SAR, for example where the solicitor has overdrawn money from that particular client's client account;

4. The bookkeeping entries required to record the transfer from office account to client account—a double entry will be required for the payment out of office account and then a double entry for receipt into client account;

5. When transfers are permitted between client accounts;

6. The entries required on the clients' accounts and the separate record required for the transfer (journal or transfer sheet), note also that there are no entries on the Cash Book;

7. The options available for dealing with the receipt of mixed office/client money:

(a) option 1—pay the total into client account and then transfer the office money to office account within 14 days;

(b) option 2—split the receipt between office and client account;

(c) option 3—available only if office money and the client money is in respect of a professional disbursement incurred but not yet paid, when the total can be paid into office account and by the end of the second day either pay the disbursement from office account or transfer the money to client account.

Now try the self-test exercises at the end of this chapter. These include elements from Chapter 11 as well as this chapter, and there are the online multiple choice questions available through your tutor via the Online Resource Centre that accompanies this book. Then move on to VAT in Chapter 13.

12.5 Exercises on basic ledger entries

In the following questions draw up the clients' ledger accounts to record the transactions. Assume in all cases that no money is held on client account for the client unless otherwise stated.

1 Allow 5 to 10 minutes.

Pay counsel's fee £188 on behalf of Nadal. Deliver a bill for £120 plus £21 VAT and disbursement. Receive payment from Nadal.

2 Allow 5 to 10 minutes.

You act for Mari. Pay search fee £10 by cash. Pay for office copy entries by cheque £15. Receive £100 from Mari in respect of disbursements.

3 Allow 10 minutes.

Levi pays you £75 on account of costs generally. Pay £5 out of petty cash on Levi's behalf for inspection of deeds. Deliver a bill of costs for £100 plus VAT. Receive payment of balance from Levi and close her account.

4 Allow 5 to 10 minutes.

Receive £235 from Jones in respect of an agreed fee for property work, which includes VAT.

5 Allow 5 to 10 minutes.

Miller's account shows a balance in hand of £500. Miller asks you to transfer £300 to Day, another client of the firm.

Allow 5 to 10 minutes each for exercises 6 and 7.

6 Knowles asks you to pay a premium of £75 on his behalf to the Star Insurance Co. for whom you act. He pays £75 to you one week later, by agreement.

7 You act for Allen. Pay counsel's fee £94 (including VAT £14). Deliver a bill of costs to Allen for £120 plus VAT. Receive moneys due from Allen.

8 Allow about 10 minutes.

You act for Collins: 1 September pay counsel's fee £235 (including VAT £35); 19 September receive £450 from Collins; 23 September pay disbursement £47 and deliver a bill of costs £120 plus £21 VAT. Transfer sum due from client to office account. Pay balance due to Collins.

9 Allow about 10 minutes.

The firm's client, Shaw, asks the firm to carry out a number of transactions whilst he is abroad. Shaw promises to send a cheque for £800 to cover expenditure. The following events take place with regard to Shaw's account.

1 June	Pay £30 to enquiry agent.
4 June	Pay counsel's fee £115.
8 June	Receive Shaw's cheque for £600. The cheque is to be split between office and client account.
9 June	Send a bill of costs to Shaw for £360 plus £63 VAT. Transfer costs and pay Shaw the balance due to him.

Prepare Shaw's account to record the above transactions.

10 Allow 20 to 25 minutes.

Your firm is acting for John Berger who is purchasing a house for £90,000. The following events occur:

4 September	Pay search fee £80.
20 September	Receive cheque for £9,000 from client for deposit.
21 September	Contracts exchanged—pay deposit of £9,000 to seller's solicitor.
29 September	Pay search fee £4.
9 October	Deliver a bill for £200 plus £35 VAT.
13 October	Receive a cheque from client for £81,319, the balance of the purchase money and costs.
14 October	Complete purchase—pay £81,000 to seller's solicitors. Transfer amount due to office account.

Prepare the client ledger card for John Berger and the Cash account to record the above transactions.

11 Allow 20 to 30 minutes.

Your firm is acting for the executors of Olive White in the administration of her estate. The following events occur:

5 October	Pay probate fees of £80.
31 October	Receive £1,000 from the Leigh Insurance Co. in respect of a policy which the deceased held with them.
	Pay £535 to the executors' bank to repay a loan.
5 November	Receive £2,000 from the deceased's building society account.
6 November	Receive £400 from sale of household contents.
	Pay legacy of £1,500.
10 November	Deliver a bill of costs £240 plus £42 VAT.
11 November	Pay residuary beneficiary £1,003.
	Transfer £362 from client to office account.

Prepare the ledger account for the executors of Olive White and the cash account to record the above.

12.6 Suggested answers to exercises on basic ledger entries

1 Nadal

Date	Details	Office account			Client account		
		DR	CR	Balance	DR	CR	Balance
	Cash: counsel's fee	188		188 DR			
	Profit costs	120					
	VAT	21		329 DR			
	Cash: you—balance due		329	—			

The cheque from Nadal must be paid into office account. See SAR rule 13, note (xi)(c)(A) and (B).

2 Mari

Date	Details	Office account			Client account		
		DR	CR	Balance	DR	CR	Balance
	Petty cash: search fee	10		10 DR			
	Cash: office copies	15		25 DR			
	Cash: you—split cheque		25	—		75	75 CR

Note that you could pay £100 into client account and then transfer £25 to office account. See SAR rule 20.

3 Levi

Date	Details	Office account			Client account		
		DR	CR	Balance	DR	CR	Balance
	Cash: you					75	75 CR
	Petty cash: inspection fee	5		5 DR			
	Profit costs	100					
	VAT	17.50		122.50 DR			
	Cash: you—balance due		47.50	75 DR			
	Cash: transfer: balance due		75	—	75		—

Note that Petty cash must be drawn from office account. The balance due from Levi is office money. See SAR rule 13, note (xi)B.

4 Jones

Date	Details	Office account			Client account		
		DR	CR	Balance	DR	CR	Balance
	Profit costs (agreed fee)	200					
	VAT	35		235 DR			
	Cash: you		235	—			

Note: a bill has been drawn up when the agreed fee is received, as the receipt of the agreed fee is the tax point for VAT, and the agreed fee must be paid into office account. See SAR rule 13, note (xi)(D).

5 Miller

Date	Details	Office account			Client account		
		DR	CR	Balance	DR	CR	Balance
	Balance						500 CR
	Day: transfer						
	(transfer sheet)				300		200 CR

Day

Date	Details	Office account			Client account		
		DR	CR	Balance	DR	CR	Balance
	Miller: transfer						
	(transfer sheet)					300	300 CR

See SAR rule 22(1)(d).

6 Knowles

Date	Details	Office account			Client account		
		DR	CR	Balance	DR	CR	Balance
	Cash: transfer premium to Star Insurance Co.	75		75 DR			
	Cash: you		75	—			

Star Insurance Co.

Date	Details	Office account			Client account		
		DR	CR	Balance	DR	CR	Balance
	Cash Knowles: transfer premium					75	75 CR

The transfer had to be from office account to client account and when Knowles pays, this is office money. See SAR rule 13, note (xi)(c)(B).

7 Allen

Date	Details	Office account			Client account		
		DR	CR	Balance	DR	CR	Balance
	Cash: counsel's fee	94		94 DR			
	Profit costs	120					
	VAT	21		235 DR			
	Cash: you—balance due		235	—			

8 Collins

Date	Details	Office account			Client account		
		DR	CR	Balance	DR	CR	Balance
1 Sept	Cash: counsel's fee	235		235 DR			
19 Sept	Cash: you					450	450 CR
23 Sept	Cash: disbursement				47		403 CR
23 Sept	Profit costs	120					
	VAT	21		376 DR			
	Cash: transfer:						
	profit costs		376	—	376		27 CR
	Cash: you—balance due				27		—

For counsel's fee see also Chapter 13, 13.4.6.1. The £450 is mixed office/client money. See SAR rule 20.

9 Shaw

Date	Details	Office account			Client account		
		DR	CR	Balance	DR	CR	Balance
1 June	Cash—enquiry agent	30		30 DR			
4 June	Cash—counsel	115		145 DR			
8 June	Cash: you—split cheque	145		—		455	455 CR
9 June	Profit costs	360		360 DR			
	VAT	63		423 DR			
	Cash: transfer:						
	profit costs		423	—	423		32 CR
	Cash: you—balance due				32		—

10 John Berger: matter—property

Date	Details	Office account			Client account		
		DR	CR	Balance	DR	CR	Balance
4 Sept	Cash: search fee	80		80 DR			
20 Sept	Cash: you					9,000	9,000 CR
21 Sept	Cash: deposit				9,000		—
29 Sept	Cash: search fee	4		84 DR			
9 Oct	Profit costs	200		284 DR			
	VAT	35		319 DR			
13 Oct	Cash: you					81,319	81,319
14 Oct	Cash: completion				81,000		319 CR
	Cash: transfer profit costs		319	—	319		—

Cash account

Date	Details	Office account			Client account		
		DR	CR	Balance	DR	CR	Balance
4 Sept	Berger: search fee		80	80 CR			
20 Sept	Berger:				9,000		9,000 DR
21 Sept	Berger: deposit					9,000	—
29 Sept	Berger: search fee		4	84 CR			
13 Oct	Berger				81,319		81,319 DR
14 Oct	Berger: completion					81,000	319 DR
	Berger: transfer						
	profit costs	319		235 DR		319	—

11   Executors of Olive White deceased

Date	Details	Office account			Client account		
		DR	CR	Balance	DR	CR	Balance
5 Oct	Cash: probate fees	80		80 DR			
31 Oct	Cash: Leigh						
	Insurance Co.					1,000	1,000 CR
	Cash: bank loan				535		465 CR
5 Nov	Cash: Building						
	Society					2,000	2,465 CR
6 Nov	Cash: sale of						
	household contents					400	2,865 CR
	Cash: legacy				1,500		1,365 CR
10 Nov	Profit costs	240		320 DR			
	VAT	42		362 DR			
	Cash: residuary						
	Beneficiary				1,003		362 CR
	Cash: transfer						
	profit costs		362	—	362		—

Cash account

Date	Details	Office account			Client account		
		DR	CR	Balance	DR	CR	Balance
5 Oct	Olive White:						
	probate fee		80	80 CR			
31 Oct	Olive White:						
	Leigh						
	Insurance Co.				1,000		1,000 DR
	Olive White: Bank						
	loan					535	465 DR
5 Nov	Olive White:						
	Building Society				2,000		2,465 DR
	Olive White: re						
	household contents				400		2,865 DR
	Olive White: legacy					1,500	1,365 DR
11 Nov	Olive White: legacy					1,003	362 DR
	Olive White:						
	transfer profit costs	362		282 DR		362	—

Note on the Cash account the £282 DR balance on office account represents the amount for payment of profit costs of £240 and VAT of £42.

13

Value added tax

13.1 Introduction

This chapter contains the following:

1. VAT—an overview;
2. Registering for VAT;
3. Accounting to HM Revenue & Customs for VAT, including input tax and output tax;
4. How to deal with disbursements paid on behalf of clients, the agency, and principal methods;
5. VAT relief for bad debts;
6. Reminder of key points;
7. Self-test exercises.

You may find the website for HM Revenue & Customs (HMRC) useful, see <http://www.hmrc.gov.uk>.

! **INTENDED OUTCOME**

An understanding of:

1. VAT being charged on goods or services by a taxable person in the course of a business, with some supplies being exempt, and the three rates of tax charged;
2. Registering and accounting for VAT to HMRC, input tax and output tax;
3. Bookkeeping entries for VAT on payments made by the firm (input tax);
4. Bookkeeping entries for VAT on billing the client (output tax);
5. Bookkeeping entries when making payments out on behalf of a client:
   (a) when the invoice is made out to the client—the agency method;
   (b) when the invoice is made out to the firm of solicitors—the principal method;
6. VAT relief available for bad debts.

The above evidenced by the ability to draw up the relevant accounts.

13.2 VAT—an overview

Many businesses in the UK will have to charge VAT (Value Added Tax) on the goods or services they supply to their customers or clients. VAT is a wide-ranging tax charged on the supply of most goods and services. The main rate of VAT is 17.5% (reduced to 15% from 1 December 2008 to 31 December 2009 because of the recession), and there is a reduced rate of 5% (for example for domestic fuel). Also some businesses are zero rated for VAT. All businesses that have to be registered for VAT will have to account to HM Revenue & Customs for the VAT they charge their clients, but will this will be less any VAT they may have paid in the course of the business. This is an advantage for zero-rated suppliers, who will charge their customers VAT at 0%, but will be able to claim back the VAT they pay in the course of the business. Contrast an exempt supplier, who will not charge customers VAT, but is unable to claim back the VAT paid in the course of the business.

Solicitors will charge VAT, where applicable, at the standard rate of 17.5% (15%).

When accounting for VAT the tax charged by a business is known as output tax (being the tax on goods or services going OUT of the business). The tax paid by a business is known as input tax (being the tax paid on goods or services coming IN to the business).

13.3 Registering for VAT

Solicitors whose taxable supplies exceed the VAT threshold set under the Valued Added Tax Act 1994 (at the time of writing £68,000) must register for VAT purposes. This threshold is changed from time to time to take account of inflation. In practice most solicitors will need to register for VAT.

13.4 Accounting to HM Revenue & Customs for VAT

Solicitors will need to keep accounting records of all VAT charged and all VAT paid and account to HMRC for the balance. They will need an account for HMRC VAT; note that this is a personal account and NOT an expense account.

The HMRC VAT account would normally show the tax charged on goods or services going out of the firm (output tax) less the tax paid on goods or services coming into the firm (input tax). Provided the tax charged is greater than the tax paid then the balance on the account is the amount payable to HMRC.

Tax is normally paid to HMRC quarterly. Within one month of the end of the quarter, a firm must send a completed return form and payment to HMRC. However, there are provisions for small and medium-sized firms to account yearly.

13.4.1 Tax points

The tax point determines the date on which the solicitors' firm must account to HMRC. Normally VAT becomes payable when a bill of costs is sent to the client, whether the client pays the bill or not. Note that if the firm receives payment in respect of an agreed fee before a bill has been sent, then this becomes the tax point for VAT. The firm will therefore usually record the bill and VAT immediately on receipt of the agreed fee.

13.4.2 Tax invoices

Solicitors must provide a tax invoice to clients who are themselves registered for VAT. In practice solicitors will usually supply invoices to all their clients. For an example of a tax invoice, see the end of the example at paras 13.4.7.1 and 13.4.7.2 below.

13.4.3 Account used

A HMRC VAT account will be required. This must be an office account, and it is a personal account with HMRC, showing the amount due to (or from) HMRC, it is **not** an expense account. The debit column will record all tax paid, the credit column will record all tax charged.

   Normally, at the end of each quarter the firm will account to HMRC for the tax charged less the tax paid.

HMRC VAT account	Office account		
	DR	CR	Balance
	Tax paid	Tax charged	

When VAT due is paid to HMRC then you would debit the HMRC (office) account and credit the Cash account (office account)

13.4.4 Overview of recording VAT for solicitors

Like other businesses solicitors will record on their accounts the VAT they have paid on supplies made to the firm, such as computers or office stationery. As stated previously this VAT can be offset against the VAT that the firm charges its clients. However, there is an extra complication for solicitors, as they often make payments on behalf of their clients. There are two ways these payments should be dealt with. If the tax invoice is addressed directly to the client, then the VAT is the client's concern, not the solicitors' firm. Thus the solicitors' firm will just pay the total, including the VAT, and no separate record of the VAT will be kept. If, however, the tax invoice is made out to the solicitors' firm, the firm must record the VAT paid on its HMRC VAT account as input tax, and then when it bills the client it will charge the client the VAT on the disbursement as output tax, as well as on its own profit costs. The paragraphs below give more detail on the accounts used.

13.4.5 Recording VAT on payments made by the firm (input tax)

When solicitors pay VAT on supplies made to the firm they must use office money. The Cash account office account will be credited, broken down into 2 entries, the net amount and the VAT, and then the relevant real or expense account will be debited with the net amount and the HMRC account will be debited with the VAT.

EXAMPLE

The firm buys a computer on 1 March and pays £800 plus £140 VAT.

Cash account

Date	Details	Office account		
		DR	CR	Balance
	Balance, say			2,000 DR
1 Mar	Office computer		800	1,200 DR
	HMRC VAT		140	1,060 DR

Office computer account

Date	Details	Office account		
		DR	CR	Balance
1 Mar	Cash	800		800 DR

HMRC VAT account

Date	Details	Office account		
		DR	CR	Balance
		Tax paid	Tax charged	
1 Mar	Cash	140		140 DR

Note that the debit balance on HMRC VAT account will offset any tax charged later.

13.4.6   Recording VAT on billing the client (output tax)

As you have seen in Chapter 11 (para 11.5), when the firm bills the client for work done, VAT will be charged on the bill. As a reminder, the entries are as follows:

EXAMPLE

On 20 September the firm delivers a bill of costs to its client Farrell in respect of litigation for £600 plus £105 VAT.

Farrell: re litigation

Date	Details	Office account			Client account		
		DR	CR	Balance	DR	CR	Balance
20 Sept	Profit costs	600		600 DR			
	HMRC VAT	105		705 DR			

Profit Costs account

Date	Details	Office account		
		DR	CR	Balance
20 Sept	Farrell		600	600 CR

HMRC VAT account

Date	Details	Office account		
		DR	CR	Balance
		Input tax paid	Output tax charged	
20 Sept	Farrell		105	105 CR

Note that the credit balance on the HMRC VAT account is the amount due to HMRC in respect of the tax charged, as this is a personal account.

13.4.7 Making payments out on behalf of a client (disbursements)

As previously stated, if a solicitor makes a payment on behalf of a client which includes VAT, then how this is treated on the accounts will depend on who the invoice is made out to.

13.4.7.1 Invoice made out to the client (agency method)

This is the easy method. If the invoice is made out to the client, then the solicitor is just making a payment on behalf of the client as agent and is not involved with the VAT. Thus the solicitor will merely make a payment of the **total** amount, including the VAT, in the normal way. The HMRC VAT account is not used at all. This means that the solicitor can use either office account or client account, if funds are available. The solicitor is acting merely as agent for the client. Thus you would debit the client ledger account in the normal way, with the total amount, including the VAT and credit the cash account with the total including the VAT.

With this method it is the client who will be able to offset the VAT paid against any VAT charged, but only if the client is a taxable person.

Note that there is an agreement with HMRC that fee notes from counsel addressed to the firm can be amended and treated as addressed to the client. If so, then the payment will be made using the agency method.

EXAMPLE

The firm receives an invoice from estate agents, addressed to its client Breen, for their fees £6,000 plus VAT £1,050.

The firm is holding £10,000 on client account for Breen and pays the amount due from client account.

Client ledger account for Breen

Date	Details	Office account			Client account		
		DR	CR	Balance	DR	CR	Balance
	Balance on account						10,000 CR
	Cash paid estate agents inc. VAT				7,050		2,950 CR

Cash account

Date	Details	Office account			Client account		
		DR	CR	Balance	DR	CR	Balance
	Breen—balance						10,000 DR
	Breen—paid estate agents inc. VAT					7,050	2,950 DR

Set out below is an example of a tax invoice sent to the client, showing the above disbursement only, and assuming that the firm charges profit costs of £600 plus VAT of £105. This should aid your understanding of the difference between the agency and principal methods, particularly if you compare it with the tax invoice at the end of the example following in respect of the principal method.

TAX INVOICE

	Supply	VAT
Name of client: Breen		
Address of client:		
VAT number (the solicitors' VAT registration number)		
To supply of legal services (Profit Costs)	600	
VAT at 17.5%		105
Total supply and VAT	600	105
Add disbursement paid by us		
Estate agents fee (inc. VAT)	7,050	
Total due from you 7,050		
705		
7,755		

13.4.7.2 Invoice made out to the firm (principal method)

Stage 1 Payment of disbursement

If the invoice is made out to the firm, then the firm is acting as principal and the HMRC VAT account must be used to record the VAT paid as input tax (see para 13.4.4 above). Because of this, the payment must always be made out of office account. The payment out will be broken down in the Cash account office account into two credit entries, showing the net amount and the VAT separately. The client ledger account office account will be debited with the net amount only, and the HMRC VAT (office) account will be debited with the VAT.

Note from the above that, at the time of payment, only the NET amount will be shown as debited to the client ledger account office account.

Note in the example shown below that the firm MUST use office account, even though there is money available on client account, as the principal method is being used and the VAT paid must be recorded on the HMRC VAT account which is an office account.

EXAMPLE

1. The firm pays an expert a fee of £800 plus £140 VAT on behalf of their client, Leith. The invoice from the expert was made out to the firm. The firm are holding £1,000 on general account of costs on client account.

Cash account

Date	Details	Office account			Client account		
		DR	CR	Balance	DR	CR	Balance
	Leith balance						1,000 DR
	Leith—expert		800	800 CR			
	HMRC VAT		140	940 CR			

Client ledger account for Leith

Date	Details	Office account			Client account		
		DR	CR	Balance	DR	CR	Balance
	Balance on a/c					1,000	1,000 CR
	Cash—expert	800		800 DR			
	(*Note*: VAT 140)						

HMRC VAT account

Date	Details	Office account		
		DR	CR	Balance
		Tax paid	Tax charged	
	Cash—VAT paid	140		140 DR

A note has been placed in the details column to remind you to charge the client the VAT on the disbursement as well as on the profit costs when the client is sent the bill.

Stage 2 Billing the client and charging VAT

When the client is billed, the firm will then charge the client VAT on the profit costs AND on the disbursement. The client ledger account will therefore record the profit costs and then the VAT on both the profit costs and the disbursement previously paid.

The Client ledger account will be debited with the Profit Costs and then the VAT on BOTH the Profit Costs and the disbursement. The Profit Costs account will be credited with the profit costs, and the HMRC VAT account will be credited with the total VAT charged to the client, ie on BOTH the profit costs and the disbursement.

Continuing the example:

---

2. The firm sends a bill to Leith for £400 plus VAT.

Cash account

Date	Details	Office account			Client account		
		DR	CR	Balance	DR	CR	Balance
	Leith balance						1,000 DR
	Leith—expert		800	800 CR			
	HMRC VAT(2)(b)		140	940 CR			

Client ledger account for Leith

Date	Details	Office account			Client account		
		DR	CR	Balance	DR	CR	Balance
	Balance on a/c					1,000	1,000 CR
	Cash expert	800		800 DR			
	(*Note*: VAT 140)						
	Profit Costs	400		1,200 DR			
	HMRC VAT						
	(140 + 70)	210		1,410 DR			

HMRC VAT account

Date	Details	Office account		
		DR	CR	Balance
	Cash—VAT paid	140		140 DR
	Leith—tax charged		210	70 CR

Profit Costs account

Date	Details	Office account		
		DR	CR	Balance
	Leith—bill		400	400 CR

Note from the HMRC VAT account that the solicitors have already paid the £140 VAT which is off-set against the amount of VAT charged, leaving a balance due to HMRC of £70.

Below is set out an example of the tax invoice to the client in respect of the above transaction.

TAX INVOICE

	Supply	VAT	
Name of client Leith			
Address of client			
VAT number (the solicitors' VAT registration number)			
To supply of legal services (Profit Costs)	400		
VAT at 17.5%		70	
Taxable disbursement paid by us			
Expert fee	800		
VAT at 17.5% on fee		140	
TOTAL DUE	1,200	210	1,410

Note: contrast this invoice with the invoice using the agency method in para 13.4.7.1 above.

13.5 Agency method on payment of a disbursement—summary

(a) The invoice is made out to the client.

(b) OFFICE or CLIENT account may be used (if funds are available on client account).

(c) On payments show the TOTAL figure paid, including the VAT. Do not show the VAT separately, as the HMRC VAT account is not used.

13.6 Principal method on payment of a disbursement—summary

(a) The invoice is made out to the firm of solicitors.

(b) OFFICE account must be used.

(c) On the client ledger account show the NET amount paid only. (The VAT paid will be shown on the HMRC VAT account.) Make a note of the VAT paid on the disbursement in the details column of the client ledger account to remind you to charge the VAT on the disbursement when the client is billed.

(d) When the bill is sent to the client, debit the Profit Costs and debit the VAT on BOTH the Profit Costs and the disbursement previously paid on the client ledger OFFICE account.

13.7 VAT relief for bad debts

As the HMRC VAT account is credited when a bill is sent to the client, then this sum will have to be accounted for to HMRC. If the client is unable to pay, then the firm may write off the total bad debt including the VAT. This is hard on a business and so VAT relief is available where the debt has not been paid for at least 6 months. For further details on writing off Bad debts, see Chapter 17 para 17.5.

13.8 Reminder of key points

1. Most solicitors will have to charge their clients VAT;

2. The main rate of VAT is 17.5% (15%), although there is a reduced rate of 5% for domestic fuel and some types of suppliers are zero rated;

3. Solicitors will have to account to HM Revenue & Customs (HMRC) for the tax they charge their clients (output tax) less the tax they have paid in the course of their business (input tax). They will therefore need an account for HMRC. This will be an office account only and is a personal account not an expense account;

4. Any VAT on payments made by the firm in the course of its business (for example office stationery) must be recorded on the HMRC account:

   (a) on the Cash account office account—Credit the amount paid net of VAT and then Credit the VAT paid separately;

   (b) (i) on the relevant account (for example office stationery) office account— Debit the net amount;

       (ii) on the HMRC VAT account office account—Debit the VAT paid;

5. Charging VAT on the client's bill of costs:

   (a) on the client's ledger account office account—Debit the Profit Costs and Debit the VAT separately underneath;

   (b) (i) on the Profit Costs account office account—Credit the Profit Costs;

       (ii) on the HMRC VAT account office account—Credit the VAT;

6. Disbursements paid on behalf of client:

   (1) Agency method—invoice made out to the client:

       You will just show the total paid out including VAT;

       (a) on the Cash account—Credit the total amount paid;

       (b) on the client ledger account—Debit the total amount paid;

       Note that office account or client account (if money is available on client account) can be used for the agency method;

(2) Principal method—invoice made out to the firm of solicitors:

You must always use office account;

(a) on the Cash account office account—Credit the net amount and then the VAT separately;

(b) (i) on the client ledger account office account—Debit the net amount paid (make a reminder note in the Details column about the VAT);

(ii) on the HMRC VAT account office account—Debit the VAT paid;

Note that when the client is finally billed, the client will be charged VAT on the Profit Costs AND on the disbursement;

(c) When the client is billed;

(i) on the client ledger account office account—Debit Profit Costs and then Debit the VAT on both the Profit Costs AND on the disbursement;

(ii) Credit the Profit Costs account with the profit costs and Credit the HMRC VAT account office account with the VAT on the Profit Costs AND on the disbursement;

7. Note when VAT relief is available for bad debts written off.

online resource centre   Now try the self-test exercises at the end of this chapter and the multiple choice questions available online through your tutor via the Online Resource Centre that accompanies this book. Then move on to the next chapter.

13.9 Exercises on ledger accounts including VAT

1 Allow 5 to 10 minutes.

You are acting for Lucy Bell. A surveyor has been instructed by Lucy to prepare a report. The surveyor sends a bill addressed to Lucy Bell for £120 plus £21 VAT. You are holding £200 on account of costs and disbursements for Lucy in client account. On 7 November you pay the surveyor's bill. On 1 December you deliver a bill of costs to Lucy for £200 plus VAT.

Show Lucy Bell's ledger account.

2 Allow 15 to 20 minutes.

You are acting in litigation for your client Jenny Gough. You instruct a consulting engineer to prepare a report. The engineer sends you a bill for £200 plus £35 VAT addressed to your firm. You are holding £300 in client account for Jenny Gough. On 23 September you pay the engineer's bill. In November the case is concluded and on 21 November you send a bill of costs to Jenny Gough for £120 plus VAT.

Show Jenny Gough's ledger account, the cash account, the HMRC account, and the Profit Costs account to record the above.

3 Allow around 15 minutes.

You are acting for Jack Taylor. In the month of October the following events occur:

1 October   Pay enquiry agent's fee £75. The enquiry agent is not registered for VAT.

3 October   Pay surveyor's fee £160 plus £28 VAT. The bill is made out to Jack Taylor.

4 October	Pay expert's fee £200 plus £35 VAT. The fee note is made out to your firm.
8 October	Receive a payment on account of costs and disbursements of £600 from Jack Taylor.
9 October	Deliver a bill of costs to Jack Taylor for £80 plus VAT. Transfer moneys due to you from client to office account and account to Jack Taylor for the balance.

Show Jack Taylor's ledger account to record the above transactions.

13.10   Suggested answers to exercises on ledger accounts including VAT

1   Lucy Bell account

Date	Details	Office account			Client account		
		DR	CR	Balance	DR	CR	Balance
	Balance					200	200 CR
7 Nov	Cash: surveyor				141		59 CR
1 Dec	Profit costs	200					
	VAT	35		235 DR			

The agency method has been used here, as the invoice was made out to Lucy. The HMRC VAT account will not be used for the disbursement.

2   Jenny Gough account

Date	Details	Office account			Client account		
		DR	CR	Balance	DR	CR	Balance
	Balance					300	300 CR
23 Sept	Cash: engineer	200		200 DR			
	(*Note*: VAT £35)						
21 Nov	Profit costs	120		320 DR			
	VAT (£21 + £35)	56		376 DR			

The principal method has been used here, as the invoice was made out to the firm. The £300 on the client account cannot be used as the payment must go through office account.

Cash account

Date	Details	Office account			Client account		
		DR	CR	Balance	DR	CR	Balance
23 Sept	Jenny Gough:						
	engineer's fee		200	200 CR			
	HMRC VAT (JG)		35	235 CR			

HMRC VAT account

Date	Details	Office account		
		DR tax paid	CR tax charged	Balance
23 Sept	Cash—engineer (JG) VAT	35		35 DR
21 Nov	Jenny Gough bill VAT		56	21 CR

Profit Costs account

Date	Details	Office account		
		DR	CR	Balance
21 Nov	Jenny Gough		120	120 CR

3 Jack Taylor account

Date	Details	Office account			Client account		
		DR	CR	Balance	DR	CR	Balance
1 Oct	Cash: enquiry agent	75		75 DR			
3 Oct	Cash: surveyor's fee	188		263 DR			
4 Oct	Cash: expert (*Note*: VAT £35)	200		463 DR			
8 Oct	Cash: you					600	600 CR
9 Oct	Profit costs	80					
	VAT (£14 + £35)	49		592 DR			
	Cash: transfer costs		592	—	592		8 CR
	Cash: you—balance due				8		—

Note the principal method was used on 3 October and the agency method on 4 October.

14

Financial statements and property transactions

14.1 Introduction

This chapter includes the following:

1. Financial statements to clients;

2. A summary of the basic financial transactions in respect of a client's sale and purchase of property;

3. Receipt of deposit on exchange of contracts, as agent for the seller or as stakeholder and the entries required on the accounts;

4. Treatment of mortgage advances and mortgage repayment;

5. Completion of a sale and purchase and the financial statement sent to the client;

6. Entries required on the accounts on completion of a sale and purchase;

7. Reminder of key points;

8. Exercises.

> **INTENDED OUTCOME**
>
> 1. An appreciation that a financial statement to a client should be clear and comprehensive evidenced by the ability to draw up a financial statement in respect of a property sale and purchase;
>
> 2. An understanding of:
>
>   (a) the financial steps in a property transaction and entries required on the accounts;
>
>   (b) the difference between receipt of deposit as agent for the seller and as stakeholder;
>
>   (c) the requirements on recording the receipt of a mortgage advance in various circumstances;
>
>   (d) the entries on the accounts on completion of a sale and purchase; evidenced by the ability to draw up the relevant accounts.

14.2 Financial statements to clients

Solicitors dealing with receipts of money and payments out on behalf of clients will have to account to the client for such receipts and payments. These will be shown on a financial statement or statement of account, which will often be sent to the client at the same time as the bill of costs. This is common in property transactions, or probate or trust matters. Other examples would be in respect of debt collection for a client, or any matter where funds have been received and held for a client.

Although there is no set form for such statements of account, they must be clear, contain a record of all receipts and payments, be relatively easy for the client to understand, and show at the end the amount due to or from the client.

In property transactions it can be useful for the client to see a clear distinction between receipts and payments regarding the purchase of property, and receipts and payments regarding the sale of property. In probate and trust matters, a clear distinction between capital and interest should be made.

Later in this chapter some examples are given of financial statements in respect of property transactions.

14.3 Property transactions—a summary of sale and purchase

Note that where a client is selling one property and buying another, rather than have two ledger cards for the client, one for the sale and one for the purchase, it is more convenient to deal with both purchase and sale on one client ledger card, as the proceeds of sale will be used towards the purchase of the new property. However, solicitors may have accounting systems where separate accounts are set up for the sale and purchase. A summary of the most common financial transactions found in respect of a client's sale and purchase is set out below. This is a guide only, as obviously these will vary.

A. Before exchange of contracts

1. Discuss finance with the client, giving details of solicitor's own charges, disbursements, for example home information pack (HIP) fees (now required before the property is marketed), search fees, stamp duty land tax (SDLT), land registry fees, and estate agent's commission. If there is a mortgage on the property to be sold, obtain details of the amount required to pay off the mortgage. If there is a mortgage on the purchase, discover how much will be available, less any costs.

2. Money may be received from the client on account of costs generally.

3. Pay any HIP/search fees, any fees for official copies, etc.

4. If the client has instructed a surveyor to check the property in respect of the purchase, the surveyor's fees may be paid.

5. Money may be received from the client or a third party, for example the bank, to meet the deposit payable on the purchase.

B. Exchange of contracts

6. On exchange of contracts on sale, a deposit will be received in respect of the sale. This may be held as stakeholder, when a separate stakeholder client ledger card will

be opened—it cannot be used towards the deposit payable regarding the purchase—or it may be held as agent for the seller, when it may be credited direct to the client ledger card and can be used towards the deposit payable regarding the purchase. (Note that a solicitor should now account for interest on stakeholder money held, where appropriate. See Chapter 15 on deposit interest generally.)

On exchange of contracts on purchase, payment of the deposit will usually be made to the seller's solicitors, either as agent for the seller, or as stakeholder.

C. After exchange of contracts

7. Completion statements will be sent in respect of the sale and the purchase, showing how much money will be required on completion, taking account of the deposit already paid, and any other adjustments, for example additional amounts in respect of carpets, fittings, etc. Note that these are merely for information—no entries will be made on the accounts until the sale and purchase are completed.

8. A financial statement will be sent to the client, showing all the receipts and payments out in respect of the sale and purchase, together with the solicitor's bills of costs and the amount that will either be due to the client, or needed from the client to complete. Note that at this stage, as the bills have been sent out, the solicitor's costs and VAT will be debited to the client ledger card. Note that all other disbursements, receipts, etc are entered only when actually paid or received.

9. Any mortgage money in respect of the purchase will be received before completion as will any money required from the client, if applicable.

D. Completion of sale and purchase

10. Complete the sale first, receive the net proceeds, ie the purchase price less any deposit paid, together with any other adjustments regarding fittings, etc.

    If the deposit on the sale was held as stakeholder, then the money should be transferred from the stakeholder account to the client ledger card. This should also be separately recorded on a transfer sheet or journal.

    Pay out the amount needed to redeem the mortgage.

    Complete the purchase. Ensure that mortgage moneys are available before paying out the amount required to complete the purchase, again less the deposit which has been paid, and take account of any other adjustments needed.

E. After completion of sale and purchase

11. Pay the estate agent's commission on sale if instructed to do so. There should be sufficient money on client account to do this.

12. Pay stamp duty land tax (SDLT) regarding purchase, again from client account if the money is available. The rates at present are 0–£125,000 nil (0–£175,000 until the end of 2009); over £125,000 (£175,000) to £250,000 1%; over £250,000 to £500,000 3%; and over £500,000 4%.

13. Pay Land Registry fees, from client account if possible.

14. Transfer costs and disbursements due to the firm from client account to office account.

15. Pay any balance to the client.

14.4 Receipt of deposit on exchange of contracts

A solicitor receiving a deposit on behalf of a client may hold the deposit as:

(a) agent; or

(b) stakeholder.

14.4.1 Receipt of deposit as agent

If a solicitor receives a deposit on exchange of contracts which is to be held as agent, it is held on behalf of the client seller. To record the receipt of a deposit as agent, the solicitor will make entries in the accounts to record a receipt of clients' money on behalf of the client seller.

EXAMPLE

The firm acts for Taylor, the seller of 5 Farm Road, which is being sold for £90,000. On 23 September the firm receives a 10% deposit to hold as agents for the seller.

Taylor: sale of 5 Farm Road

Date	Details	Office account			Client account		
		DR	CR	Balance	DR	CR	Balance
23 Sept	Cash: purchaser's solicitor, deposit					9,000	9,000 CR

Cash account

Date	Details	Office account			Client account		
		DR	CR	Balance	DR	CR	Balance
23 Sept	Taylor Cash: purchaser's solicitor, deposit				9,000		9,000 DR

14.4.2 Receipt of deposit as stakeholder

When a solicitor receives a deposit as stakeholder, it is not held on deposit for the client seller, or for the buyer, but held between the parties, therefore the receipt of a stakeholder deposit should not be recorded in the client seller's ledger account.

A separate account, the stakeholder account, is opened to record dealings with deposits held by a solicitor as stakeholder. The deposit is held in the stakeholder account until completion, when it belongs to the seller.

The stakeholder account only records dealings with client money; the money belongs to the client(s) not the solicitor.

When the firm receives a deposit as stakeholder, the following entries are made:

(a) CREDIT the Stakeholder ledger account, client column.

(a) DEBIT the Cash account, client column.

Assume that in the example in para 14.4.1 above the firm receives the 10% deposit as stakeholder.

Stakeholder account

Date	Details	Office account			Client account		
		DR	CR	Balance	DR	CR	Balance
23 Sept	Cash: deposit re Taylor sale of 5 Farm Road					9,000	9,000 CR

The double entry will be in the Cash account as in the example in para 14.4.1 above.

On completion of the sale the deposit is transferred from the stakeholder account to the client seller's account. The bookkeeping entries are those to record a transfer from one client ledger account to another.

Continuing the example, assume that completion takes place on 24 October.

Stakeholder account

Date	Details	Office account			Client account		
		DR	CR	Balance	DR	CR	Balance
23 Sept	Cash: deposit re Taylor sale of 5 Farm Road					9,000	9,000 CR
24 Oct	Taylor: transfer sheet				9,000		—

Taylor: re sale of 5 Farm Road

Date	Details	Office account			Client account		
		DR	CR	Balance	DR	CR	Balance
24 Oct	Stakeholder: transfer sheet					9,000	9,000 CR

14.5 Mortgage advances

14.5.1 Acting for mortgagee and purchaser

Rule 32(6) of the Solicitors' Accounts Rules 1998 provides that a solicitor acting for a borrower and lender on a mortgage advance in a property transaction shall not be required to open separate ledger accounts for the borrower and lender provided that:

(a) the funds belonging to each client are clearly identifiable; and

(b) the lender is an institutional lender which provides mortgages on standard terms in the normal course of its business, for example, a building society or bank.

Thus, if the solicitor is acting for a buyer and a building society provides the mortgage advance, the transactions can all be recorded in the client buyer's ledger account, without the need to open a separate ledger account for the building society.

However, if the solicitor is acting for a buyer and a private lender, then separate ledger accounts must be opened for each.

In (a) above, 'clearly identifiable' requires the solicitor to ensure that the buyer's ledger account states unambiguously the nature and owner of the mortgage advance. Care therefore needs to be taken in completing the details entry. For example, if the Kent Building Society makes an advance of £50,000 to Smith who is purchasing Greenway, Smith's ledger account should state, when the advance is received:

'Cash: mortgage advance from Kent Building Society: £50,000.'

Note that the mortgage money credited to the account still belongs to the lender, not the borrower, until completion takes place.

EXAMPLE (INSTITUTIONAL LENDER)

The firm acts for Rocca who is purchasing Bank House for £150,000. Rocca has obtained a mortgage advance of £100,000 from the Highgate Building Society for which the firm also acts. Rocca is providing the balance from his own funds. The firm receives the mortgage advance on 16 October, with the usual instruction that the cheque is not to be negotiated until completion. Rocca has been informed that he will be required to pay £50,517 prior to completion. He brings a cheque to the office on 17 October. Completion takes place on 18 October and on the same date the firm sends two bills of costs to Rocca, one for £400 plus VAT for the conveyancing and one for £40 plus VAT for acting on behalf of the building society in respect of the mortgage, which is to be paid by Rocca. The transactions will be recorded as follows.

Rocca: re purchase of Bank House

Date	Details	Office account			Client account		
		DR	CR	Balance	DR	CR	Balance
17 Oct	Cash: you					50,517	50,517 CR
18 Oct	Cash: mortgage advance from Highgate Building Society					100,000	150,517 CR
	Cash: seller's solicitor				150,000		517 CR
	Profit costs	400					
	VAT	70		470 DR			
	Profit costs (Highgate Building Society re mortgage)	40					
	VAT	7		517 DR			
	Cash: transfer costs		517	—	517		—

EXAMPLE (PRIVATE LENDER)

In the above example assume that Rocca is borrowing £100,000 from his uncle G. Rocca, for whom the firm also acts. On 16 October G. Rocca pays the firm £100,000 and both give written authority for that money to be transferred and used towards Rocca's purchase of Bank House. The costs of the mortgage are to be paid by Rocca. The transactions will be recorded as follows:

Rocca: re purchase of Bank House

Date	Details	Office account			Client account		
		DR	CR	Balance	DR	CR	Balance
18 Oct	Cash: you					50,517	50,517 CR
	G. Rocca: transfer mortgage advance					100,000	150,517 CR
	Cash: seller's solicitors				150,000		517 CR
	Profit costs	400					
	VAT	70		470 DR			
	G. Rocca: transfer costs	47		517 DR			
	Cash: transfer costs		517	—		517	—

G. Rocca: re mortgage advance

Date	Details	Office account			Client account		
		DR	CR	Balance	DR	CR	Balance
16 Oct	Cash: you					100,000	100,000
18 Oct	Profit costs	40					
	VAT	7		47 DR			
	Rocca: transfer sheet mortgage advance				100,000		—
	Rocca: transfer costs		47	—			

Note that G. Rocca is billed first and then the amount payable by Rocca is transferred.

When this method is used the lender's costs are transferred from the buyer's account to the lender's account by making the following entries:

(a) DEBIT purchaser's ledger card office account with costs and VAT.
(b) CREDIT lender's ledger card office account with costs and VAT.

As an alternative to transferring the gross advance from G. Rocca to Rocca, the solicitor could have transferred the net advance, after deducting costs, in which case G. Rocca's account would have appeared as follows:

G. Rocca: re mortgage advance

Date	Details	Office account			Client account		
		DR	CR	Balance	DR	CR	Balance
16 Oct	Cash: you					100,000	100,000 CR
18 Oct	Profit costs	40					
	VAT	7		47 DR			
	Rocca: transfer net advance				99,953		47 CR
	Cash: transfer costs		47	—	47		—

A further alternative is that the solicitors could have paid the net advance to the seller's solicitors out of G. Rocca's account. No entry would be made in Rocca's account in respect of the payment of the net advance.

14.5.2 Solicitor acting for mortgagee only

The accounting entries when the solicitor acts for the mortgagee only are:

(a) The solicitor opens an account for the mortgagee.

(b) When the mortgage advance is received, the solicitor makes entries in the mortgagee's account to record a receipt of client money.

(c) On completion, the solicitor makes entries in the mortgagee's account to record the delivery of a bill of costs to the mortgagee.

(d) On completion, the solicitor pays the net advance to the purchaser's solicitor and records this in the mortgagee's account as a payment of client money.

(e) Following completion, the solicitor transfers the costs from client to office account.

EXAMPLE

The firm acts for the Highgate Building Society which is making a mortgage advance of £100,000 to Rocca in connection with his purchase of Bank House. Rocca's solicitors are Barlows. The firm's costs for acting for the building society are £120 plus £21 VAT. The mortgage advance is received on 16 October and completion takes place on 18 October. Costs are transferred on 18 October.

Highgate Building Society

Date	Details	Office account			Client account		
		DR	CR	Balance	DR	CR	Balance
16 Oct	Cash: you					100,000	100,000 CR
18 Oct	Profit costs	120					
	VAT	21		141 DR			
	Cash: Barlows				99,859		141 CR
	Cash: transfer: costs			141	—	141	—

14.5.3 Solicitor acting for buyer/borrower only

The accounting entries when the solicitor acts for the buyer/borrower only are:

(a) An account is opened for the buyer. No account is opened for the mortgagee because the mortgagee is not a client.

(b) On completion the firm records the receipt of the net advance as a receipt of client's money in the buyer's ledger account.

(c) On completion the firm records the payment of the net advance to the seller's solicitor, as a payment of clients' money, in the buyer's ledger account.

(d) Entries are made in the cash account and the buyer's ledger account to record receipt and payment of client money, even if the cheque from the mortgagee is endorsed in favour of the seller's solicitor.

EXAMPLE

The firm acts for Rocca with regard to his purchase of Bank House. Rocca is obtaining a mortgage advance of £100,000 from the Highgate Building Society. The solicitors acting for the building society have stated that their costs, which are to be paid by Rocca, will be £120 plus £21 VAT.

It has been agreed that these costs will be deducted from the mortgage advance. On completion on 18 October, the building society's cheque for £99,859 is received by the firm and a cheque for that amount is paid to Gibsons, the seller's solicitor.

Rocca

Date	Details	Office account			Client account		
		DR	CR	Balance	DR	CR	Balance
18 Oct	Cash: Highgate					99,859	99,859
	Cash: Gibsons				99,859		—

14.6 Mortgage repayment

14.6.1 Usual method

The firm will treat the repayment as a normal payment out of client money, like any other disbursement.

14.6.2 Acting for the seller and a lender

Rule 32(6) of the Solicitors' Accounts Rules 1998 may not apply on redemption of a mortgage. Thus, if the solicitor acts for the seller and a lender, separate accounts will need to be opened for the seller and the lender. Note that this will be uncommon in practice.

(a) *Entries on completion.* When completion takes place the sale proceeds belong to the seller and are shown as a receipt of client money in the client seller's account.

EXAMPLE

The firm acts for Grady with regard to the sale of 1 Linwood Avenue. Completion takes place on 28 January when £140,000 is received.

Grady: re sale of 1 Linwood Avenue

Date	Details	Office account			Client account		
		DR	CR	Balance	DR	CR	Balance
28 Jan	Cash: sale proceeds					140,000	140,000 CR

(b) *Costs.* The solicitor's costs for acting on the redemption will be recorded in the lender's account, although in practice they will be paid by the seller client.

EXAMPLE

The firm's costs for acting on behalf of Andover Building Society, which has a mortgage on 1 Linwood Avenue of £55,000, and for whom the firm also acts, are £40 plus £7 VAT.

Andover Building Society: re mortgage redemption (Grady)

Date	Details	Office account			Client account		
		DR	CR	Balance	DR	CR	Balance
28 Jan	Profit costs	40					
	VAT	7		47 DR			

As the redemption costs will be paid by the borrower, a transfer of the costs and VAT will be made from the borrower's account to the lender's account. The transfer will be effected by making the following entries in the accounts.

(i) DEBIT the seller's ledger account office column.

(ii) CREDIT the lender's ledger account office column.

(c) *Redemption.* When the mortgage is redeemed a transfer of the redemption money is made from the seller's account to the lender's account. The payment of the redemption money to the lender is then shown as a payment of client money from the ledger account.

EXAMPLE

The firm's costs for acting for Grady on the sale of 1 Linwood Avenue are £200 plus £35 VAT. The redemption figure for the mortgage is £55,000. The mortgage is redeemed and costs transferred on 28 January. On the same date a cheque is sent to Grady for the balance due to him. The entries in the ledger accounts for Grady and Andover Building Society will be as follows:

Grady: re sale of 1 Linwood Avenue

Date	Details	Office account			Client account		
		DR	CR	Balance	DR	CR	Balance
28 Jan	Cash: sale proceeds					140,000	140,000 CR
	Andover: transfer mortgage redemption				55,000		85,000 CR
	Profit costs	200					
	VAT	35		235 DR			
	Andover: transfer costs	47		282 DR			
	Cash: transfer costs		282	—	282		84,718 CR
	Cash: you				84,718		—

Andover: re mortgage redemption (Grady)

Date	Details	Office account			Client account		
		DR	CR	Balance	DR	CR	Balance
28 Jan	Profit costs	40					
	VAT	7		47 DR			
	Grady: transfer redemption money					55,000	55,000 CR
	Grady: transfer costs		47	—			
	Cash: you— mortgage redemption				55,000		—

14.7 Completion

14.7.1 Financial statement

Before completion of a sale or purchase on behalf of a property client, a financial statement will be sent to the client. This will show the amount which the client will have to provide for completion or the balance due to the client following completion. As stated previously there is no set form of financial statement, but whichever form is used it is essential that the statement should show all moneys received from and on behalf of the client and all payments made on his or her behalf.

The following is a suggested method of presentation of a financial statement when a solicitor is acting for a client selling and buying property simultaneously. It does have the advantage for the client of showing net proceeds of sale, after repayment of mortgage and expenses, and the total required on the purchase. However, firms may use different methods of presentation, all of which are valid.

FINANCIAL STATEMENT
TO: AWAN
SALE OF 3, BADGERS CLOSE AND PURCHASE OF 54, CAMBRIDGE ROAD
SALE OF 3, BADGERS CLOSE

Sale price		180,000	
LESS mortgage repayment		40,200	
		139,800	
LESS payments			
Estate agents' fees inc. VAT	4,230		
Official copies and search fees	170		
Profit costs on sale inc. VAT	235		
		4,635	
NET SALE PROCEEDS		135,165	
PURCHASE OF 54, CAMBRIDGE ROAD			
PURCHASE PRICE		220,000	
LESS mortgage advance		80,000	
		140,000	
LESS paid by you in advance		4,000	
		136,000	
ADD			
Payments out			
SDLT	2,200		
Land Registry fees	300		
Profit costs on purchase inc. VAT	470		
Profit costs on mortgage inc. VAT	94		
		3,064	
Balance due on purchase		139,064	
Amount required to complete purchase			139,064
LESS net amount received on sale			135,165
			3,899

OR (if net sale proceeds are more than amount required on purchase)
            Net amount received on sale
            LESS amount required to complete purchase.

14.7.2 Exercises on financial statements

1. You act for Walker who is selling 6 Conway Road for £50,000. On 1 April you receive a 10% deposit as stakeholder; 6 Conway Road is subject to a mortgage of £15,000. You receive an account from the estate agent for £600 plus £105 VAT. Your costs for acting on the sale are £200 plus £35 VAT. Prepare a financial statement for Walker.

2. You act for Sadler who is buying 60 Manor Crescent for £180,000. He is borrowing £140,000 from the building society for whom you also act. You receive a bridging loan of £18,000 from your client's bank for the deposit. You exchange contracts and pay the deposit. Your costs for acting for the building society are £80 plus VAT and these are to be paid by Sadler. Your costs are £400 plus £70 VAT, the Land Registry fee is £90, and stamp duty land tax is £1,800. Sadler's bank informs you that the interest on the bridging loan is £75. Prepare a financial statement for Sadler.

3. Black and Co. solicitors acted for Hall in respect of the purchase of a house, 10 Arden Way, for £100,000 and the sale of her existing house, 25 James Street, for £80,000. The mortgage repayment on 25 James Street was £40,000 and a new mortgage was taken out on 10 Arden Way for £60,000. Black and Co. paid the following disbursements: estate agents' charges on the sale £1,200 plus VAT, search fee of £10, and Land Registry fee of £200. Their profit costs on the sale were £200 plus VAT, on the purchase £400 plus VAT and on the mortgage £80 plus VAT.

   Draw up a financial statement for Hall, showing the amount required from her on completion.

14.7.3 Answers to exercises on financial statements

1. FINANCIAL STATEMENT DATE

TO: WALKER
SALE OF 6 CONWAY ROAD

Sale price	50,000	
LESS mortgage repayments	15,000	
	35,000	
LESS payments		
Estate agents' fees inc. VAT	705	
Profit costs on sale inc. VAT	235	
		940
NET SALE PROCEEDS		34,060

2. FINANCIAL STATEMENT DATE

TO: SADLER
PURCHASE OF 60 MANOR CRESCENT

PURCHASE PRICE	180,000
LESS mortgage advance	140,000
	40,000

ADD

Payments out

SDLT	1,800	
Land Registry fees	90	
Bank loan interest	75	
Profit costs on purchase inc. VAT	470	
Profit costs on mortgage inc. VAT	94	
		2,529
Balance due on purchase		42,529

3. FINANCIAL STATEMENT DATE

TO: HALL

SALE OF 25 JAMES STREET AND PURCHASE OF 10 ARDEN WAY

SALE OF 25 JAMES STREET

Sale price		80,000	
LESS mortgage repayment		40,000	
		40,000	
LESS payments			
Estate agents' fees inc. VAT	1,410		
Profit Costs on sale inc. VAT	235		
		1,645	
NET SALE PROCEEDS		38,355	
PURCHASE OF 10 ARDEN WAY			
purchase price		100,000	
LESS mortgage advance		60,000	
		40,000	
ADD			
Payments out			
Land Registry fees	200		
Search fee	10		
Profit costs on purchase inc. VAT	470		
Profit costs on mortgage inc. VAT	94		
		774	
Balance due on purchase		40,774	
Amount required to complete purchase			40,774
LESS net amount received on sale			38,355
Balance due from you			2,419

14.7.4 Entries on sale completion

The solicitor's accounts must reflect all the transactions involved in completing the sale of a property on the client's behalf. The following entries will usually have to be made on the completion of a sale:

(a) Entries to record the delivery of a bill of costs to the client for acting on the client's behalf with regard to the sale.

EXAMPLE

The firm acts for Ali with regard to the sale of 'Church Cottage' at a price of £160,000. On 3 May a bill of costs is delivered to Ali in the sum of £400 plus £70 VAT. Ali's account will appear as follows:

Ali

Date	Details	Office account			Client account		
		DR	CR	Balance	DR	CR	Balance
3 May	Profit costs	400					
	VAT	70		470 DR			

(b) Entries to record the receipt of the sale proceeds from the purchaser's solicitor (ie entries to record a receipt of client money).

Continuing the example:

Completion of Ali's sale takes place on 3 May. The firm receives a bank draft for £144,000. A deposit of £16,000 was paid to the firm as stakeholders on 3 April. Ali's account will appear as follows:

Ali

Date	Details	Office account			Client account		
		DR	CR	Balance	DR	CR	Balance
3 May	Profit costs	400					
	VAT	70		470 DR			
	Cash: purchaser's solicitor on completion					144,000	144,000 CR

(c) Entries to record the transfer of the deposit from stakeholder account to the client's ledger account if the deposit was paid to the seller's solicitor as stakeholder on exchange of contracts.

Continuing the example:

Stakeholder account

Date	Details	Office account			Client account		
		DR	CR	Balance	DR	CR	Balance
3 Apr	Cash: deposit re Ali					16,000	16,000 CR
3 May	Ali: transfer sheet				16,000		—

Stakeholder account

Date	Details	Office account DR	CR	Balance	Client account DR	CR	Balance
May 3	Profit costs	400					
	VAT	70					
	Cash: purchaser's solicitor on completion			470 DR		144,000	144,000 CR
	Stakeholder: transfer sheet					16,000	160,000 CR

(d) Entries to record the redemption of a mortgage.

Continuing the example:

Assume that there is a mortgage to the Abbey Bank on 'Church Cottage'. The mortgage of £98,000 is redeemed on 4 May. Ali's account would appear as follows:

Ali

Date	Details	Office account DR	CR	Balance	Client account DR	CR	Balance
May 3	Profit costs	400					
	VAT	70					
	Cash: purchaser's solicitor			470 DR		144,000	144,000 CR
	Stakeholder: transfer sheet					16,000	160,000 CR
May 4	Cash: Abbey Bank				98,000		62,000 CR

(e) Entries to record the payment of any outstanding disbursements, for example estate agents' fees.

Continuing the example:

Assume that on 6 May the firm pays an estate agent's charges of £1,880. Ali's account would appear as follows:

Ali

Date	Details	Office account DR	CR	Balance	Client account DR	CR	Balance
May 3	Profit costs	400					
	VAT	70					
	Cash: purchaser's solicitor			470 DR		144,000	144,000 CR
	Stakeholder: transfer sheet					16,000	160,000 CR
May 4	Cash: Abbey Bank: redemption				98,000		62,000 CR
May 6	Cash: estate agent				1,880		60,120 CR

(f) Entries to record the transfer of costs from client to office account and to record the payment to the client of any balance owed.

Continuing the example:

Assume that on 6 May costs are transferred and the balance remaining in client account is paid to Ali.

Ali's account will appear as follows:

Ali

Date	Details	Office account DR	CR	Balance	Client account DR	CR	Balance
3 May	Profit costs	400					
	VAT	70		470 DR			
	Cash: purchaser's solicitor					144,000	144,000 CR
	Stakeholder: transfer sheet					16,000	160,000 CR
4 May	Cash: Abbey Bank: redemption				98,000		62,000 CR
6 May	Cash: estate agent				1,880		60,120 CR
	Cash: transfer: costs		470	—	470		59,650 CR
	Cash: you				59,650		—

14.7.5 Purchase completions

The solicitor's accounts must reflect all the transactions involved in completing the purchase of a property on the client's behalf. The following entries will usually have to be made on the completion of a purchase:

(a) Entries to record the delivery of a bill of costs to the client for acting with regard to the purchase.

EXAMPLE

The firm acts for Agha with regard to the purchase of 15 Hunters Lane at a price of £195,000. On 3 May a bill of costs is delivered to Agha in the sum of £320 plus £56 VAT. The firm also acted for the mortgagee, the Chelsea Building Society, and its costs are £160 plus £28 VAT. Agha's account will appear as follows:

Agha

Date	Details	Office account			Client account		
		DR	CR	Balance	DR	CR	Balance
200—							
3 May	Profit costs	320					
	VAT	56		376 DR			
	Profit costs:						
	Building Society	160					
	VAT	28		564 DR			

(b) Entries to record the receipt of the balance of the purchase money from the client, if required, as shown on the financial statement.

Continuing the example:

A financial statement has been delivered to Agha, showing a balance due from him on completion of £3,164. On 3 May Agha pays the sum of £3,164 to the firm. Agha's account will appear as follows:

Agha

Date	Details	Office account			Client account		
		DR	CR	Balance	DR	CR	Balance
200—							
3 May	Profit costs	320					
	VAT	56		376 DR			
	Profit costs:						
	Building Society	160					
	VAT	28		564 DR			
	Cash: you					3,164	3,164 CR

(c) Entries to record the receipt of the mortgage advance from the building society. Note that if the mortgage was from a private lender for whom the firm was acting, a separate ledger account would be opened for the lender and the mortgage advance would be shown as a transfer from the lender's account.

Continuing the example:

Agha has obtained a mortgage advance of £175,000 from the Chelsea Building Society for whom the firm also acts.

Agha

Date	Details	Office account			Client account		
		DR	CR	Balance	DR	CR	Balance
3 May	Profit costs	320					
	VAT	56		376 DR			
	Profit costs:						
	Building Society	160				3,164	3,164 CR
	VAT	28		564 DR			
	Cash: Chelsea						
	Building Society, mortgage advance					175,000	178,164 CR

(d) Entries to record the payment of the balance of the purchase moneys to the seller's solicitors.

Continuing the example:

Completion takes place on 3 May. On 3 April a 10% deposit of £19,500 had been paid by Agha to the seller's solicitors, Rowlands. The balance payable to Rowlands on completion is £175,500. Agha's account would appear as follows:

Agha

Date	Details	Office account			Client account		
		DR	CR	Balance	DR	CR	Balance
3 May	Profit costs	320					
	VAT	56		376 DR			
	Profit costs:						
	Building Society	160				3,164	3,164 CR
	VAT	28		564 DR			
	Cash: you						
	Cash: Chelsea					175,000	178,164 CR
	Building Society, mortgage advance						
	Cash: Rowlands				175,500		2,664 CR

(e) Entries to record the payment of any disbursements after completion, for example SDLT or Land Registry fees.

Continuing the example:

On 5 May the firm pays SDLT of £1,950 and on 16 May Land Registry fees of £150. Agha's account will appear as follows:

Agha

Date	Details	Office account			Client account		
		DR	CR	Balance	DR	CR	Balance
3 May	Profit costs	320					
	VAT	56		376 DR			
	Profit costs:						
	Building Society	160					
	VAT	28		564 DR			
	Cash: you					3,164	3,164 CR
	Cash: Chelsea						
	Building Society, mortgage advance					175,000	178,164 CR
	Cash: Rowlands				175,500		2,664 CR
5 May	Cash: SDLT				1,950		714 CR
16 May	Land Registry fees				150		564 CR

(f) Entries to record the transfer of costs from client to office account.

Continuing the example:

Costs are transferred to office account on 7 May. Agha's account will appear as follows:

Agha

Date	Details	Office account			Client account		
		DR	CR	Balance	DR	CR	Balance
3 May	Profit costs	320					
	VAT	56		376 DR			
	Profit costs: Chelsea						
	Building Society	160				3,164	3,164 CR
	VAT	28		564 DR			
	Cash: you						
	Cash: Chelsea						
	Building Society, mortgage advance					175,000	178,164 CR
	Cash: Rowlands				175,500		2,664 CR
5 May	Cash: SDLT				1,950		714 CR
	Cash: Land Registry fees				150		564 CR
7 May	Cash: transfer: costs		564	—	564		—

14.7.6 Simultaneous sale and purchase

When acting for a client with regard to a simultaneous sale and purchase, entries will be made in the accounts as in paras 14.7.4 and 14.7.5 above.

In the examples following, for convenience, a single ledger account will be shown for both the sale and the purchase, although in practice you may find that firms use separate accounts for the sale and the purchase.

14.7.6.1 **Example**

Swift & Co., solicitors, acted for Griffiths in the purchase of 'Meadow Court' for £350,000 and the sale of 7 Princess Road for £300,000 and for the Cheshire Building Society in respect of an advance. The following events took place.

200—

2 September	Paid search fee of £165.
9 September	Paid survey fee of £940 including VAT in respect of the purchase of 'Meadow Court'.
10 September	The Cheshire Building Society instructed the firm to act in respect of an advance of £125,000.
15 September	Received from NatWest Bank PLC a cheque for £35,000, being a bridging loan in respect of 'Meadow Court'.
17 September	Exchanged contracts for the sale of Griffiths' house, 7 Princess Road, the deposit of 10% (£30,000) having been paid to the estate agent by the buyer. On the same day contracts were exchanged for the purchase of 'Meadow Court' and the deposit of £35,000 was paid to the seller's solicitor to hold as stakeholder.
24 September	Received completion statement from the seller's solicitor in respect of 'Meadow Court', showing £315,000 due on completion.
27 September	Sent completion statement to the solicitors acting for the buyer of 7 Princess Road, showing the balance due of £270,000.
2 October	Received cheque for £125,000 from the building society. The profit costs to be charged regarding the advance are £120 plus VAT.
5 October	Sent financial statement to Griffiths showing the balance of money required from him on completion of the sale and purchase, together with bills of costs in respect of the sale, purchase, and mortgage advance. The statement includes, amongst other items, the following information:
	Solicitors' costs on sale £400 plus VAT;
	Solicitors' costs on purchase £600 plus VAT;
	Estate agent's commission inc. VAT £7,050;
	Stamp duty land tax £10,500;
	Land Registry fees £250;
	Amount to redeem mortgage £60,500.
7 October	Cheque received from Griffiths, being the balance of purchase money and payment of costs.
12 October	Completed the sale and purchase. The amount due to redeem the mortgage is paid the same day. A cheque for £22,950 is received from the estate agents, being the deposit less their charges.
14 October	The bridging loan of £35,000 is paid to NatWest Bank PLC. Griffiths has paid the interest due on the loan direct to NatWest Bank PLC.
15 October	Paid stamp duty land tax.
25 October	Paid Land Registry fees. Transferred costs and disbursements from client account to office account.

Draw up the ledger account of Griffiths, showing all entries necessary to deal with the above events, and prepare a financial statement, suitable for presentation to Griffiths on 5 October 200—, showing the balance due from him on completion.

FINANCIAL STATEMENT 5 OCTOBER 200—

TO: GRIFFITHS

SALE OF 7 PRINCESS ROAD AND PURCHASE OF 'MEADOW COURT'

SALE OF 7 PRINCESS ROAD

Sale price		300,000
LESS mortgage repayment		60,500
		239,500
LESS payments		
Estate agents' fees inc. VAT	7,050	
Search fee	165	
Profit costs on sale inc. VAT	470	
		7,685
NET SALE PROCEEDS		231,815
PURCHASE OF 'MEADOW COURT'		
Purchase price		350,000
LESS mortgage advance		125,000
		225,000
ADD		
Payments out		
Survey fee	940	
Stamp duty land tax	10,500	
Land Registry fees	250	
Profit costs on purchase inc. VAT	705	
Profit costs on mortgage inc. VAT	141	
	12,536	
Balance due on purchase	237,536	
Amount required to complete purchase		237,536
LESS net amount received on sale		231,815
Balance due from you		5,721

Griffiths

Sale of 7 Princess Road, purchase of 'Meadow Court'

Date	Details	Office account			Client account		
		DR	CR	Balance	DR	CR	Balance
200—							
2 Sept	Cash: search fee	165		165 DR			
9 Sept	Cash: survey fee	940		1,105 DR			
15 Sept	Cash: NatWest Bank PLC re deposit					35,000	35,000 CR
17 Sept	Cash: deposit on purchase				35,000		—
2 Oct	Cash: mortgage advance Cheshire Building Society					125,000	125,000 CR

Date	Details	Office account		Client account		
5 Oct	Costs on sale	400				
	VAT	70	1,575 DR			
	Costs on purchase	600				
	VAT	105	2,280 DR			
	Costs re advance	120				
	VAT	21	2,421 DR			
7 Oct	Cash: you—to complete				5,721	130,721 CR
12 Oct	Cash: balance proceeds sale				270,000	400,721 CR
	Cash: estate agent's deposit on sale less their commission				22,950	423,671 CR
	Cash: re purchase			315,000		108,671 CR
	Transfer re redemption			60,500		48,171 CR
14 Oct	Cash: bridging loan			35,000		13,171 CR
15 Oct	Cash: stamp duty land tax			10,500		2,671 CR
25 Oct	Cash: Land Registry fee			250		2,421 CR
	Cash: transfer costs and disbursements	2,421	—	2,421		—

14.8 Reminder of key points

1. A financial statement to the client should be clear, containing a full record of all receipts and payments;

2. The basic financial stages in a property transaction on simultaneous sale and purchase:

    (a) **before exchange of contracts**—information required, possible receipt of money on account of costs from the client, payment of any HIP fees/search fees, surveyor's fees, receipt of any deposit required on purchase;

    (b) **on exchange of contracts**—receive deposit on sale, pay deposit on purchase;

    (c) **after exchange of contracts**—completion statements on sale and purchase, financial statement to the client, bill of costs to the client, receipt of mortgage money for purchase;

    (d) **completion of sale and purchase**—complete sale first, receive balance on sale price, including any deposit held, pay off any mortgage, then complete purchase, pay balance of purchase price;

    (e) **post completion**—pay estate agent if instructed to do so, pay stamp duty land tax, pay Land Registry fees, and, finally, transfer costs and disbursements due to the firm from client account to office account, if not already done so. Pay any balance to the client.

3. The difference between the receipt of a deposit as agent for the seller and as stakeholder—check the relevant entries on the accounts; if received as agent show

receipt on the client ledger account; if received as stakeholder, receipt must be on the stakeholder account client account and the money transferred back to the client ledger account client account on completion;

4. Note the special requirements where a firm records the receipt of a mortgage advance on the borrower's/purchaser's account and check the relevant entries on the accounts; if received from an institutional lender money can be paid into borrower's account, provided funds clearly identified;

5. Note the entries required for a mortgage advance if acting for both a private lender and a borrower—separate accounts must be opened for borrower and private lender;

6. Note the entries required for a mortgage advance if acting for the lender only, or if acting for the borrower only—open account for mortgagee, record receipt of mortgage advance, record bill of costs and VAT, pay net advance to purchaser's solicitor on completion and then transfer costs due from client to office account;

7. Note the entries required for repayment of a mortgage—treat as normal payment out of client money;

8. The form of a financial statement to be sent to a client before completion of a sale and purchase; the example given is designed to be clear for the client, but different firms use different forms of financial statement, all equally valid;

9. Check all the entries required in respect of the completion of sale and purchase of properties on behalf of a client; record bills of costs; record receipt of sale proceeds; transfer any deposit held on stakeholder account; record redemption of mortgage payment; record any receipt of money required from client towards purchase; record receipt of any mortgage advance for the purchase; pay the balance of the purchase price; pay stamp duty land tax and Land Registry fees; transfer costs due from client account to office account.

online resource centre Now try the self-test exercises at the end of the chapter, and you may wish to try the online multiple choice questions available through your tutor via the Online Resource Centre that accompanies this book.

14.9 Exercises on property transactions

1 Allow 5 to 10 minutes.

Kumar and Co. act for Jain in respect of the sale of his property, 1 Langdale Close, for £180,000, and the purchase of 23 Harwood Grove, for £250,000. On 2 April the firm receives a cheque for £25,000 from Jain for the deposit on the purchase.

On 10 April the firm exchanges contracts on the sale and purchase, receiving the 10% on the sale as stakeholder and paying the 10% deposit on the purchase. Show the entries on the client ledger account for Jain.

2 Allow around 10 minutes.

Your firm acts for Sinclair in respect of the sale of 2 Athens Avenue for £300,000 and the purchase of 1 Beech Park for £400,000. The firm has exchanged contracts on the sale and purchase. Sinclair paid the 10% deposit on the purchase and the firm received the 10% deposit on the sale as stakeholder. Show the entries required on Sinclair's client ledger account in respect of the following transactions:

1 March	The firm receives a mortgage for £150,000 from Wakefield Building Society.
3 March	The firm completes the sale of 2 Athens Avenue, transferring the amount due from stakeholder account and receiving the balance of the sale proceeds. It also completes the purchase of 1 Beech Park, paying the balance of the purchase price. It redeems the mortgage on 2 Athens Avenue by paying £35,625.

3 Allow about 15 minutes.

Farrell and Co. acted for Keeble in the sale of his house 'Rosewood' for £500,000 and for the Burnley Building Society who were owed approximately £15,000 by way of mortgage on the house. The following events took place:

200—

8 May	Received cheque for £450,000 from the buyer's solicitors, being the balance of purchase moneys. The amount required to redeem the mortgage including interest is £150,325. The amount due to the building society is paid by cheque.
9 May	Mann and Co., estate agents, acting for Keeble, send a cheque for £44,125, being the deposit less their commission of £5,000 plus VAT £875.
10 May	Sent cheque for £594 including VAT to Oliver in respect of pre-sale repairs to the property.
13 May	Bill of costs sent to Keeble for £400 plus VAT.
15 May	Costs and disbursements are transferred to office account and the balance due to Keeble is paid to him.

Write up the client's ledger account for Keeble, showing all necessary entries to record the above transactions. VAT is to be calculated at 17.5%.

4 Allow about 30 minutes.

Your firm acts for Andrew Hooper who is purchasing 18 Vale Road for £100,000 with a private mortgage of £80,000 from Peter Lloyd, for whom the firm also acts. The following events take place:

2009

16 December	Receive cheque for £10,000 from Andrew for the deposit.
17 December	Contracts exchanged. Paid £10,000 to the seller's solicitors.
20 December	Receive completion statement from seller's solicitors showing £90,000 payable on completion.
31 December	Send statement to Andrew showing amount required for completion including:

Costs on purchase: £200 plus VAT

Costs on mortgage: £80 plus VAT

Bill of costs also sent.

2010

12 January	Receive mortgage advance and Andrew's cheque for the balance of the completion money.
15 January	Complete the purchase.
16 January	Transfer costs and disbursements to office account.

Prepare the ledger accounts for Andrew and Peter Lloyd and the cash account, together with the financial statement sent to Andrew on 31 December.

5 Allow about 1 hour.

Hargreaves, solicitors, acted for Simpson in respect of the purchase of 22 Morton Road and the sale of his existing house 4 Oak Avenue. 22 Morton Road was being purchased for £180,000 and 4 Oak Avenue was to be sold for £140,000.

200—

8 May	Paid local search fees of £150.
14 May	Instructions received from the Dudley Building Society to act in connection with the advance to Simpson of £28,000 regarding 22 Morton Road.
20 May	Received £18,000 from Simpson, being the deposit on 22 Morton Road.
25 May	Exchanged contracts for the sale of 4 Oak Avenue and received 10% deposit as stakeholder. Also exchanged contracts for purchase of 22 Morton Road and paid 10% deposit to the seller as stakeholder.
10 June	Seller's solicitors sent completion statement showing the balance of purchase money due, being the purchase price less the deposit paid.
15 June	Sent financial statement to Simpson, showing the amount due from him on completion, together with bills of costs in respect of the sale and the purchase. Costs on sale were £280 plus VAT, costs on the purchase were £360 plus VAT, and costs in respect of the mortgage advance were £80 plus VAT.
23 June	Simpson sent a cheque for the amount shown as due on the financial statement.
24 June	Paid petty cash search fees of £10.
25 June	Received advance cheque from Dudley Building Society.
27 June	Completed the sale and purchase of the properties.
30 June	Paid the estate agent's charges, being £2,800 plus VAT. Paid stamp duty land tax of £1,800.
10 July	Paid Land Registry fees of £400. Transferred costs and disbursements from client account to office account.

Draw up the financial statement for Simpson and the client ledger card.

6 Allow about 1 hour.

Thorn Ashley & Co. act for Mr and Mrs Edhi in respect of the sale of their property 8 Ashley Avenue for £450,000 and the purchase of 'Greenway' for £600,000. There is a mortgage of approximately £100,000 on 8 Ashley Avenue, due to the Leeds Building Society.

The Abbey Bank has agreed to advance £200,000 in respect of the new purchase. The bank will also assist with bridging finance in respect of the deposit due on the purchase. The balance required for the purchase will come from a bonus that Mr Edhi is expecting.

200—

1 June	HIP fee £400 paid.
9 June	Bridging loan in respect of the balance required for the deposit on the purchase is received in the sum of £15,000.
14 June	Contracts are exchanged in respect of the sale of 8 Ashley Avenue, the deposit of £45,000 being received as agents for the sellers. Contracts are also exchanged in respect of the purchase of Greenway and a cheque for £60,000 is forwarded to the solicitors for the sellers who are holding as stakeholders.
20 June	A completion statement is sent to the buyer's solicitors in respect of the sale of 8 Ashley Avenue showing the balance due of £405,000 and a sum of £10,000 in respect of carpets, curtains, and furnishings. The solicitors acting for the seller of Greenway confirm that the balance due on the purchase will be £540,000.
21 June	An invoice is received from the estate agents acting for Mr and Mrs Edhi showing the commission due to them of £9,000 plus VAT.
24 June	The firm sends bills of costs in respect of the sale and purchase to Mr and Mrs Edhi. Profit costs on the purchase are £1,200 plus VAT, profit costs on the sale are £800 plus VAT. Profit costs in respect of the mortgage advance amount to £200 plus VAT.
25 June	Mr Edhi sends a a cheque to cover the balance required on purchase and all costs and disbursements. The Abbey Bank sends a draft for £200,000 in respect of the mortgage advance.
4 July	Completed sale of 8 Ashley Avenue and purchase of Greenway. The bridging loan is repaid to the bank, together with interest of £140. The mortgage on 8 Ashley Avenue is redeemed in the sum of £99,500. Costs and disbursements due are transferred from client account to office account.
	Stamp duty land tax of £24,000 is paid.
10 July	Paid the estate agent's commission plus VAT. Paid the Land Registry fees of £300.

Draw up a financial statement showing the amount required from Mr and Mrs Edhi to complete the transactions, and show the account of Mr and Mrs Edhi.

14.10 Suggested answers to exercises on property transactions

1 Jain—sale of 1 Langdale Close; purchase of 23 Harwood Grove

Date	Details	Office account			Client account		
		DR	CR	Bal	DR	CR	Bal
2 Apr	Cash: you—deposit					25,000	25,000 CR
10 Apr	Cash: deposit on purchase				25,000		—

Note that the £18,000 deposit paid as stakeholder will be credited to the stakeholder account, not Jain's account, and then it will be transferred back to Jain's account on completion of the sale.

2 Sinclair—sale of 2 Athens Avenue; purchase of 1 Beech Park

Date	Details	Office account			Client account		
		DR	CR	Bal	DR	CR	Bal
1 Mar	Cash: Wakefield Building Society, mortgage advance					150,000	150,000 CR
3 Mar	Transfer sheet—stakeholder deposit					30,000	180,000 CR
	Cash: balance sale proceeds					270,000	450,000 CR
	Cash: balance purchase moneys				360,000		90,000 CR
	Cash: repay mortgage				35,625		54,375 CR

3 Farrell and Co

Keeble: re sale of 'Rosewood'

Date	Details	Office account			Client account		
		DR	CR	Balance	DR	CR	Balance
200—							
8 May	Cash: sale proceeds					450,000	450,000 CR
	Cash: Burnley Building Society, mortgage redemption				150,325		299,675 CR
9 May	Cash: Mann & Co. (less commission £5,875)					44,125	343,800 CR
10 May	Cash: Oliver				594		343,206 CR
13 May	Profit costs	400					
	VAT	70		470 DR			
15 May	Cash: transfer: costs		470	—	470		342,736 CR
	Cash: you				342,736		—

4 Hooper

FINANCIAL STATEMENT

TO: ANDREW HOOPER
PURCHASE OF 18 VALE ROAD

Purchase price	100,000
LESS mortgage advance	80,000
	20,000
LESS deposit paid by you	10,000
	10,000

ADD
Payments out

Profit costs on purchase inc. VAT	235	
Profit costs on mortgage inc. VAT	94	
		329
Balance due on purchase		10,329

Client: Andrew Hooper

Matter: purchase of 18 Vale Road

Date	Details	Office account			Client account		
		DR	CR	Balance	DR	CR	Balance
2009							
16 Dec	Cash you					10,000	10,000 CR
17 Dec	Cash: deposit				10,000		—
31 Dec	Profit costs (purchase)	200					
	VAT	35		235 DR			
2010							
12 Jan	Cash: you					10,329	10,329 CR
15 Jan	Peter Lloyd transfer advance					80,000	90,329 CR
	Cash: completion				90,000		329 CR
	Peter Lloyd transfer costs	94		329 DR			
	Cash: transfer costs		329	—	329		—

Peter Lloyd

Date	Details	Office account			Client account		
		DR	CR	Balance	DR	CR	Balance
2009							
31 Dec	Profit costs	80					
	VAT	14		94 DR			
2010							
12 Jan	Cash: you					80,000	80,000 CR
15 Jan	Hooper: transfer sheet				80,000		—
	Hooper: transfer costs		94	—			—

Cash account

Date	Details	Office account			Client account		
		DR	CR	Balance	DR	CR	Balance
2009							
16 Dec	Hooper				10,000		10,000 DR
17 Dec	Hooper: deposit					10,000	—
2010							
12 Jan	Peter Lloyd, mortgage advance				80,000		80,000 DR
	Hooper				10,329		90,329 DR
15 Jan	Hooper: completion					90,000	329 DR
16 Jan	Hooper: transfer: costs	329		329 DR		329	—

5   Simpson

FINANCIAL STATEMENT DATE

TO: SIMPSON

SALE OF 4 OAK AVENUE AND PURCHASE OF 22 MORTON ROAD

SALE OF 4 OAK AVENUE

Sale price		140,000
LESS payments		
Search fee	150	
Estate agents' fees inc. VAT	3,290	
Profit costs on sale inc. VAT	329	
		3,769
NET SALE PROCEEDS		136,231
PURCHASE OF 22 MORTON ROAD		
Purchase price		180,000
LESS mortgage advance		28,000
		152,000
LESS paid by you in advance		18,000
		134,000
ADD		
Payments out		
SDLT	1,800	
Land Registry fees	400	
Search fees	10	
Profit costs on purchase inc. VAT	423	
Profit costs on mortgage inc. VAT	94	
		2,727
Balance due on purchase		136,727

Amount required to complete purchase		136,727
LESS net amount received on sale		136,231
		496

Simpson: re sale of 4 Oak Avenue and purchase of 22 Morton Road

Date	Details	Office account			Client account		
		DR	CR	Balance	DR	CR	Balance
200—							
8 May	Cash: local search fee	150		150 DR			
20 May	Cash: you—re deposit					18,000	18,000 CR
25 May	Cash: deposit on sale				18,000		—
15 June	Profit costs on sale	280		430 DR			
	VAT	49		479 DR			
	Profit costs on purchase	360		839 DR			
	VAT	63		902 DR			
	Profit costs re advance	80		982 DR			
	VAT	14		996 DR			
23 June	Cash: you—to complete					496	496 CR
24 June	Petty cash search fees	10		1,006 DR			
25 June	Cash: Dudley Building Society, mortgage advance					28,000	28,496 CR
27 June	Cash: sale proceeds					126,000	154,496 CR
	Transfer stakeholder					14,000	168,496 CR
	Transfer sheet						
	Cash: seller's solicitors				162,000		6,496 CR
30 June	Cash: estate agents inc. VAT				3,290		3,206 CR
	Cash: SDLT				1,800		1,406 CR
10 July	Cash: Land Registry fees				400		1,006 CR
	Cash: transfer from client to office		1,006	—	1,006		—

6   Edhi

FINANCIAL STATEMENT DATE

TO: MR AND MRS EDHI

SALE OF 8 ASHLEY AVENUE AND PURCHASE OF 'GREENWAY'

SALE OF 8 ASHLEY AVENUE

Sale price		450,000
ADD re carpets curtains, etc		10,000
		460,000
LESS mortgage repayment		99,500
		360,500
LESS payments		
Estate agents' fees inc. VAT	10,575	
HIP fee	400	
Profit costs on sale inc. VAT	940	
		11, 915
NET SALE PROCEEDS		348,585
PURCHASE OF 'GREENWAY'		
Purchase price		600,000
LESS mortgage advance		200,000
		400,000
ADD		
Payments out		
SDLT	24,000	
Land Registry fees	300	
Interest on bridging loan	140	
Profit costs on purchase inc. VAT	1,410	
Profit costs on mortgage inc. VAT	235	
		26,085
Balance due on purchase		426,085

Amount required to complete purchase	426,085
LESS net amount received on sale	348,585
Amount due from you	77,500

Client: Mr and Mrs Edhi
Matter: sale of 8 Ashley Avenue and purchase of 'Greenway'

Date	Details	Office account			Client account		
		DR	CR	Balance	DR	CR	Balance
200—							
1 June	Cash: HIP fee	400		400 DR			
9 June	Cash: Abbey Bank deposit					15,000	15,000 CR
14 June	Cash: deposit on sale					45,000	60,000 CR
	Cash: deposit on purchase				60,000		—
24 June	Profit costs on purchase	1,200		1,600 DR			
	VAT	210		1, 810 DR			
	Profit costs on sale	800		2,610 DR			
	VAT	140		2,750 DR			
	Profit costs on mortgage	200		2,950 DR			
	VAT	35		2,985 DR			
25 June	Cash: you—balance due					77,500	77,500 CR
	Cash: mortgage advance					200,000	277,500 CR
4 July	Cash: balance on sale					415,000	692,500 CR
	Cash: balance on purchase				540,000		152,500 CR
	Cash: repay bridging loan plus interest				15,140		137,360 CR
	Cash: mortgage redemption				99,500		37,860 CR
	Cash: SDLT				24,000		13,860 CR
	Cash: transfer costs from client to office account		2,985	—	2,985		10,875 CR
10 July	Cash: estate agents				10,575		300 CR
	Cash: Land Registry fee				300		—

15

Deposit interest and interest payable to clients

15.1 Introduction

This chapter includes:

1. The two methods of paying interest to clients on money held on their behalf;

2. Entries required when placing money on a special designated deposit account for a client;

3. When solicitors should pay a client interest from office account if the money has not been placed on a special deposit account;

4. Example of entries made to record interest payable to the client;

5. Earning interest on client money on a general deposit account;

6. Reminder of key points;

7. Exercises on deposit interest and interest payable to the client.

! INTENDED OUTCOME

An appreciation of the following:

1. When interest should be paid to a client;

2. The two methods of paying interest to clients:

   (a) transfer to a deposit account—evidenced by the ability to make the entries recording transfer to a deposit account, receipt of interest on the deposit account, transfer back to general client bank account, and payment to the client;

   (b) paying interest to the client from office account—evidenced by the ability to make the entries to record interest payable, either with a separate cheque drawn on office account in favour of the client, or a transfer to client account;

3. That interest earned on a general client deposit account is office money and the entries required to transfer money to general client deposit account, and for the receipt of interest on that account—evidenced by the ability to make such entries.

15.2 Paying interest to the client (SAR rules 24 and 25)

As solicitors often hold large sums of money on behalf of their clients for some time, in many cases they are obliged to pay interest to their clients on the sums held. There are two ways of doing this:

1. by placing the sum held for an individual client on a special designated deposit account for that client (in the name of the firm) to earn interest, all of which must be paid to the client;

    OR

2. by paying the client a fair sum as interest equivalent to that which would have been earned had they placed the money on a designated deposit account. Note that this sum must come out of office account. (See SAR rule 24.)

Clearly the first method can only be used if the solicitors know that the money will be held for some time. Its advantage for solicitors is that the bank will calculate the interest payable. This method may also be useful where trust money is involved.

The second method may be used by solicitors where they have placed a substantial part of client moneys on a general deposit account; this will earn interest for the firm, and the interest earned must be paid into office account. The firm can then pay individual clients interest out of this office money. Usually a higher rate of interest will be earned on this general client account than the amount payable on the individual accounts for clients, and so the solicitors and their clients can benefit from the difference.

15.2.1 Placing money on special designated deposit account

Solicitors must aim to obtain a reasonable amount of interest on money held in designated deposit account (SAR rule 25). The solicitor will ask the bank to transfer the client's money from the firm's client account at the bank to a separate deposit account in the client's name (see SAR rule 14(5)). The solicitor must account to the client for all the interest earned on this account (see SAR rule 24(1)). The money, together with interest, will be transferred back to the ordinary client account before paying the client.

Basic steps

Entries on the accounts to record placing money on designated deposit account can seem quite complex. The basic steps are as follows:

1. **Pay out of main client account**—the money to be transferred to the designated deposit account for the client must be paid out of client account, so a normal double entry for payment out of client account will be made.

2. **Pay into designated deposit account**—the money paid into the designated deposit account must then be recorded by a double entry on a client ledger account for the deposit account (or an additional column on the ordinary client ledger account recording the amount held on deposit (SAR rule 32(3)(b)) and on a combined cash account for all the designated deposit accounts.

3. **Record the interest earned on the designated deposit account**—when interest is earned on the designated deposit account this must be recorded by a double entry on the client ledger account—deposit account (or additional column) and on the combined cash account for the designated deposit accounts.

4. **Take the money off designated deposit account and then pay back into main client account**—when the money is returned to the client, then the money must be taken off deposit; a double entry must be made on the client ledger account—deposit account (or additional column) and the combined cash account, showing the payment out of the deposit account, then a double entry will be made to show the receipt into the ordinary client account.

EXAMPLE

The firm acts for Madden in a personal injury claim and received £50,000 in settlement of the claim on 3 September. Madden is not sure how to invest the money and on 5 September asks you to hold it for some time. The firm transfers the £50,000 to a designated deposit account.

1. **The entries on the accounts will show a receipt into client account:**

Cash account

Date	Details	Office account			Client account		
		DR	CR	Bal	DR	CR	Bal
3 Sept	Madden: settlement of claim (1)				50,000		50,000 DR

Madden account

Date	Details	Office account			Client account		
		DR	CR	Bal	DR	CR	Bal
3 Sept	Cash: settlement of claim (1)					50,000	50,000 CR

Then the entries on the accounts will show a payment out of the client account and a receipt into the deposit account.

2. **Payment out of the firm's client account:**
    CREDIT the Cash account Client account.
    DEBIT the Client ledger account Client account.

Cash account

Date	Details	Office account			Client account		
		DR	CR	Bal	DR	CR	Bal
3 Sept	Madden: settlement of claim (1)				50,000		50,000 DR
5 Sept	**Madden: transfer to Deposit account (2)**					50,000	—

Madden account

Date	Details	Office account			Client account		
		DR	CR	Bal	DR	CR	Bal
3 Sept	Cash: settlement of claim (1)					50,000	50,000 CR
5 Sept	**Cash: Transfer to Deposit (2)**				50,000		—

3. **Receipt into the firm's designated deposit account for the client:**
    DEBIT the Deposit Cash account (this will be a combined account for all the designated deposit accounts; see SAR rule 32(3)(a)).
    CREDIT a separate Client ledger account for the Deposit Client account. (See SAR rule 32(3)(b)).

Deposit Cash account

Date	Details	Office account			Client account		
		DR	CR	Bal	DR	CR	Bal
5 Sept	Madden: held on deposit (3)				50,000		50,000 DR

Madden
Held on deposit

Date	Details	Office account			Client account		
		DR	CR	Bal	DR	CR	Bal
5 Sept	Deposit Cash account (3)					50,000	50,000 CR

All that has happened is that the money has been moved from the main client bank account to the deposit account, and a separate client ledger account for Madden has been opened to record this.

4. **When the interest is earned the entries are:**
    DEBIT the Deposit Cash account Client account.
    CREDIT Madden Held on deposit Client ledger Client account.
    Continuing the example—interest earned on 1 December is £120.

Deposit Cash account

Date	Details	Office account			Client account		
		DR	CR	Bal	DR	CR	Bal
5 Sept	Madden: held on deposit (3)				50,000		50,000 DR
1 Dec	**Madden: deposit interest (4)**				**120**		**50,120 DR**

Madden
Held on deposit account

Date	Details	Office account			Client account		
		DR	CR	Bal	DR	CR	Bal
5 Sept	Deposit cash (3)					50,000	50,000 CR
1 Dec	**Deposit cash: interest (4)**					**120**	**50,120 CR**

When the firm wants to pay Madden the total amount, as the deposit account will not have a cheque book, the total money held on deposit will be transferred back to the ordinary client bank account before paying Madden.

The entries for transferring the money back from deposit account are:

5. **Payment out of deposit account:**
    CREDIT the Deposit Cash account.
    DEBIT Madden Held on deposit account Client account.

6. **Receipt into ordinary client bank account:**
    DEBIT Cash account Client account.
    CREDIT Madden Client ledger account Client account.

Deposit Cash account

Date	Details	Office account			Client account		
		DR	CR	Bal	DR	CR	Bal
5 Sept	Madden: held on deposit (3)				50,000		50,000 DR
1 Dec	Madden: deposit interest (4)				120		50,120 DR
	Madden: held on deposit (5)					**50,120**	**—**

Madden
Held on deposit account

Date	Details	Office account			Client account		
		DR	CR	BAL	DR	CR	BAL
5 Sept	Deposit Cash (3)					50,000	50,000 CR
1 Dec	Deposit Cash: interest (4)					120	50,120 CR
1 Dec	**Deposit Cash account transfer back (5)**				**50,120**		—

Cash account

Date	Details	Office account			Client account		
		DR	CR	BAL	DR	CR	BAL
3 Sept	Madden: settlement of claim (1)				50,000		50,000 DR
5 Sept	Madden: transfer to Deposit account (2)					50,000	—
1 Dec	**Madden: transfer from Deposit account (6)**				**50,120**		**50,120 DR**

Madden account

Date	Details	Office account			Client account		
		DR	CR	BAL	DR	CR	BAL
3 Sept	Cash: settlement of claim (1)					50,000	50,000 CR
	Cash account transfer to Deposit (2)				50,000		—
1 Dec	**Cash account: back from Deposit (6)**					**50,120**	**50,120 CR**

7. **Then a normal payment out of client money to Madden can be made:**
    CREDIT the Cash account.
    DEBIT Madden account.

Cash account

Date	Details	Office account			Client account		
		DR	CR	Bal	DR	CR	Bal
3 Sept	Madden: settlement of claim (1):				50,000		50,000 DR
	Madden: transfer Deposit account (2)					50,000	—
1 Dec	Madden: transfer back from Deposit account (6)				50,120		50,120 DR
	Madden: balance due (7)					**50,120**	—

Madden account

Date	Details	Office account			Client account		
		DR	CR	Bal	DR	CR	Bal
3 Sept	Cash—						
	settlement of claim (1)					50,000	50,000 CR
	Cash account transfer						
	to Deposit (2)				50,000		—
1 Dec	Cash account: back						
	from Deposit (6)					50,120	50,120 CR
	Cash account: you (7)				**50,120**		—

As mentioned previously SAR rule 32(3)(b) gives an alternative to opening a separate Client ledger account for the deposit money held. The firm may have an additional column on the client ledger card recording the amount held on deposit. Using the information in the above example the client ledger account for Madden would be as follows:

Madden account

Date	Details	Office account			Client account			Deposit client account		
		DR	CR	Bal	DR	CR	Bal	DR	CR	Bal
3 Sept	Cash:									
	settlement					50,000	50,000 CR			
	of claim									
5 Sept	Cash account									
	transfer to									
	Deposit				50,000		—			
5 Sept	Deposit Cash								50,000	50,000 CR
1 Dec	Deposit Cash								120	50,120 CR
	interest									
1 Dec	Deposit Cash									
	transfer back							50,120		—
1 Dec	Cash account:									
	back from					50,120	50,120 CR			
	deposit									
	Cash account:				50,120		—			
	you									

15.2.2 Paying the client a fair sum in lieu of interest from office account (SAR rules 24 and 25)

If the firm does not place money held for the client on deposit, then the solicitor should account for a fair sum in lieu of interest, but not if:

(a) the amount of interest calculated is £20 or less; or

(b) the sum of money held does not exceed the amount shown below for a time not exceeding the period shown:

    £1,000 for 8 weeks;

    £2,000 for 4 weeks;

    £10,000 for 2 weeks;

    £20,000 for 1 week.

If a sum over £20,000 is held for less than a week, a firm need only account for interest if it is fair and reasonable to do so.

Note that there are other exceptions to the payment of interest in SAR rule 24.

If clients have not been paid interest they may apply to the Law Society Legal Complaints Service for a certificate as to whether interest should have been paid, and the amount payable.

If a firm pays a sum out of office account as interest to the client, a business expense has been paid. To record payments of interest, an expense account, the Interest Payable account, is opened. This is an office account only. The firm may pay the interest by a cheque drawn on office account, and send a separate cheque, drawn on client account, for the money held. Alternatively the firm may transfer the interest payable from office account to client account, and pay one cheque to the client for the balance together with the interest.

EXAMPLES

A. The firm has held £10,000 for its client Floyd for one month and on 10 December pays a cheque from office account for interest of £25, together with a cheque from client account for the £10,000. Note that the interest payable will also have to be recorded on the Client ledger account Office account column under SAR rule 32(4).

1. Thus the entries to show the interest payable are:
   DEBIT the Interest Payable account Office account and CREDIT Floyd's Client ledger account Office account.
   Then when the two cheques are sent the entries would be:
2. Payment of interest payable: CREDIT the Cash account Office account and DEBIT Floyd's Client ledger account Office account.
3. Payment of amount held on Client account: CREDIT the Cash account Client account and DEBIT Floyd's Client ledger account Client account.
   Note that the numbers in the details columns refer to the matching double entries in the order that they take place.

Interest Payable account—Expense account

Date	Details	Office account		
		DR	CR	Balance
10 Dec	Floyd (1)	25		25 DR

Floyd account

Date	Details	Office account			Client account		
		DR	CR	Balance	DR	CR	Balance
	Balance held						10,000 CR
10 Dec	Interest Payable (1)		25	25 CR			
	Cash: you—interest (2)	25		—			
	Cash: you—						
	balance due (3)				10,000		—

Cash account

Date	Details	Office account			Client account		
		DR	CR	Balance	DR	CR	Balance
	Balance						10,000 DR
	Floyd interest (2)		25	25 CR			
	Floyd balance due (3)					10,000	—

B. Alternatively, if the solicitor decides to send one cheque drawn on client account, then the entries will be as follows:

1. Record the interest payable as before: DEBIT the Interest Payable account Office account and CREDIT Floyd's Client ledger account Office account.
2. Transfer the interest payable to Client account: CREDIT the Cash account Office account and DEBIT Floyd's Client ledger account Office account. Then DEBIT the Cash account Client account and CREDIT Floyd's Client ledger account Client account.
3. Pay the client the total due from Client account: CREDIT the Cash account Client account and DEBIT Floyd's Client ledger account Client account. The accounts would therefore be as follows:

Interest Payable account—Expense account

Date	Details	Office account		
		DR	CR	Balance
10 Dec	Floyd (1)	25		25 DR

Floyd account

Date	Details	Office account			Client account		
		DR	CR	Bal	DR	CR	Balance
	Balance held						10,000 CR
10 Dec	Interest Payable (1)		25	25 CR			
	Cash transfer—interest (2)	25				25	10,025 CR
	Cash: you—balance due (3)				10,025		—

Cash account

Date	Details	Office account			Client account		
		DR	CR	Bal	DR	CR	Balance
	Balance						10,000 DR
	Floyd: transfer interest (2)		25	25 CR	25		10,025 DR
	Floyd: balance due (3)					10,025	—

15.3 Earning interest on client money on a general deposit account

As stated in para 15.2 above solicitors may transfer part of their client money to a general deposit account. Any interest earned on this is office money (see SAR rule 13, note (xi)(b)) and will be credited direct to office account. This can then be used to pay interest to individual clients, where appropriate.

When a solicitor transfers client money from current account to deposit account the following entries in the accounts are made:

(a) CREDIT the cash account client column.

(b) DEBIT the deposit cash account client column.

EXAMPLE

The firm has a balance of £100,000 on its client current account. The partners decide to place £30,000 of this on deposit on 9 September.

Cash account

Date	Details	Office account			Client account		
		DR	CR	Bal	DR	CR	Balance
	Balance						100,000 DR
9 Sept	Deposit cash:						
	general deposit					30,000	70,000 DR

Deposit Cash account

Date	Details	Office account			Client account		
		DR	CR	Balance	DR	CR	Balance
9 Sept	Cash: general						
	deposit, client						
	money				30,000		30,000 DR

Interest earned on the general deposit account is practice income and the firm will open an income account, the Interest Received account, to record this income.

When the bank notifies the firm that interest has been earned on the client deposit account, the following bookkeeping entries will be made:

(a) Credit the Interest Received account.

(b) Debit the Cash account office column.

EXAMPLE

On 8 May the bank credits £1,000 interest to office account on money held on general deposit.

Interest Received account/office account

Date	Details	DR	CR	Balance
8 May	Cash (general deposit)		1,000	1,000 CR

Cash account

Date	Details	Office account			Client account		
		DR	CR	Balance	DR	CR	Balance
8 May	Cash (general						
	deposit): interest						
	receivable	1,000		1,000 DR			

15.4 Reminder of key points

1. Interest should be paid to a client in accordance with SAR rules 24 and 25;

2. The two methods of paying interest to clients are:

   (a) placing the money held for the individual client on a designated deposit account for that client and accounting for all the interest earned;

OR

(b) paying the client a fair sum in lieu of interest from office account;

3. If placed on a designated deposit account, then entries will be required for:

(a) the transfer from general client account to a designated deposit account;

(b) the receipt of interest earned on the designated deposit account;

(c) the transfer back from the designated deposit account to the general client bank account;

(d) finally payment of the total including the interest earned to the client;

4. If the money is not placed on a designated deposit account, then entries are required to show the interest payable to the client from office account;

EITHER

(a) when a separate cheque drawn on office account is sent to the client, entries will be made to show the interest payable on office account, before the client is paid from office account;

OR

(b) when the interest payable is transferred to client account before being paid to the client, entries must be made to show the interest payable on office account before transferring the interest payable to client account and then paying the client;

5. Note that if money from client account is placed on general client deposit account, any interest earned is office money;

6. Entries will be made in respect of the transfer to a general client deposit account and for the receipt of interest earned on the general client deposit account (note that the interest is office money as stated in 5. above);

Now try the self-test exercises at the end of the chapter, and the multiple choice questions available online through your tutor via the Online Resource Centre that accompanies this book.

15.5 Exercises on deposit interest and interest payable

1 Allow up to 25 minutes.

On 1 March Cooper asked his solicitors to hold the net proceeds of sale of his cottage, previously received by them, being £100,000, until he had taken full investment advice. The money was placed on a designated deposit account immediately, and on 1 October the sum of £102,000, including interest earned, was transferred back to the client current account, before a cheque was sent to Cooper for the total. Draw up all the relevant accounts for the above.

2 Allow up to 15 minutes.

A firm of solicitors acted for Booth in respect of debt collection. The firm received £14,000 from a debtor on behalf of Booth on 5 January, and Booth asked the firm to hold this until 20 March. The firm then allowed interest of £100 and paid a cheque drawn on client account for the total of £14,100 to Booth on that date.

15.6 Suggested answers to exercises on deposit interest and interest payable

1. Cooper—sale of cottage

Date	Details	Office account			Client account		
		DR	CR	Bal	DR	CR	Bal
	Balance (sale proceeds)						100,000 CR
1 Mar	Cash: transfer to deposit (1)				100,000		—
1 Oct	Cash: from deposit (5)					102,000	102,000 CR
	Cash: you (6)				102,000		—

Cooper
Held on deposit account

Date	Details	Office account			Client account		
		DR	CR	Bal	DR	CR	Bal
1 Mar	Deposit Cash (2)					100,000	100,000 CR
1 Oct	Deposit Cash— interest (3)					2,000	102,000 CR
1 Oct	Deposit Cash account (4)				102,000		—

Deposit Cash account

Date	Details	Office account			Client account		
		DR	CR	Bal	DR	CR	Bal
1 Mar	Cooper: held on deposit (2)				100,000		100,000 DR
1 Oct	Cooper: deposit interest (3)				2,000		102,000 DR
	Cooper: deposit transfer back (4)					102,000	—

Cash account

Date	Details	Office account			Client account		
		DR	CR	Bal	DR	CR	Bal
	Cooper: balance						100,000 DR
1 Mar	Cooper: transfer to deposit account (1)					100,000	—
1 Oct	Cooper: transfer from deposit account (5)				102,000		102,000 DR
	Cooper: balance due (6)					102,000	—

2. Booth account—debt collection

Date	Details	Office account			Client account		
		DR	CR	Bal	DR	CR	Bal
5 Jan	Cash: debtor (1)					14,000	14,000 CR
20 Mar	Interest payable (2)		100	100 CR			
	Cash transfer interest (3)	100		—		100	14,100 CR
	Cash: you—balance due (4)				14,100		

Interest Payable account

Date	Details	Office account			Client account		
		DR	CR	Bal	DR	CR	Bal
20 Mar	Booth—interest (2)	100		100 DR			

Cash account

Date	Details	Office account			Client account		
		DR	CR	BAL	DR	CR	BAL
5 Jan	Booth: debtor (1)				14,000		14,000 DR
20 Mar	Booth: transfer interest (3)		100	100 CR	100		14,100 DR
	Booth: balance due (4)					14,100	—

Probate transactions

16.1 Introduction

This chapter includes:

1. A summary of common probate financial transactions;
2. Reminder of key points;
3. Self-test exercises on probate transactions.

! **INTENDED OUTCOME**

An appreciation of common probate financial transactions, evidenced by the ability to draw up the relevant ledger accounts.

16.2 Summary of common probate financial transactions

These occur when a firm acts in connection with the administration of an estate. A summary is set out below:

(a) A grant of probate or letters of administration will be required, probate fees will be paid, and, where applicable, inheritance tax. It may be necessary to obtain a loan from the bank to the executors in respect of any inheritance tax payable. This may be paid direct from the loan account to HM Revenue & Customs, or the money may be paid into the firm's client account before payment is made to HMRC.

(b) Payments will be made regarding advertisements.

(c) Once probate has been obtained the firm will use it to collect all the assets of the deceased, such as bank account moneys, building society moneys, and life policy proceeds. Some of this may be used to pay back the bank loan for inheritance tax, together with any interest due on the loan.

(d) Property belonging to the deceased may be sold, for example house and household contents.

(e) Debts due from the estate of the deceased will be paid, as will funeral expenses.

(f) Pecuniary legacies will be paid.

(g) The firm will charge costs (plus VAT) regarding administration and any sale of property, and transfer such costs from client account to office account with the agreement of the executors.

(h) The balance of the estate will be distributed to the beneficiary/beneficiaries, together with any interest due from the firm, either from moneys held on designated deposit or interest in lieu.

16.3 Reminder of key points

online resource centre

As in para 16.2 above. Now try the self-test exercises following. There are also the online multiple choice questions available through your tutor via the Online Resource Centre that accompanies this book.

16.4 Exercises on probate transactions

1 O'Malley & Co., solicitors, are instructed by the executors of Parry, deceased, to administer the estate on their behalf. The estate consists of a house valued at £162,000 (subject to a mortgage of approximately £12,000) and personalty valued at £17,000. There are various debts due by the estate amounting to £1,892. The following events take place:

7 October	Probate fees of £50 are paid by the firm's cheque.
15 October	A cheque for £16 is drawn in respect of the statutory advertisements, the cost of the local advertisement (£8) being met by a payment out of petty cash.
18 October	The balance remaining in the Scottish Building Society (£223) is paid into client account.
21 October	Proceeds of life policy received, being £5,000.
28 October	The household contents are sold and a cheque for £5,890 is received from the auctioneer. Commission of £620 had already been deducted.
4 November	Contracts for the sale of the house (£162,000) are exchanged, and a deposit of £16,200 is received by O'Malley & Co. for them to hold as stakeholders.
18 November	Debts amounting to £1,927 are paid.
25 November	Paid funeral expenses £432.
4 December	The sale of the house is completed and £145,800 for the balance of the purchase money is received. The mortgage is redeemed by the payment of £12,367 which is inclusive of accrued interest.
11 December	A pecuniary legacy of £5,000 is paid to a legatee.
12 December	Bill of costs re sale of the house is prepared and agreed with the executors, profit costs being £440 plus VAT, and cash disbursements £20 (no VAT) are paid by the firm. The estate agents are paid their commission, £1,600 plus VAT.
16 December	Bill of costs for the administration of the estate, profit costs £520 (plus VAT) and disbursements, sent to executors, and

after receiving their agreement, all moneys due to the firm from the estate are transferred to office account.

17 December   The balance of moneys now held by O'Malley & Co., on behalf of the executors, is paid over to Richards, the residuary legatee, in accordance with their instructions. This includes the interest allowed on the money held by the firm on behalf of the executors of £208.

Show the client ledger card of the executors of Parry deceased. The rate of VAT is to be taken as 17.5%.

2 The firm is informed that Sheldon died on 26 February, and the executors appointed in the will instruct the firm to act in the administration of the estate generally. The estate consists of a house 'The Elms' valued at £70,000 and personalty valued at £47,500. There are various debts due by the estate (£1,500) together with a loan from an insurance company (secured on a life insurance policy) amounting to £5,000. The residue of the estate has been left to Newton, a nephew, who is in the process of buying 'Rose Cottage', a matter which is being dealt with by the firm.

During the administration, the following events take place:

8 March   House insurance premium (£95) on 'The Elms', now due, and the firm debits the Executors' account, the amount being transferred to the account of the insurance company, for whom the firm acts.

14 March   Probate fees of £70 are paid by cheque.

19 March   The grant is received and registered with the bank.

26 March   The amount invested by the deceased with the Cambridge Building Society is, after registration of the grant, withdrawn, the balance amounting to £590 being paid into client account.

27 March   The firm draws a cheque in respect of statutory advertisements (£22), and pays £12 out of petty cash in respect of the local advertisement.

29 March   Received cheque from the Zurich Insurance Co. Ltd for the sum of £6,342, being the net sum receivable from the company after the deduction of £5,158 in respect of the loan together with accrued interest.

1 April   Debts amounting to £1,500, together with funeral expenses of £1,000, are paid out of client account.

The executors have agreed to an interim distribution of £4,000 to Newton, which is transferred to Newton's client account. The firm then sends a cheque (£4,000) to the solicitors acting for the seller of 'Rose Cottage', for them to hold as stakeholders, contracts being exchanged the same day.

5 April   Exchanged contracts for the sale of 'The Elms', the deposit of £7,000 having been received by the firm for them to hold as stakeholders.

| 12 April | Sundry fees (£3) paid from office account re the transmission of shares to Vernon, a beneficiary in the estate of Sheldon, deceased. |

26 April   Received completion statement in respect of 'Rose Cottage', showing £36,000 due, being the balance of purchase money. Sent financial statement to Newton same day, showing profit costs of £280 excluding VAT (as per bill of costs attached thereto), Land Registry fees £70. Paid £10 from petty cash, in respect of bankruptcy search.

30 April   Completed purchase of 'Rose Cottage', the balance of purchase moneys being received by the firm from the Bank of Scotland as a loan, an undertaking having been given that the sum would be repaid to them from the proceeds of sale of 'The Elms'. The executors had previously agreed to this arrangement.

2 May   Completed sale of 'The Elms', receiving a bank draft (£63,000) in respect of the balance of purchase moneys.

Paid Land Registry fees re 'Rose Cottage'.

9 May   The firm agrees the bills of cost for the sale of the house and the administration of the estate with the executors. Profit costs with regard to the sale amount to £440 (excluding VAT), and with regard to the administration £680 (excluding VAT), together with disbursements in both cases. With the executors' agreement, a sum amounting to £36,146 is transferred from the account of the executors to the account of Newton, and a cheque for this amount is sent to the Bank of Scotland in accordance with the firm's undertaking.

16 May   All moneys due to the firm from the estate are transferred to office account.

17 May   The balance of moneys held by the firm on behalf of the executors is transferred to the account of Newton at the request of the executors, such sum being inclusive of interest allowed by the firm of £567.

All moneys due to the firm from Newton are transferred to office account, the balance due to Newton being held pending further instructions.

You are required to show the ledger accounts of:

(i) Newton;

(ii) the executors of Sheldon, deceased.

The rate of VAT is to be taken as 17.5%.

In making the necessary entries, it is important that the account in which the corresponding entry would be made is clearly identified by the appropriate entry in the details column.

                                              (Solicitors' Final Examinations, amended.)

16.5 Suggested answers to exercises on probate transactions

1   Executors of Parry deceased

Date	Details	Office account			Client account		
		DR	CR	Balance	DR	CR	Balance
7 Oct	Cash: probate fees	50		50 DR			—
15 Oct	Cash: advertisements	16		66 DR			
	Petty cash: advertisements	8		74 DR			
18 Oct	Cash: Scottish Building Society					223	223 CR
21 Oct	Cash: life policy					5,000	5,223 CR
28 Oct	Cash: auctioneer (less commission £620)					5,890	11,113 CR
18 Nov	Cash: debts				1,927		9,186 CR
25 Nov	Cash: funeral expenses				432		8,754 CR
4 Dec	Cash: sale proceeds					145,800	154,554 CR
	Stakeholder: transfer					16,200	170,754 CR
	Cash: mortgage redemption				12,367		158,387 CR
11 Dec	Cash: legacy				5,000		153,387 CR
12 Dec	Costs: sale	440					
	VAT	77		591 DR			
	Petty cash: disbursements	20		611 DR			
	Cash: estate agent inc. VAT				1,880		151,507 CR
16 Dec	Costs: re estate	520					
	VAT	91		1,222 DR			
	Cash: transfer: costs		1,222	—	1,222		150,285 CR
17 Dec	Interest payable		208	208 CR			
	Cash transfer interest payable	208		—		208	150,493 CR
	Cash: Richards				150,493		—

2   Executors of Sheldon deceased re administration of estate

Date	Details	Office account			Client account		
		DR	CR	Balance	DR	CR	Balance
8 Mar	Cash: transfer: insurance premium: client account: 'The Elms',	95		95 DR			
14 Mar	Cash: probate fees	70		165 DR			
26 Mar	Cash: Combridge Building Society					590	590 CR
	Cash: statutory advertisement				22		568 CR
	Petty cash: local advertisement	12		177 DR			
29 Mar	Cash: Zurich Insurance Co. Ltd					6,342	6,910 CR
1 Apr	Cash: debts				1,500		5,410 CR
	Cash: funeral expenses				1,000		4,410 CR
	Newton: transfer				4,000		410 CR
12 Apr	Cash: fees: transmission of shares to Vernon	3		180 DR			
2 May	Cash: purchaser's of 'The Elms'					63,000	63,410 CR
	Stakeholder: transfer sheet					7,000	70,410 CR
9 May	Costs: sale	440					
	VAT	77		697 DR			
	Costs: administration	680					
	VAT	119		1,496 DR			
	Newton: transfer			—	36,146		34,264 CR
16 May	Cash: transfer: costs		1,496	—	1,496		32,768 CR
	Interest payable		567	567 CR			
17 May	Cash: transfer: from office account in lieu of interest	567		—		567	33,335 CR
	Newton: transfer residue				33,335		—

Newton: re purchase of 'Rose Cottage'

Date	Details	Office account			Client account		
		DR	CR	Balance	DR	CR	Balance
1 Apr	Executors of Sheldon, deceased: transfer					4,000	4,000 CR
	Cash: deposit re 'Rose Cottage'				4,000		—
26 Apr	Costs	280					
	VAT	49		329 DR			
	Petty cash: bankruptcy search	10		339 DR			
30 Apr	Cash: Bank of Scotland					36,000	36,000 CR
	Cash: purchase of 'Rose Cottage'				36,000		—
2 May	Cash: Land Registry	70		409 DR			
9 May	Executors of Sheldon, deceased: transfer					36,146	36,146 CR
	Cash: Bank of Scotland				36,146		—
17 May	Executors of Sheldon, deceased: transfer: residue					33,335	33,335 CR
	Cash: transfer: costs		409	—	409		32,926 CR

Further transactions

17.1 Introduction

This chapter includes:

1. Reducing the client's bill and VAT (abatements);
2. Dishonoured cheques on:
    (a) office account;
    (b) client account;

    including drawing against uncleared cheques and entries required to correct any breach of the Solicitors' Accounts Rules.
3. Small transactions;
4. Bad debts—a reminder; VAT relief
5. Reminder of key points.

The following transactions are further examples of the operation of the Solicitors' Accounts Rules 1998.

! INTENDED OUTCOME

An understanding of:

1. The entries required in respect of the reduction (abatement) of a client's bill, evidenced by the ability to make the relevant entries on the accounts;
2. The entries required in respect of a dishonoured cheque, evidenced by the ability to make the relevant entries on the accounts;
3. The entries required where a payment had been made from client account against a cheque which is later dishonoured, evidenced by the ability to make the relevant entries on the accounts;
4. Dealing with small transactions;
5. VAT relief available on bad debts.

17.2 Abatements—reduction of profit costs

After a bill of costs has been delivered to the client, a solicitor may decide to reduce the profit costs.

When an abatement of costs is made, a credit note is sent to the client, showing the reduction in costs and VAT.

The solicitor will make the following entries in the accounts to record an abatement:

(a) CREDIT the Client ledger account Office column with the reduction in profit costs and VAT (on separate lines).

(b) DEBIT the Profit Costs account with the costs reduction/abatement.

(c) DEBIT the HMRC VAT account with the reduction in VAT.

EXAMPLE

On 30 June 200— the firm delivers a bill of costs to Cross, the executor of Farrell, deceased, for £600 plus VAT. After discussing the matter with Cross, the firm agrees to reduce its bill to £400 and records the abatement in its account on 31 July 200—.

Executor of Farrell deceased

Date	Details	Office account			Client account		
		DR	CR	Balance	DR	CR	Balance
200—30 June	Profit costs	600					
	VAT	105		705 DR			
31 July	Costs: abatement		200				
	VAT: abatement		35	470 DR			

Profit Costs account (Office account)

Date	Details	DR	CR	Balance
200—30 June	Profit costs: executor of Farrell deceased		600	600 CR
31 July	Profit costs: abatement: executor of Farrell deceased	200		400 CR

HMRC VAT account (Office account)

Date	Details	DR	CR	Balance
200—30 June	Executor of Farrell deceased		105	105 CR
31 July	Executor of Farrell deceased: VAT: abatement	35		70 CR

Note that the balance on the Executor's account showing the executor owes £470, being the reduced profit costs of £400 and £70 VAT.

17.3 Dishonoured cheques

17.3.1 Dishonoured cheque which has been paid into office account

If a cheque paid into office account is later dishonoured, the solicitor will have to cancel out the original receipt by making the following entries in the accounts:

(a) DEBIT the Client ledger account Office column with the value of the dishonoured cheque.

(b) CREDIT the Cash account Office column.

EXAMPLE

There is a debit balance of £235 on Payne's Office account on 1 November 200— in respect of profit costs and VAT previously charged to Payne. On 21 November Payne pays the costs by cheque. On 26 November the firm's bank notifies it that Paynes' cheque has been returned by the paying banker. To record the above transactions, the following entries will be made in Payne's account.

Payne

Date	Details	Office account			Client account		
		DR	CR	Balance	DR	CR	Balance
200—							
1 Nov	Balance b/d			235 DR			
21 Nov	Cash: you		235	—			
26 Nov	Cash: dishonoured cheque	235		235 DR			

The cash account will appear as follows:

Cash account

Date	Details	Office account			Client account		
		DR	CR	Balance	DR	CR	Balance
200—							
21 Nov	Payne	235		235 DR			
26 Nov	Payne (dishonoured cheque)		235	—			

17.3.2 Dishonoured cheque which has been paid into client account

If a cheque paid into client account is later dishonoured, again the solicitor will have to cancel out the original receipt by making the following entries in the accounts:

(a) DEBIT the Client ledger account Client column with the value of the cheque.

(b) CREDIT the Cash account Client column.

EXAMPLE

On 4 February 200— Jones paid the sum of £200 on account of costs and disbursements by cheque. On 7 February the firm's bankers notified it that Jones' cheque had been returned. The following entries will be made in the accounts to record these events.

Jones

Date	Details	Office account			Client account		
		DR	CR	Balance	DR	CR	Balance
200—							
4 Feb	Cash: you					200	200 CR
7 Feb	Cash: dishonoured cheque				200		—

Cash account

Date	Details	Office account			Client account		
		DR	CR	Balance	DR	CR	Balance
200—							
4 Feb	Jones				200		200 DR
7 Feb	Jones (dishonoured cheque)					200	—

17.3.3 Drawing against uncleared cheques in client account

The Solicitors' Accounts Rules 1998 (SAR) do not prevent a solicitor from drawing against an uncleared cheque paid into client account, but, if the cheque is later dishonoured, the solicitor is in breach of SAR rules 1(c) and 22(5) and must make an immediate transfer from office to client account of the amount by which the client account is overdrawn. See SAR rule 7(1).

When a solicitor has drawn on client account against a cheque which is later dishonoured, the following entries will be made in the accounts:

(a) Entries to record the dishonour of a client account cheque (ie those entries in para 17.3.2 above).

(b) Entries to record the transfer from office account to client account of the amount by which client account is overdrawn.

Note: it is not necessary to transfer the full value of the cheque which has been dishonoured unless the client account is overdrawn by this amount.

Continuing the example from para 17.3.2 above:

Assume that after the receipt of the cheque from Jones on 5 February the firm drew a cheque on client account for £55 in respect of court fees. The cheque from Jones was then dishonoured on 7 February.

Jones

Date	Details	Office account			Client account		
		DR	CR	Balance	DR	CR	Balance
200—							
4 Feb	Cash: you					200	200 CR
5 Feb	Cash: court fee				55		145 CR
7 Feb	Cash: dishonoured cheque				200		55 DR
	Cash: transfer to remedy breach	55		55 DR		55	—

Cash account

Date	Details	Office account			Client account		
		DR	CR	Balance	DR	CR	Balance
200—							
4 Feb	Jones				200		200 DR
5 Feb	Jones (court fee)					55	145 DR
7 Feb	Jones (dishonoured cheque)					200	55 CR
	Jones (transfer to client account)		55	55 CR	55		—

17.4 Small transactions

When a solicitor does work which involves only one accounting transaction—the charging of costs, for example, for drafting a will—the solicitor may open a ledger account for the client and record the delivery of a bill of costs and receipt of payment of profit costs in the usual way.

Alternatively the solicitor may make entries only to record the receipt of profit costs, as follows:

(a) DEBIT the Cash account Office column with profit costs and VAT (on separate lines).

(b) CREDIT the Profit Costs account with costs.

(c) CREDIT the HMRC VAT account with VAT.

17.5 Bad debts and VAT relief

If no VAT relief is available the firm will have to write off the total amount due, including VAT. If VAT relief is available (see Chapter 13, para 13.7) the VAT element can be debited to the HMRC VAT account, thus offsetting the VAT due to HMRC. The firm will then only lose the net amount.

EXAMPLE

A bill delivered to Hardy for £235 (including £35 VAT) has not been paid. At the end of the financial year 31 December the debt is written off.

Hardy account

Date	Details	DR	CR	Balance
	Balance: amount due			235 DR
31 Dec	Bad debt: written off		235	—

Bad Debts account

Date	Details	DR	CR	Balance
31 Dec	Hardy: debt written off	235		235 DR

Contrast the entries to write off a bad debt where VAT is recoverable:

The client ledger account will be credited with the Profit Costs and the VAT written off (shown as separate entries) on office account, and then the Bad Debts account will be debited with the Profit Costs written off (office account) and the HMRC VAT account will be debited with the VAT (office account).

EXAMPLE VAT RELIEF

The firm delivered a bill to its client Hardy for £200 plus £35 VAT. Hardy was then adjudicated bankrupt and the debt was written off after 6 months.

Hardy

Date	Details	Office account			Client account		
		DR	CR	Balance	DR	CR	Balance
	Profit Costs	200		200 DR			
	HMRC VAT	35		235 DR			
	Bad debt written off		200	35 DR			
	HMRC VAT		35	—			

HMRC VAT account

Date	Details	Office account		
		DR	CR	Balance
	Hardy VAT on Profit Costs		35	35 CR
	Hardy VAT written off	35		—

Profit Costs account

Date	Details	Office account		
		DR	CR	Balance
	Hardy bill		200	200 CR

Bad Debts account

Date	Details	Office account		
		DR	CR	Balance
	Hardy written off	200		200 CR

The above example shows that when the bad debt is written off with VAT relief, the firm will only lose the profit costs element, and not the VAT.

17.6 Reminder of key points

1. Note the entries required in respect of a reduction (abatement) of a client's bill of costs on the relevant accounts—the client ledger account will be credited with the reduction and VAT on the reduction separately, and the Profit Costs account will be debited with the reduction and the HMRC VAT account debited with the VAT on the reduction.

2. Note the entries required in respect of a dishonoured cheque (entries will be made to cancel the original receipt): if on office account, then debit the client ledger account office account and credit the cash account office account; if on client account, debit the client ledger account client account and credit the cash account client account.

3. Note the entries required where a payment has been made from client account against a cheque which is then dishonoured—as well as the entries above cancelling out the receipt, a transfer of the amount spent (effectively overdrawn) on client account must be transferred from office account.

4. Note small transactions—solicitors may open a client ledger account in the normal way or not open an account and just record the receipt of the profit costs and VAT.

5. Note on bad debts, unless VAT relief is available, the firm will have to write off the total including the VAT.

online resource centre Now try the online multiple choice questions available through your tutor via the Online Resource Centre that accompanies this book, and the exercises following.

17.7 Exercises on further transactions

1 On 12 February 2008 a firm of solicitors receives £100 from its client Green on account of his pending divorce action costs. On 13 February the sum of £75 is paid out of moneys received from Green to an enquiry agent. On 17 February the bank notifies the firm that the cheque from Green for £100 has been returned by the paying bankers. Prepare the account of Green.

2 You act for Allen who is purchasing a house:

1 May   Receive a cheque from Allen for £6,000 for the deposit.

2 May   Send a cheque for £6,000 to seller's solicitors.

6 May   Bank notifies you that Allen's cheque has been returned.

Prepare the account for Allen and the cash account to record the above.

3 (a)   On 20 January you deliver a bill of costs to Cowell for £200 plus £35 VAT. On 27 January you agree to reduce the cost to £160 plus VAT.

(b)   On 20 January Adams sends a cheque for £500: £141 is in payment of a bill you have delivered to him and the balance is for payment to the Wilshire County Court for an action which he lost. On 21 January you pay the money due to the county court. On 22 January Adams' cheque is dishonoured. On 28 January Adams brings in cash to replace the dishonoured cheque.

Show the client ledger accounts and the Cash account to record the above.

4 During the month of November, Davies & Platt, solicitors, deal with the following events, and you are required to show all the relevant entries on the client ledger accounts, showing all balances. The rate of VAT is to be taken as 17.5%.

1 November   £6,000 is being held as stakeholder for Lomas. Cheque received (£4,000) from Poole, who is not a client of the firm, being the deposit on the sale of a house by Miller, for whom the firm acts. The firm is to hold the money as stakeholders. Exchanged contracts for the sale of Miller's house, and paid petty cash disbursements of £6 (no VAT) on his behalf, on the same day.

4 November   Banker's draft received (£54,000) on completion of the sale of Lomas's house, stake money of £6,000 being transferred from stakeholder account. The mortgagee of Lomas's house, Alexander, had already instructed the firm to act on his behalf in the redemption of his charge on Lomas's house, and the redemption money (£9,675) is transferred to his account. It has been agreed that the mortgagee's costs (£40 plus VAT) will be borne by Lomas. (Assume that Alexander is not an institutional lender.)

5 November   Paid by cheque the sum of £10,000 in respect of a debt which had been incurred by Lomas to Peters, Lomas having previously agreed to this action.

The amount due to Alexander the mortgagee of Lomas' house is paid by cheque, and Lomas' estate agent's fee (£1,200 plus VAT) is paid by the firm since the invoice was addressed to them.

A bill of costs is sent to Lomas, showing profit costs of £800 plus VAT.

The firm writes off the sum of £70.50 (inclusive of VAT £10.50) as a bad debt, the amount having been owed to the firm by Shaw since March 2007. Shaw has now been adjudicated bankrupt.

11 November
The designated deposit account opened by the firm re Oakes, in respect of an amount of £10,000 held by them for the period of six months, is closed, and a cheque for the sum, together with interest of £150 credited by the bank, is sent to Oakes.

14 November
Cheque sent to Lomas in respect of balance of moneys held on his behalf, including interest allowed of £124. The amount due to the firm is transferred to office account and Lomas' account is then closed.

25 November
Bill of costs is sent to Miller, showing profit costs (£320 plus VAT) together with the disbursements already incurred.

29 November
The sale of Miller's house is completed, a banker's draft for £36,000 being received from the purchaser's solicitors. The amount due to the firm is transferred to office account, and a cheque for the balance due to Miller is sent to him.

(Solicitors' Final Examination, amended.)

17.8 Suggested answers to exercises on further transactions

1 Green

Date	Details	Office account			Client account		
		DR	CR	Balance	DR	CR	Balance
12 Feb	Cash: you					100	100 CR
13 Feb	Cash: enquiry agent				75		25 CR
17 Feb	Cash: returned cheque				100		75 DR
	Cash: transfer	75		75 DR		75	—

2 Allen

Date	Details	Office account			Client account		
		DR	CR	Balance	DR	CR	Balance
1 May	Cash: you					6,000	6,000 CR
2 May	Cash: deposit paid				6,000		—
6 May	Cash: dishonoured cheque				6,000		6,000 DR
	Cash: transfer to correct breach	6,000		6,000 DR		6,000	—

Cash account

Date	Details	Office account			Client account		
		DR	CR	Balance	DR	CR	Balance
1 May	Allen: moneys received				6,000		6,000 DR
2 May	Allen: deposit paid					6,000	—
6 May	Allen: dishonoured cheque					6,000	6,000 CR
	Allen: transfer to correct breach		6,000	6,000 CR	6,000		—

3 (a) Cowell

Date	Details	Office account			Client account		
		DR	CR	Balance	DR	CR	Balance
20 Jan	Profit costs	200					
	VAT	35		235 DR			
27 Jan	Profit costs abatement		40				
	VAT abatement		7	188 DR			

Note the balance of £188 represents profit costs of £160 and VAT of £28.

(b) Adams

Date	Details	Office account			Client account		
		DR	CR	Balance	DR	CR	Balance
20 Jan	Balance			141 DR			
	Cash: you—split cheque		141	—		359	359 CR
21 Jan	Cash: Wilshire County Court				359		—
22 Jan	Cash: dishonoured cheque	141		141 DR	359		359 DR
	Cash: transfer to correct breach	359		500 DR		359	—
28 Jan	Cash: you		500	—			

Cash account

Date	Details	Office account			Client account		
		DR	CR	Balance	DR	CR	Balance
	Adams split cheque	141		141 DR	359		359 DR
21 Jan	Adams: Wilshire County Court					359	—
22 Jan	Adams: dishonoured cheque		141	—		359	359 CR
	Adams: transfer to correct breach		359	359 CR	359		—
28 Jan	Adams:	500		141 DR			

4 Davies & Platt

Stakeholder account

Date	Details	Office account			Client account		
		DR	CR	Balance	DR	CR	Balance
	Balance					6,000	6,000 CR
1 Nov	Cash: Miller					4,000	10,000 CR
4 Nov	Lomas: transfer				6,000		4,000 CR
29 Nov	Miller: transfer				4,000		—

Miller

Date	Details	Office account			Client account		
		DR	CR	Balance	DR	CR	Balance
1 Nov	Petty cash: disbursement	6		6 DR			
25 Nov	Profit costs	320		326 DR			
	HMRC VAT	56		382 DR			
29 Nov	Cash: sale proceeds					36,000	36,000 CR
	Stakeholder: transfer: deposit					4,000	40,000 CR
	Cash: transfer: costs from client to office account		382	—	382		39,618 CR
	Cash: you				39,618		—

Lomas

Date	Details	Office account			Client account		
		DR	CR	Balance	DR	CR	Balance
4 Nov	Cash: sale proceeds					54,000	54,000 CR
	Stakeholder: transfer: deposit					6,000	60,000 CR
	Alexander: transfer: redemption				9,675		50,325 CR
	Alexander: transfer: redemption costs	47		47 DR			
5 Nov	Cash: Peters				10,000		40,325 CR
	Cash: estate agent	1,200		1,247 DR			
	Profit Costs	800		2,047 DR			
	HMRC VAT (210 + 140)	350		2,397 DR			
	Interest allowed		124	2,273 DR			
14 Nov	Cash: transfer interest allowed	124		2,397 DR		124	40,449 CR
	Cash: transfer: costs		2,397	—	2,397		38,052 CR
	Cash: you				38,052		—

Alexander

Date	Details	Office account			Client account		
		DR	CR	Balance	DR	CR	Balance
4 Nov	Profit costs	40					
	VAT	7		47 DR			
	Lomas: transfer: redemption					9,675	9,675 CR
	Lomas: transfer: redemption costs		47	—			
5 Nov	Cash: you				9,675		—

Shaw

Date	Details	Office account			Client account		
		DR	CR	Balance	DR	CR	Balance
	Balance			70.50 DR			
8 Nov	Bad debt		60				
	HMRC VAT		10.50	—			

Note: VAT bad debt relief available here.

Oakes

Date	Details	Office account			Client account		
		DR	CR	Balance	DR	CR	Balance
	Cash account: back from deposit					10,150	10,150 CR
11 Nov	Cash: you				10,150		

Oakes
Held on deposit

Date	Details	Office account			Client account		
		DR	CR	Balance	DR	CR	Balance
	Balance						10,000 CR
	Deposit interest					150	10,150 CR
11 Nov	Deposit cash: transfer back to client account				10,150		

Short-answer questions and revision questions on solicitors' accounts

18.1 Introduction

This chapter includes the following questions on solicitors' accounts:

1. Set A. These questions require a statement of the principles or rules involved;

2. Set B. These questions require a statement of the principles or rules involved and the entries on the accounts;

3. Two long questions requiring you to make entries in a series of transactions.

! **INTENDED OUTCOME**

Consolidation of your understanding of the operation of the Solicitors' Accounts Rules 1998 (SAR) and the entries required on the accounts.

18.2 Revision questions—Set A

Explain how a firm of solicitors should deal with the following. You should just state the principles/rules involved. There is no need to state the debit and credit entries involved.

Allow 5 to 10 minutes for each question.

1 The firm is dealing with a probate matter and the deceased's bank agrees to advance £20,500 to the executors in respect of inheritance tax. A loan account is opened by the bank for the executors and a cheque for £20,500 is drawn by the executors, payable to HMRC, and handed to the firm of solicitors.

2 The firm has held the net proceeds of sale of a house on behalf of its client Davies for the past two months. Davies now asks for the net proceeds, totalling £10,000, to be sent to him.

3 Jackson, a client, owes the firm £940, being £800 re costs and £140 re VAT. Seven months after the bill was delivered the firm writes off the debt.

4 The firm receives cash of £600 on behalf of its client Clarke in settlement of a claim. Clarke has asked that the firm pay this cash over to Boswell in payment of a debt due from Clarke to Boswell.

5 The firm acts for Rule, a partner in the firm, and her friend Johnson, who is a legal executive in the firm. They are selling a cottage and purchasing a larger house in town. The firm receives a cheque for £30,000 to hold as agent for the seller.

6 The firm receives a cheque for £400 on general account of costs from their client Irwin. A disbursement of £415 (no VAT payable) is paid by the firm on behalf of Irwin.

7 The firm receives a cheque for £770 from their client Latham. This is in respect of the firm's bill for £400 plus VAT, which had been sent to Latham, and counsel's fees of £300 (no VAT) which have not yet been paid.

18.3 Suggested answers to revision questions—Set A

1 No entries need be shown on the solicitors' accounts at all, as the loan account at the bank belongs to the executors and not the firm. The cheque is made out to HMRC, so it does not belong to the firm and it should merely be forwarded to HMRC.

2 As £10,000 has been held for two weeks or more, here two months, then the money should have been placed on a designated deposit account to earn interest for Davies. The proceeds plus the interest should be paid to him. See SAR rule 24(2). If the money has not been placed on a designated deposit account for Davies then the firm should pay a fair sum in lieu of interest that would have been earned on a designated deposit account. The interest payable must come from the firm's office account.

3 As the debt is at least six months old the firm may claim bad debt relief. Thus the amount of £800 will be recorded as a bad debt, and the VAT of £140 can be debited to the HMRC VAT account, thus reducing the VAT payable by the firm to HMRC.

4 Although normally a firm of solicitors must pay money received on behalf of a client into a client bank account, under SAR rule 17(a), where money is received in cash and is without delay paid in cash in the ordinary course of business to the client or on the client's behalf there is no need to pay into the client bank account. The firm can therefore pay the money to Boswell. However, entries must be made on the accounts showing the receipt and payment out of client money. Note take care re money laundering.

5 Although money received on behalf of partners in the firm is not client money (SAR rule 13, note (xii)), where the money is received on behalf of a partner together with a non-partner, then the money will be client money and as this is held as agent for the seller, it can be recorded on a client ledger card for Rule and Johnson.

6 The £400 on general account of costs should have been paid into client account (SAR rule 13, note (i)(d)). The firm cannot pay the total disbursement of £415 from client account (SAR rule 22(5)). Although it would be technically possible for the firm to pay two cheques, one for £400 from client account and one for £15 from office account, this would seem odd, and the better course would be to pay £415 from office account, and then transfer £400 from client account. It is also possible for the firm to advance money to fund the payment under SAR rule 15(2)(b). It may be necessary to ask the client for further funds if these are needed for other disbursements.

7   This is mixed office/client money (SAR rules 19 and 20). The sum of £470, being £400 plus £70 VAT, is office account money. The remaining £300 should be held on client account until counsel's fees are paid. The cheque may be split or, more usually, the whole amount paid into client account, and then £470 transferred to office account within 14 days. Alternatively the entire sum may be paid into office account and counsel's fees paid or the money transferred to client account by the end of the second working day following receipt (SAR rule 19).

18.4 Self-assessment questions—Set B

Decide whether the following transactions should be dealt with through client account or office account, and show or explain the entries that would be made on the accounts.

Allow about 10 minutes for each question.

1   A solicitor receives £400 on general account of costs from Javed.

2   A solicitor receives £470 as an agreed fee in respect of work to be done for Hughes. The firm has not yet sent a bill to Hughes.

3   The solicitor holds £200 on general account of costs from Ellis. An enquiry agent is paid £150 (no VAT is payable).

4   The firm is acting for one of the partners, Khalid, in respect of his sale of a flat in Mersey Quays. The sale price of £154,000 is received on completion from the purchaser's solicitors.

5   The firm is acting on behalf of one of its employees, Palmer, in respect of the sale of a house. Sale proceeds are received in the sum of £90,000.

6   The firm is acting for one of its partners, Janson, together with her husband in respect of the sale of a house. Sale proceeds are received in the sum of £150,000.

7   The firm has £80,000 on general client account. The office account is overdrawn at the bank. A disbursement of £50 has to be paid on behalf of their client Bashir, who has not yet sent any money on account of costs.

8   The firm sent out a bill to Anthony for £800 plus £140 VAT. Counsel's fees are due but not yet paid in the sum of £600. Anthony sends a cheque for £1,540.

9   The firm receives £30,000 in respect of Delaney's sale of 'The Gables', to hold as stakeholder.

10   The firm receives £26,000 in respect of Marsh's sale of 8 Beaumont Square, to hold as agent for the seller. The sum of £25,000 is paid out in respect of her purchase of 10 Bloxham Road.

11   A cheque made out to their client Saleem for £3,000 is received by the firm.

12   The firm receives £60 cash on behalf of its client Clark in respect of debt collection. Later that day the cash is handed to Clark who has called into the office.

13   A cheque is received made out to the firm for £9,000 in respect of a debt due from Agnes to its client Jarman.

14   The firm sent out a bill of costs for £800 plus VAT to its client, Timms. The firm later agreed with Timms to reduce the bill to £600 plus VAT.

18.5 Suggested answers to self-assessment questions—Set B

1 Money on general account of costs is client money and must be paid into client account (see SAR rule 13(d)).

Date	Details	Office account			Client account		
		DR	CR	Balance	DR	CR	Balance
	Cash: you—on account of costs					400	400 CR

Cash book

Date	Details	Office account			Client account		
		DR	CR	Balance	DR	CR	Balance
	Javed on account costs				400		400 DR

2 An agreed fee is office money and must be paid into office account (see SAR rule 19(5)). So:

(a) CREDIT Hughes Client ledger card Office account.

(b) DEBIT the Cash book Office account.

As receipt of the fee is the tax point for VAT it would be advisable to record the bill of costs £400 and the £70 VAT on the Profit Costs account and the HMRC VAT account at the same time.

3 The £200 on general account of costs would have been paid into client account. As this money is available, and VAT is not involved, the enquiry agent can be paid from client account.

Ellis

Date	Details	Office account			Client account		
		DR	CR	Balance	DR	CR	Balance
	Cash: you—on account of costs					200	200 CR
	Cash: enquiry agent				150		50 CR

Cash book

Date	Details	Office account			Client account		
		DR	CR	Balance	DR	CR	Balance
	Ellis: on a/c costs				200		200 DR
	Ellis: enquiry agent					150	50 DR

4 Client money does not include money to which the only person entitled is the solicitor himself or herself or, in the case of a firm of solicitors, one or more of the

partners in the firm: see the notes to SAR rule 13, note (xii). The money cannot be paid into client account; it must be held on an office account in the name of Khalid.

Khalid

Date	Details	Office account			Client account		
		DR	CR	Balance	DR	CR	Balance
	Cash: sale proceeds		154,000	154,000 CR			

Cash book

Date	Details	Office account			Client account		
		DR	CR	Balance	DR	CR	Balance
	Khalid: re sale	154,000		154,000 DR			

5 Palmer does not fall within the exception in **Answer 4** above: she is a client and the money will be paid into client account on her behalf. So:

(a) CREDIT Palmer Client ledger card Client account.

(b) DEBIT the Cash book Client account.

6 Provided Janson's husband is not a partner in the firm, the money is again client money: see **Answer 4** above, ie Janson is not the only person entitled. So:

(a) CREDIT Janson and husband Client ledger card Client account.

(b) DEBIT the Cash book Client account.

7 Although there are sufficient funds on client account to pay the disbursement, as the firm is not holding any money on behalf of Bashir, the payment cannot be made out of client account; it must be made out of office account. See SAR rule 22(8), which makes it clear that money drawn cannot exceed the total held on account of the client, subject only to limited exceptions. So:

(a) DEBIT Bashir Client ledger card Office account.

(b) CREDIT the Cash book Office account.

8 A solicitor may only pay money into office account in respect of, *inter alia*, 'costs', which excludes counsel's fees which have not yet been paid. On the assumption that no VAT is payable in respect of counsel's fees in this case, then £940 is office money and £600 is client money. The cheque may be split, ie £940 paid into office account and £600 into client account, or all the money may be paid into client account, and then £940 transferred to office account within 14 days, or all the money may be paid into office account and then either counsel's fees paid or transferred to client account, within two working days (see SAR rule 19).

Entries where the money is split:

Anthony

Date	Details	Office account			Client account		
		DR	CR	Balance	DR	CR	Balance
	Costs	800		800 DR			
	VAT	140		940 DR			
	Cash: you		940	—		600	600 CR

The Cash book would be debited £940 on office account, and debited £600 on client account.

Entries where the money is paid into client account and then transferred:

Anthony

Date	Details	Office account			Client account		
		DR	CR	Balance	DR	CR	Balance
	Balance re costs and VAT			940 DR			
	Cash: you					1,540	1,540 CR
	Cash: transfer costs		940	—	940		600 CR

Cash book

Date	Details	Office account			Client account		
		DR	CR	Balance	DR	CR	Balance
	Anthony				1,540		1,540 DR
	Anthony: transfer costs	940		940 DR		940	600 DR

9 The money does not belong to Delaney until completion of the sale. It must be paid into stakeholder account, a client ledger card client account. So:

(a) CREDIT the Stakeholder account Client ledger card Client account.

(b) DEBIT the Cash book Client account.

10 As this money is held for Marsh it may be paid into her client ledger card client account and used in respect of the deposit payable on the purchase.

Marsh: Sale 8 Beaumont Square; purchase 10 Bloxham Road

Date	Details	Office account			Client account		
		DR	CR	Balance	DR	CR	Balance
	Cash deposit: agent for vendor					26,000	26,000 CR
	Cash deposit on purchase				25,000		1,000 CR

Note that the other entries would have been to debit the cash book client account with £26,000, and to credit the cash book client account in respect of the deposit paid on purchase, ie £25,000.

11 As the cheque is made out to the client, it cannot be paid into the solicitors' bank accounts, whether office account or client account. No entries need be made on the accounts, although a note may be made if required.

12 Although the rules do not require this money to be paid into client account at the bank, client money has still been received and then paid out. Thus entries must be made on the accounts in respect of the receipt and payment out.

Receipt:

(a) CREDIT the Client ledger card of Clark Client account.

(b) DEBIT the Cash book Client account.

Payment out:

(a) DEBIT the Client ledger card of Clark Client account.

(b) CREDIT the Cash book Client account.

13   As the cheque is made out to the firm it can be paid into the firm's bank account. The money is received on behalf of Jarman and is client money. So:

(a)   CREDIT Jarman's Client ledger card Client account.

(b)   DEBIT the Cash book Client account.

14   **Timms**

Date	Details	Office account			Client account		
		DR	CR	Balance	DR	CR	Balance
	Profit Costs	800		800 DR			
	VAT	140		940 DR			
	Abatement		200	740 DR			
	VAT		35	705 DR			

Profit Costs account Office account

Date	Details	DR	CR	Balance
	Timms: bill of costs		800	800 CR
	Timms: abatement	200		600 CR

HMRC VAT account Office account

Date	Details	DR	CR	Balance
	Timms: bill of costs		140	140 CR
	Timms: abatement	35		105 CR

18.6 Test on further transactions

Allow about 40 to 45 minutes to complete this test.

Hart, Price, and Adams are solicitors, and they deal with the following events:

3 January   Paid by cheque the sum of £2,000 on behalf of Black and received later the same day from Black, a cheque for £1,500 as part payment. The balance is to be paid from the proceeds of the sale of his house, which will be received within a few days' time.

7 January   Received cheque, in respect of the sale of Black's house, amounting to £270,000, being the balance of purchase money. The sum of £30,000 is transferred from stakeholder account the same day. The firm sends £70,000 to the Salisbury Building Society to redeem the mortgage.

10 January   Bill of costs sent to Black (£360 plus VAT).The amount due to the firm is transferred to office account.

13 January   Hart repays by cheque made out to the firm a personal loan of £1,000 made by Price, a partner in the firm.

16 January   Grady pays £300 on account of her pending divorce action costs, and petty cash disbursements of £16 are paid in respect of this on the same day.

22 January   Paid enquiry agent, on behalf of Grady, the sum of £100 (no VAT), the cheque being drawn on client account.

24 January   The bank notifies the firm that the cheque from Grady has been returned unpaid by the paying bankers.

29 January   The sum of £1,000, which has been held on behalf of Bell for three months, is repaid to Bell, together with agreed interest of £40.

The payment is made by a cheque drawn on client account. The money was not deposited in a designated deposit account.

Draw up the client ledger accounts, showing all relevant entries. All accounts are to be balanced. The rate of VAT is to be taken as 17.5%.

(Law Society Final Examination, amended.)

18.7 Suggested answer to test on further transactions

Black

Date	Details	Office account DR	CR	Balance	Client account DR	CR	Balance
3 Jan	Cash	2,000		2,000 DR			
3 Jan	Cash: you		1,500	500 DR			
7 Jan	Cash: purchaser's solicitors					270,000	270,000 CR
	Stakeholder: transfer					30,000	300,000 CR
	Cash: Salisbury Building Society: redemption				70,000		230,000 CR
10 Jan	Profit costs	360		860 DR			
	VAT	63		923 DR			
10 Jan	Cash: transfer costs		923		923		229,077

Grady—divorce

Date	Details	Office account DR	CR	Balance	Client account DR	CR	Balance
16 Jan	Cash: you					300	300 CR
	Petty cash: disbursements	16		16 DR			
22 Jan	Cash: enquiry agent				100		200 CR
24 Jan	Cash: returned cheque				300		100 DR
	Cash: transfer to correct breach	100		116 DR		100	—

Bell

Date	Details	Office account DR	CR	Balance	Client account DR	CR	Balance
29 Jan	Balance						1,000 CR
	Interest payable		40	40 CR			
	Cash: transfer interest	40				40	1,040 CR
	Cash: you—amount due				1,040		—

Note: a client account is not opened for Price as he is a partner in the firm and it would be in breach of SAR rule 13, note (xii) to pay the money received from Hart into client account. It will be paid into office account for Price.

18.8   Test on ledger accounts including VAT

Allow approximately 1 hour to complete this test.

Except where specifically referred to in the questions, taxation (including VAT) should be ignored.

Brown, Platt, and Halson are solicitors, and they deal with the following events:

3 April	Paid £47 (including VAT £7) by cheque drawn on office account, in respect of reproduction of documents. The invoice is made out to the client, Powell, for whom the firm is acting in a tax matter before the Special Commissioners.
4 April	Received banker's draft for £450,000 from the purchaser's solicitors, being the balance of purchase money on the sale by their client Smith of his house 'Beeches'. On the same day the sum of £190,000 is sent by cheque to the mortgagees of the property, in full payment of the amount due to them.
7 April	Lloyd, Hirst and Co., the estate agents acting for Smith, send cheque to firm for £42,000, being the deposit on 'Beeches' less their commission.
8 April	Received the sum of £300 from Powell on account of costs generally.
11 April	The firm acts for Jones in the collection of a debt due to her, amounting to £5,000. The debtor sends two cheques for the debt, each cheque being for the sum of £2,500 and dated 16 May and 16 June, respectively.
14 April	Sent cheque for £587.50 (including VAT £87.50) to A. Beswick in respect of pre-sale repairs to 'Beeches'. The invoice was addressed to the firm.
28 April	Paid fee of £235 (including VAT £35) to E. Price, a witness, who appeared on behalf of Powell. The bill was addressed to Powell, and payment made out of client account.
29 April	Bill of costs sent to Smith (£600 plus VAT).
5 May	Paid from client account £65 (including VAT) in respect of transcripts obtained on behalf of Powell.
9 May	Profit costs and disbursements are transferred from client account to office account in respect of Smith.
20 May	Bill of costs in respect of tax matter is sent to Powell, showing profit costs of £700 plus VAT.
16 June	Received cheque in settlement of Powell's account with the firm.
17 June	Bill of costs for £60 plus VAT delivered to Jones.
20 June	Both cheques from the debtor of Jones, having been presented and met, the total amount due, after deduction of costs but inclusive of interest allowed by the firm (£22), was paid over to Jones. The amount due to the firm is transferred from client to office account.
30 June	The firm allows interest of £250 for Smith, before paying the total due from client account.

You are required to show the ledger accounts of Powell, Smith, and Jones, recording all the above transactions. The rate of VAT is to be taken as 17.5%.

(Law Society Final Examination, amended.)

18.9 Suggested answer to test on ledger accounts including VAT

Powell

Date	Details	Office account			Client account		
		DR	CR	Balance	DR	CR	Balance
3 Apr	Cash: production of documents	47		47 DR			
8 Apr	Cash: you					300	300 CR
28 Apr	Cash: E. Price				235		65 CR
5 May	Cash: transcripts				65		—
20 May	Profit costs	700		747 DR			
	HMRC VAT	122.50		869.50 DR			
16 June	Cash: you		869.50	—			

Smith

Date	Details	Office account			Client account		
		DR	CR	Balance	DR	CR	Balance
4 Apr	Cash: purchaser's solicitors					450,000	450,000 CR
	Cash: redemption				190,000		260,000 CR
7 Apr	Cash: estate agent (less commission)					42,000	302,000 CR
14 Apr	Cash: A. Beswick	500		500 DR			
29 Apr	Profit costs	600		1,100DR			
	HMRC VAT 87.50 + 105	192.50		1,292.50 DR			
9 May	Cash: transfer: costs		1,292.50	—	1,292.50		300,707.50 CR
30 June	Interest payable		250	250 CR			
	Cash: transfer interest	250		—		250	300,957.50 CR
	Cash: you				300,957.50		—

Jones

Date	Details	Office account			Client account		
		DR	CR	Balance	DR	CR	Balance
16 May	Cash: debtor					2,500	2,500 CR
16 June	Cash: debtor					2,500	5,000 CR
17 June	Profit costs	60					
	HMRC VAT	10.50		70.50 DR			
20 June	Interest payable		22	48.50 DR			
	Cash: transfer	22		70.50 DR		22	5,022 CR
	Cash: transfer		70.50	—	70.50		4,951.50 CR
	Cash: you				4,951.50		—

online resource centre

Now try the online multiple choice questions available through your tutor via the Online Resource Centre that accompanies this book.

Index